Oracle Data Mining

Mining Gold from your Warehous

Oracle In-Focus Series

Carolyn K. Hamm, Ph.D.

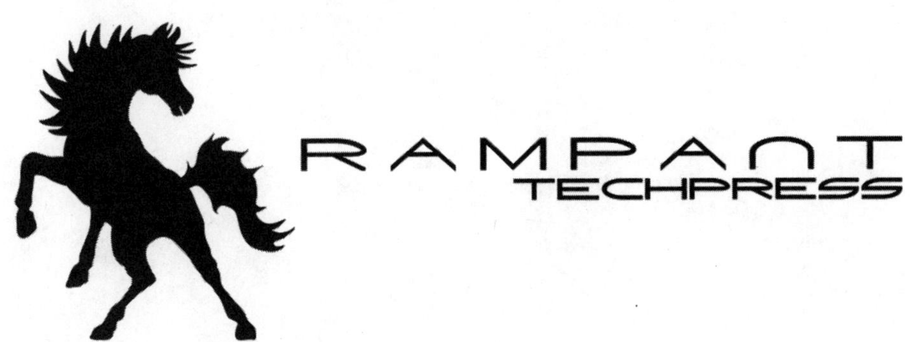

Dr. Hamm's book, "Oracle Data Mining, Mining Gold from your Warehouse" provides an easy to read, step-by-step, practical guide for learning about data mining using Oracle Data Mining. It is a must read for anyone looking to harvest insights, predictions and valuable new information from their Oracle data.

Charles Berger

Senior Director of Product Management,

Life & Health Sciences Industries and Data Mining Technologies

Oracle Corporation

To Alex, the companion of my home.

April 1985 - August 2006

An Old Russian Prayer.....

Hear our prayer, Lord, for all animals,
May they be well-fed and well-trained and happy;
Protect them from hunger and fear and suffering;
And, we pray, protect specially, dear Lord,
The little cat who is the companion of our home,
Keep him safe as he goes abroad,
And bring him back to comfort us. ....Author Unknown

Oracle Data Mining

Mining Gold from your Warehouse

By Dr. Carolyn Hamm, PhD

Printed in the United States of America.

Published in Kittrell, North Carolina, USA.

Oracle In-Focus Series: Book #25

Series Editor: Donald K. Burleson

Editors: Janet Burleson and John Lavender

Production Editor: Teri Wade

Cover Design: Janet Burleson

Printing History: September 2007 for First Edition

ISBN: 0-9744486-3-X ISBN-13: 978-0974448633

Library of Congress Control Number: 2006934081

Table of Contents

Conventions Used in this Book

It is critical for any technical publication to follow rigorous standards and employ consistent punctuation conventions to make the text easy to read. However, this is not an easy task. Within database terminology there are many types of notation that can confuse a reader. For example, some Oracle utilities such as STATSPACK and TKPROF are always spelled in CAPITAL letters, while Oracle parameters and procedures have varying naming conventions in the database documentation. Hence, all Rampant TechPress books follow these conventions:

Parameters - All database parameters will be *lowercase italics*. Exceptions to this rule are parameter arguments that are commonly capitalized (KEEP pool, TKPROF); these will be left in ALL CAPS.

Variables – All procedural language (e.g. PL/SQL) program variables and arguments will also remain in *uppercase BOLD*.

Tables & Dictionary Objects – All data dictionary objects are referenced in lowercase italics (*dba_indexes*, *v$sql*). This includes all *v$* and *x$* views (*x$kcbcbh, v$parameter*) and dictionary views (*dba_tables*, *user_indexes*).

SQL – All SQL is formatted for easy use in the code depot, and all SQL is displayed in lowercase. The main SQL terms (select, from, where, group by, order by, having) will always appear on a separate line.

Programs & Products – All products and programs that are known to the author are capitalized according to the vendor specifications (IBM, Benchmark Factory, etc). All names known by Rampant TechPress to be trademark names appear in this text as initial caps. References to UNIX are always made in uppercase.

Acknowledgements

The writing has consumed many hours of weekend and evening personal quality time normally spent with family and friends. I thank my mother Evelyn Warren for supporting my efforts with home cooked meals, housekeeping chores, and all the innumerable ways that mothers help daughters. Thanks go to Ellen Apatov for her patience over lost movie nights, and especially her encouraging words as I labored over this book. My heartfelt gratitude goes to Jim Watts, who sacrificed and suffered along with me while writing, kept me going and saved my sanity by replacing my computer's mother board when it died a few months into this book.

I thank COL David L. Jones, COL Fifi Stritmatter, and COL Jill Phillips (retired), for their support and encouragement in our data mining efforts at Walter Reed Army Medical Center. My deepest respect and admiration goes to Dr. Tim Wu for his brilliant and uncanny ability to create business intelligence systems with ease and proficiency. Thank you for your unfailing good humor and for all the data tables you made me for data mining.

Without the support and assistance of Oracle's data mining staff this book would have been impossibile. My heartfelt thanks go to Esin Yilmaz, Richard Solari, and especially Dr. Robert Haberstroh for camping out in our offices to teach us how to mine data. Oracle partnered with Walter Reed and came in as a finalist in DM Review's 2005 World Class Solution awards for Business Intelligence. Many thanks go to Charlie Berger and Jacek Myczkowski for their support and enthusiasm.

I am most grateful to Mark Hornick for his thoughtful review of this manuscript, and allowing us to include his work with ODM and BI Publisher in Chapter 7.

This type of highly technical reference book requires the dedicated efforts of many people. Though we are the authors, our work ends when we deliver the content. After each chapter is delivered, several Oracle DBAs carefully review and correct the technical content. After the technical review, experienced copy editors polish the grammar and syntax.

The finished work is then reviewed as page proofs and turned over to the production manager, who arranges the creation of the online code depot and manages the cover art, printing distribution, and warehousing.

In short, the authors play a small role in the development of this book, and we need to thank and acknowledge everyone who helped bring this book to fruition:

Janet Burleson, for her help with the production management including the coordination of the cover art, page proofing, printing, and distribution.

Teri Wade, for her help in the production of the page proofs.

John Lavender, for his assistance with the web site, and for creating the code depot and the online shopping cart for this book.

With my sincerest thanks,

Carolyn K. Hamm

Foreword by Donald K. Burleson

It took humankind 300,000 years to accumulate 12 exabytes (1 billion gigabytes) of information. It will take just under 3 years to create the next 12 exabytes, according to a study from the School of Information Management and Systems at the University of California, Berkeley. The world's total annual production of information amounts to approximately 250 MB for each man, woman, and child on earth, and that number is expected to double every year for the foreseeable future.[1] Ninety-three percent of the information that is currently produced each year is now stored in digital form.[1] Increased computing power, decreasing costs, and advances in data capture and storage technologies have resulted in massive data sets in many disciplines, including healthcare. Databases of gigabyte size are common in the humanities, social, medical, and life sciences. When one contemplates the newer units of measurement for data, exabyte, terabyte, petabyte, the volume is staggering. Healthcare has always been data-rich. As more healthcare data is captured and stored electronically, the need for new methods to derive information from large, multifaceted data sets has become more apparent. [1]

Oracle data mining and in-database analytics is one of the most promising areas of Oracle. As disk prices fall by orders of magnitude, many shops find multi-terabyte online archives of historical information. This is a virtual gold-mine of information.

---

1 "Data Mining as a Tool for Research and Knowledge Development in Nursing" Anne M. Berger, MS, MBA, RN; Charles R. Berger, MS, MBA; CIN: Computers, Informatics, Nursing; Vol. 22, No. 3, 123–131 ; © 2004 Lippincott Williams & Wilkins, Inc.

Historical Oracle information is so valuable that a typical data warehouse can pay for itself in just a few months by providing nuggets of information that saves the company millions of dollars.

Once a new data warehouse and ETL have been created, Oracle data experts implement data queries, ranging from the simple to the more powerful and insightful -- data mining queries might include:

- **Ad-hoc query:** The Discoverer 10g end-user layer will be configured to allow for the ad-hoc display of summary and detailed level data.
- **Aggregation and multidimensional display:** Develop Oracle Warehouse Builder structures to summarize, aggregate and rollup salient information for display using the Oracle 10g Discoverer interface.
- **Basic correlations:** The front-end should allow the end-user to specify dimensions and request a correlation matrix between the variables with each dimension. The system will start with one-to-one correlations and evolve to support multivariate chi-square methods.
- **Hypothesis testing:** The data warehouse is used to validate theories about the behavior of the customer universe, and curve formulation techniques allow data mining experts to derive valid formulae to describe their data. Hypothesis testing in data mining often involves simulation modeling, using the Oracle data as input.
- **Data Mining:** This is the capstone of Oracle data queries, a method for defining cohorts of related data items and tracking them over time. The basic goal of data mining is to identify hidden correlations, and the data mining expert must identify populations (e.g. Eskimo's with alcoholism) and then track this population across various external factors (e.g.

treatments and drugs). These Oracle Decision Support System (DSS) interfaces require the ability for the end-user to refine their decision rules and change the salient parameters of their domain (i.e. the confidence interval for the predictions).

Obviously, performing Oracle data mining requires special skills, and Oracle data mining requires advanced statistics skills including multivariate (chi-square) techniques for identifying hidden correlations.

Performing advanced analytics in an Oracle data warehouse requires skills that are far-beyond those of an ordinary Oracle system. Many shops employ professionals with advanced degrees in areas that are statistics-centered drawing from people with doctorates in Economics, Experimental Psychology and Sociology. To perform complex and valid studies, the warehouse team must have a statistician with these skills:

- **Multivariate statistics:** Even a simple longitudinal study required knowledge of the application of applied multivariate statistics.
- **Artificial Intelligence:** Oracle Data Mining (ODM) product is heavily-centered around the application of AI for the mining algorithms and the statistician should have a firm grounding in fuzzy logic, pattern matching and the use of advanced Boolean logic.

That is why this book on Oracle data mining was written. The Oracle data mining tools are extremely powerful and provide the hope of extracting valuable new information – predictions and greater insights. ODM professionals must understand how to best apply Oracle's powerful in-database analytical engine to harvest information from their vast Oracle databases.

Oracle Data Mining and Predictive Analytics

There has been great discussion about using the scientific method with Oracle databases, and how mathematical models are developed for Oracle. Predicting the future without historical justifications is the realm of psychics, not scientists. Virtually every predictive model in Oracle software uses the database to create the predictive model:

Data mining can sift through massive amounts of data and find hidden information — valuable information that can help you better understand your customers and anticipate their behavior.

The Oracle data mining tools scan historical data and identify statistically significant correlations (within 2 standard deviations of the mean value), and base their results on empirical truths, not theory.

For example, we might find-out that people with red hair buy a disproportionate amount of skin care products. Knowing "why" is critically important, such that just having the prediction is not actionable.

In sum, rules don't have to be proven true to be statistically reliable, and exceptions do not make the rule invalid. For example, if two out of every 1,000 read-haired people don't buy skin care products, we still have a model with a very-high predictive quality.

Why this book is important

As the first book on Oracle Data Mining, Dr. Hamm is breaking new ground and sharing her valuable insights into the complex machinations of this sophisticated tool. Dr. Hamm has done a great job in explaining the complex concepts and providing citations to get more information.

Dr. Hamm has delivered a step-by-step approach to data mining, and you should carefully download the sample data and follow her step-by-step directions. In this fashion you will learn, first-hand, how the features of ODM work with real data.

This is a book for both database analysts and business users, but it should not be targeted at dilettantes. Readers of this book will need to have some knowledge of their data, their business problems, their data, and some basic understanding or intuition about data analysis. Data mining favors the inquisitive personality.

So, join me in learning about the most exciting and challenging areas of Oracle databases, the quest to find hidden gold within massive quantities of data.

Introduction to Model Building

CHAPTER

One day you are called into the office of your boss who is struggling with a large spreadsheet he has pulled from company databases to understand how several stores in the SH[2] chain are doing. He asks you to help with a pivot table report about trends in retail sales and how each store differs from the others. There is concern that one of the stores will close because of diminishing sales, and he wants to send a promotional flyer to customers with proven buying habits.

If he can target customers most likely to respond to the sales pitch, the company will save time and money by avoiding customers who are not likely to make purchases. You look over his shoulder as he punches up trends in sales performance of the stores, and you decide to take a look at prior customer buying habits.

What is Data Mining?

You quickly realize that pivot table analyses, while interesting, will take weeks or months of examination and since time is of the essence, you decide to try your hand at data mining. Why? Data mining is great at finding patterns in huge amounts of data. The Gartner Group, the information technology research firm, defines data mining (from their web site, Jan. 2004):

---

[2] SH refers to the Sales History schema, which is installed as one of the sample schemas in the 9i and 10g databases. This schema is designed for demos with large amounts of data, and supports advanced analytic processing.

> "Data mining is the process of discovering meaningful new correlations, patterns and trends by sifting through large amounts of data stored in repositories, using pattern recognition technologies as well as statistical and mathematical techniques."

This is a wonderful but somewhat obtuse definition of data mining! How do we start? Let us explore a little bit about the Oracle data warehousing tools.

Oracle provides a powerful data mining infrastructure embedded directly into the database. This infrastructure, Oracle Data Mining (ODM), can be accessed by the graphical user interface (GUI) or Oracle Data Miner, Java API, SQL API, Predictive Analytics one-click data mining, and the Clemintine® data mining interface by SPSS, Inc. Even though data mining is based on statistics and machine learning as in artificial intelligence, you do not have to have to be a statistical genius to run your data mining analysis with Oracle. ODM automates the process of data mining.

The approach to Oracle data mining follows these straightforward steps:

- Sample from a larger database or data warehouse.
- Explore, clean, preprocess and reduce the data, including treatment of outliers and missing data.
- Develop an understanding of attributes (variables or fields) and selection of attributes for building a model.
- Partition data into training (build) and test data sets.
- Build and test several models using different techniques, choosing one on the basis of its performance on the test data. Results with the test data are an indicator of how well

the model will do with new data. Test is not used for unsupervised classification techniques. This will be covered in Chapter Four.

These steps will be explained in greater detail as we go along.

First of all, how will you obtain the customer data? Do you have to decide what attributes are important at the outset? Fortunately, one of the strengths of data mining is that there are algorithms available to help capture the important fields that are needed to build successful models of good customers. So do not worry about deciding which fields are needed, include as many as you can reasonably load into the table and let Oracle data miner help mine the gold from the data.

Components of Oracle Data Miner

To help with steps one and two above, Oracle Data Miner has an impressive array of tools for sampling, exploring, and cleaning the data. These tools include importing files, recoding existing fields, filtering using where queries, and deriving new fields. Treatment of outliers and missing data is done automatically in Data Miner, and although quite capable for almost all datasets, the do it yourselfer will find missing values, normalize, numeric, and outlier treatment wizards described in Chapter 5.

In addition, there are utilities for creating views, creating tables from views, copying tables, joining tables together, and importing text files. Displaying summary statistics and histograms assist in step three, developing an understanding of the data.

In order to build the model to predict which customers to contact for the marketing blitz, the data will need to be partitioned into build and test data sets. We will develop a model, test it, and then apply it to new data to obtain the customer mailing list. The Oracle Data Mining Activity steps through the whole process with only a few mouse clicks. This chapter will demonstrate how easy it is to do using the sample data provided by Oracle.

Because Oracle Data Miner is built into the database, we do not need to extract data from tables or import the data into another server or database for analysis, thereby enhancing security and protecting the integrity of the data. In the next section we will demonstrate connecting to Oracle's sample data.

Sampling Data from the Database

The current release of Data Miner includes sample views describing the purchasing habits of customers in a pilot marketing campaign. This view is MINING_DATA_BUILD_V. The process of installing sample data is outlined in the Appendix.

The MINING_DATA_BUILD_V will be examined in more detail now. After logging into ODM through Oracle Data Miner, expand data sources and the corresponding user name, which in this case is DMUSER. The BUILD dataset will be used to construct the classification model.

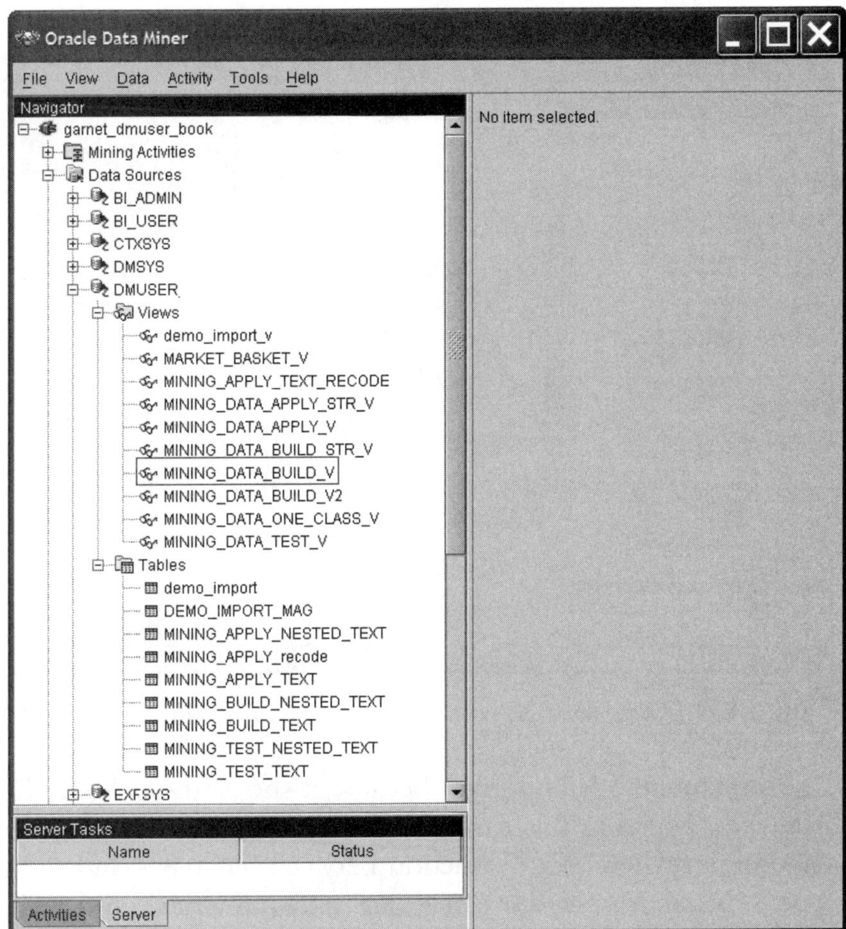

Figure 1.1: *Data Miner Navigator*

After choosing MINING_DATA_BUILD_V view, the right panel of Data Miner shows three tabs: Structure, Data, and View Lineage.

The structure tab depicts all attributes or fields in the view and their descriptors, including the primary key (PK), column name (Name), format of the data (Type), size of the field (Size), Scale and whether NULL is allowed. If any comments were added when the view was created, these will be displayed here also.

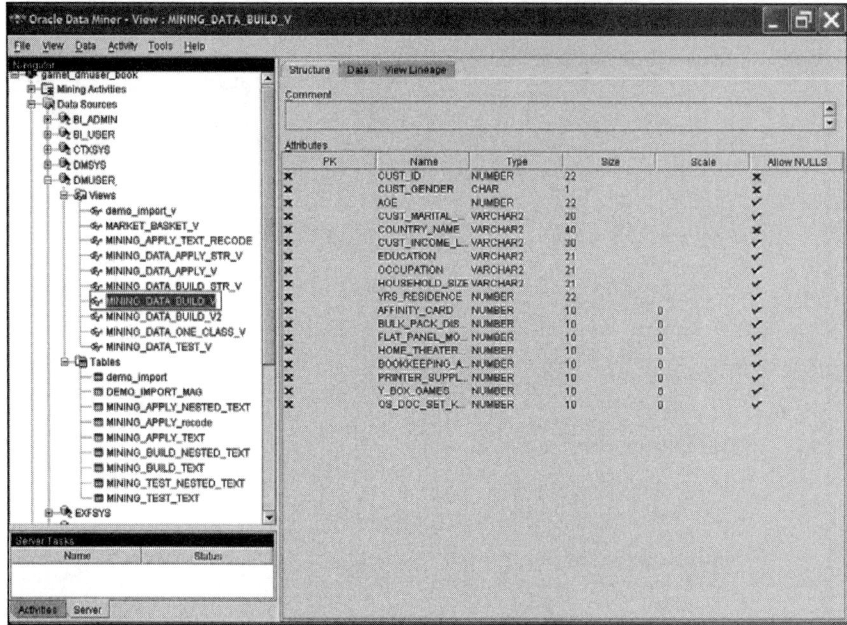

Figure 1.2: *Data Miner Navigator for MINING_DATA_BUILD_V*

The structure tab is important because it shows the fields and the datatypes, which in this case are number, char, and varchar2. In data mining, there is a distinction between datatypes and mining types. Mining types are categorical and numerical, and will be designated for each attribute when we start building the classification model.

The Data Miner Data Tab

The data tab queries the view and shows data for 100 rows. Fetch Next brings in an additional 100 rows, and so on for every time you click Fetch Next. Refresh re-runs the query.

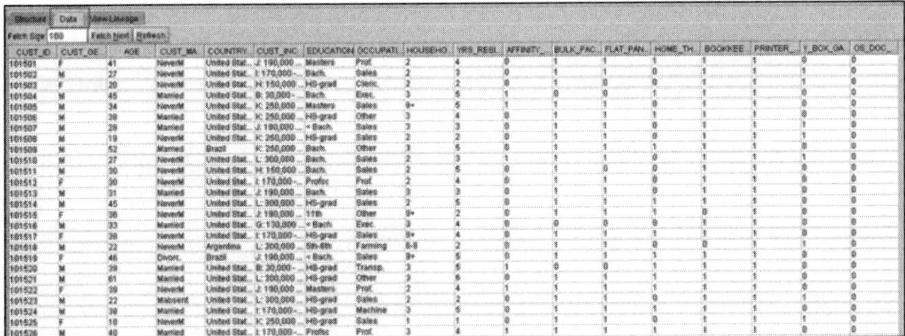

Figure 1.3: *Data in the View.*

Only views will have the View Lineage tab, and this can be used to see where the data was derived.

Figure 1.4 shows that the MINING_DATA_BUILD_V view was built using three tables from the SH schema in the Oracle database:

- CUSTOMERS
- COUNTRIES,
- SUPPLEMENTARY_DEMOGRAPHICS

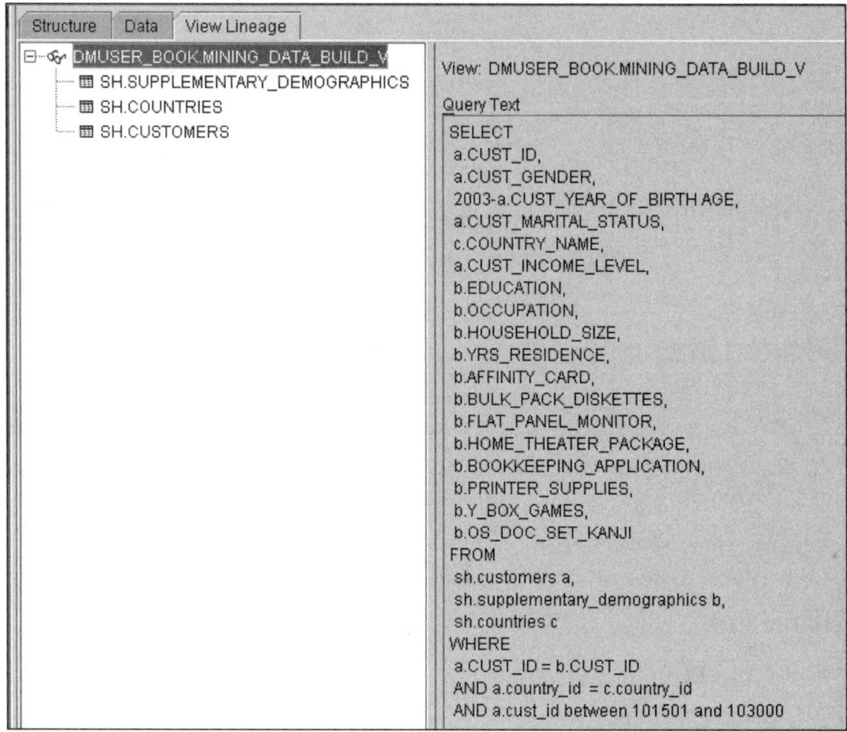

Figure 1.4: *View Lineage.*

These tables contain information about customer demographic characteristics and purchasing habits. The attribute AFFINITY_CARD is the target attribute, having a value of one for customers that increased spending more than 10% in a test marketing campaign, and zero if less than 10%. The target attribute is the attribute that is to be predicted. In supervised mining, or clustering and regression, the process of building models uses a known dependent variable, the target attribute. Unsupervised mining, or clustering techniques, has no such target attribute.

Exploring the Data

Now that we have seen how the data was generated in the view, we will begin to explore the data in more detail. Right click MINING_DATA_BUILD_V in the navigator window and select Show Summary Single-Record as shown in Figure 1.5. Because each customer's data is contained on only one row of the data set, we select Single-Record rather than Multi-Record.

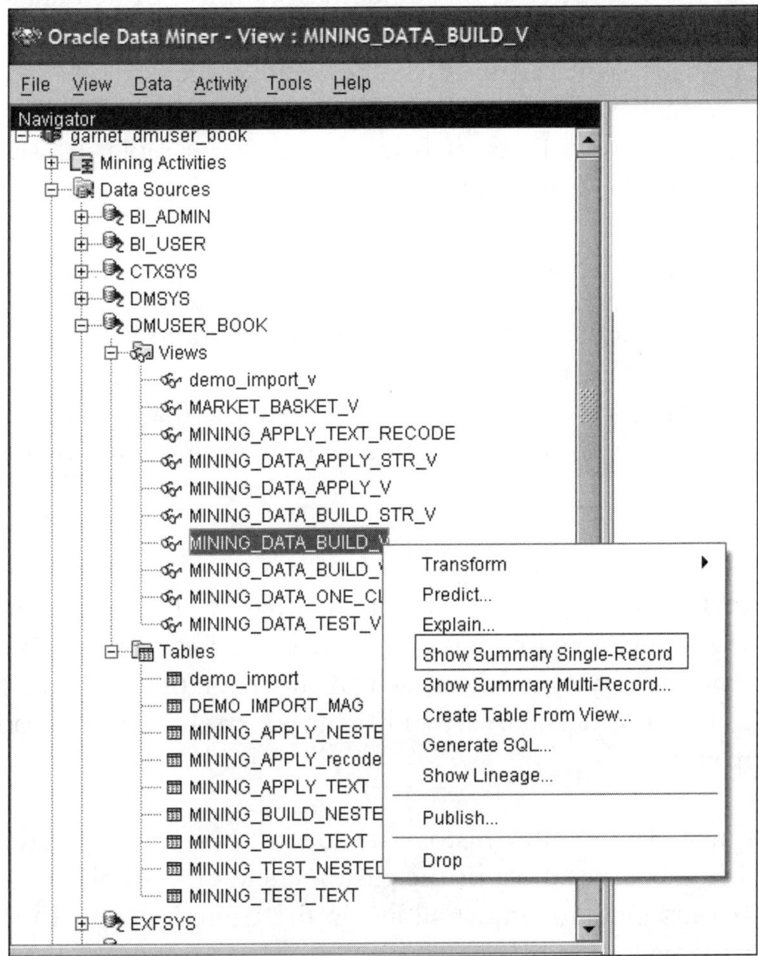

Figure 1.5: *Show Summary Single-Record.*

Using Show Summary Single Record, a new window opens up titled Data Summarization viewer. Note that in this instance the sample count is 999 records. Keep in mind that you can change the sample count by going to Tools, Preferences, and choosing the Sampling tab. You might like to try this now, and change the setting to 2000. Next time you view the Data Summarization viewer, you will notice that now the sample count is 1500, which is the entire data set. If you are reporting the summary statistics shown in the viewer, you will sometimes want the entire data set. Say for example that you need to report on the average age of your clientele. You can say that the average age is 38.89 years, ranging from 17 to 90 with a statistical variance of 185.95. These statistics are slightly different from the smaller sample displayed in Figure 1.6, where the average age is shown as 39.06 years.

Data Mining Histogram Display

Histograms are a powerful way to visually and statistically explore the data. In one glance you can see where most of your data is concentrated. You will know what country the majority of your customers reside in, and what age ranges are represented by your clientele.

The histogram will also show if the data is normally distributed. A normal distribution is the traditional bell-shaped curve described in introductory statistics courses. Histograms are very useful for identifying outliers, which are data points lying far outside the normal curve, and can adversely affect model performance.

In our raw dataset, the histograms describe un-normalized or skewed data because most of the customers in our sample are less than 40 years old and almost all live in the United States. In this section we will show how to view histograms of our customer population.

After selecting AGE as shown below, you will see a Preference and Histogram button on the right side of the screen. If you click on Preference here, you can change the number of bins in your sampling, but you cannot change the sample count, which in this case is now set to 2000.

Data Summarization Viewer: DMUSER_BOOK.MINING_DATA_BUILD_V

File Help

Sample Count: 999

Attribute Count: 18

Name	Mining ...	Attribut...	Average	Max	Min	Variance	Nulls
AFFINITY_CARD	categor...	NUMBER	0.23	1	0	0.18	0
AGE	numeri...	NUMBER	39.06	90	17	194.14	0
BOOKKEEPING_APPLICATI...	categor...	NUMBER	0.88	1	0	0.11	0
BULK_PACK_DISKETTES	categor...	NUMBER	0.61	1	0	0.24	0
COUNTRY_NAME	categor...	VARCH...					0
CUST_GENDER	categor...	CHAR					0
CUST_ID	numeri...	NUMBER	102,23...	102,999	101,502	185,64...	0
CUST_INCOME_LEVEL	categor...	VARCH...					0
CUST_MARITAL_STATUS	categor...	VARCH...					0
EDUCATION	categor...	VARCH...					0
FLAT_PANEL_MONITOR	categor...	NUMBER	0.57	1	0	0.25	0
HOME_THEATER_PACKAGE	categor...	NUMBER	0.57	1	0	0.25	0
HOUSEHOLD_SIZE	categor...	VARCH...					0
OCCUPATION	categor...	VARCH...					0
OS_DOC_SET_KANJI	categor...	NUMBER	0	1	0	0	0
PRINTER_SUPPLIES	categor...	NUMBER	1	1	1	0	0
YRS_RESIDENCE	numeri...	NUMBER	4.09	14	0	3.78	0
Y_BOX_GAMES	categor...	NUMBER	0.29	1	0	0.21	0

Preference...

Histogram

Figure 1.6: *Data Summarization View.*

We will examine the age attribute by clicking on histogram. With number of bins set to 10, the histogram will show 10 bars or groups, age values for each group, number of cases in each bin or bin count, and percent of total.

Numerical attributes like AGE and YRS_RESIDENCE are divided into bins of equal width between the minimum and maximum. The equiwidth binning strategy groups or bins the data so that each bin is the same width, irrespective of the number of cases in each bin. Quantile binning is an example of equidepth binning, where each bin contains roughly equal numbers of cases, irrespective of the width of the numerical range.

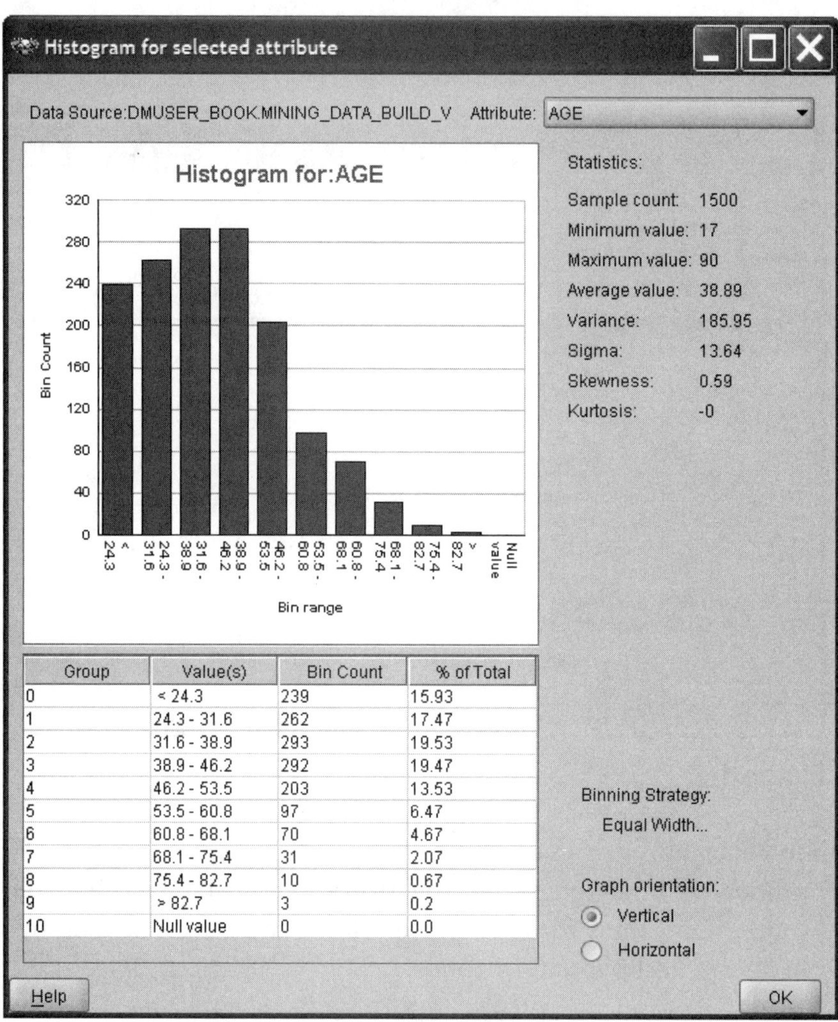

Figure 1.7: *Histogram for Age with 10 Bins.*

You can see that the proportion of young clients in this database is large. Change the number of bins to three and see what happens. Click Preference in the Data Summarization Viewer, and type 3.

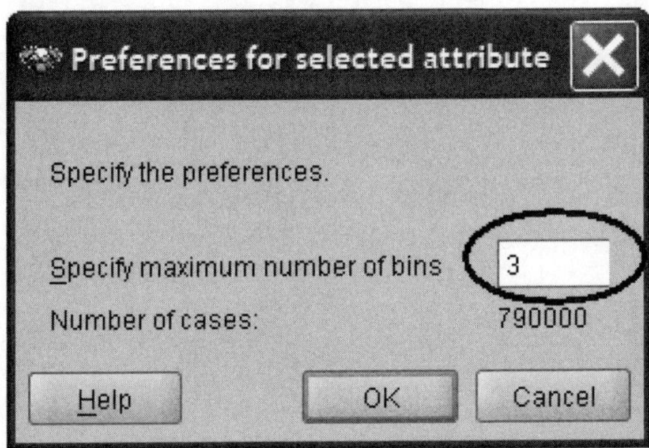

Figure 1.8: *Preferences for Selected Attribute*

Now there are three age groups, with group zero containing 904 cases less than 42 years, group one having 538 cases between 42 and 67, and group three with 58 cases over 67.

But suppose that you really wanted to divide your age groups into set age ranges, say 1 to 25, 25 to 30, and 30 to 65? Creating ranges of values will be demonstrated in Chapter 5.

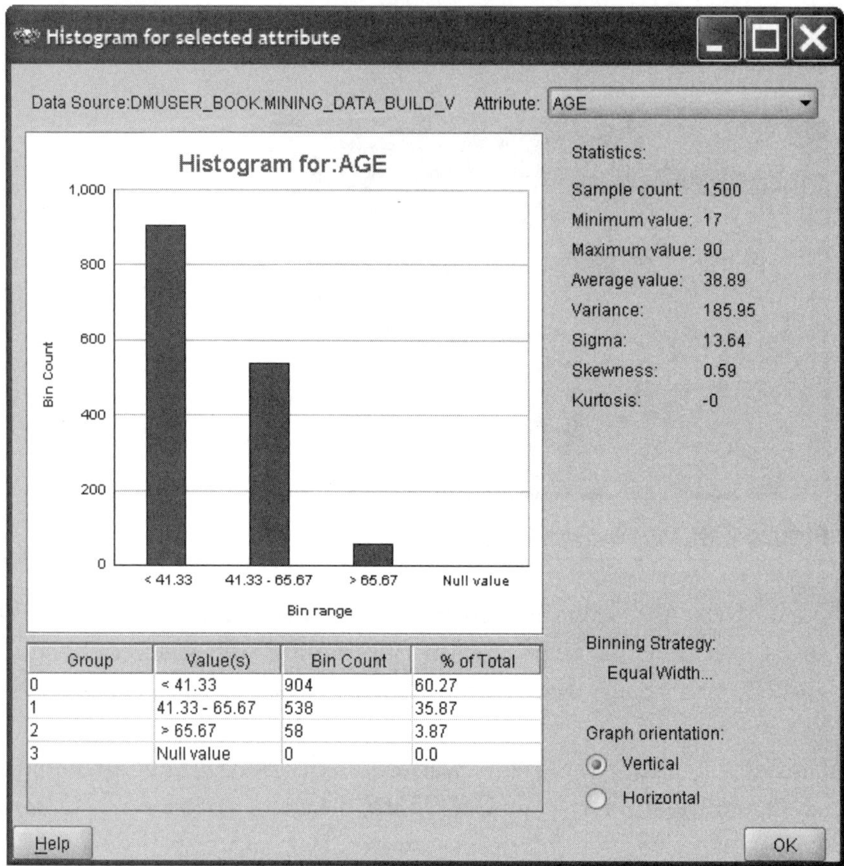

Group	Value(s)	Bin Count	% of Total
0	< 41.33	904	60.27
1	41.33 - 65.67	538	35.87
2	> 65.67	58	3.87
3	Null value	0	0.0

Figure 1.9: *Histogram for AGE with Three Bins.*

Notice that the attribute with AGE selected in the histogram window is a drop down list. You can choose each categorical and numerical field and view the histogram for each one. Categorical attributes are binned using the Top N method, where N is the number of bins. There are 19 different countries for COUNTRY_NAME, and if you leave the bins set to 10, as in top 10, the group labeled OTHER will contain South Africa, New Zealand, India, and so on. Setting the number of bins to 19 shows all countries individually. The mode is United States, where the majority of clients reside.

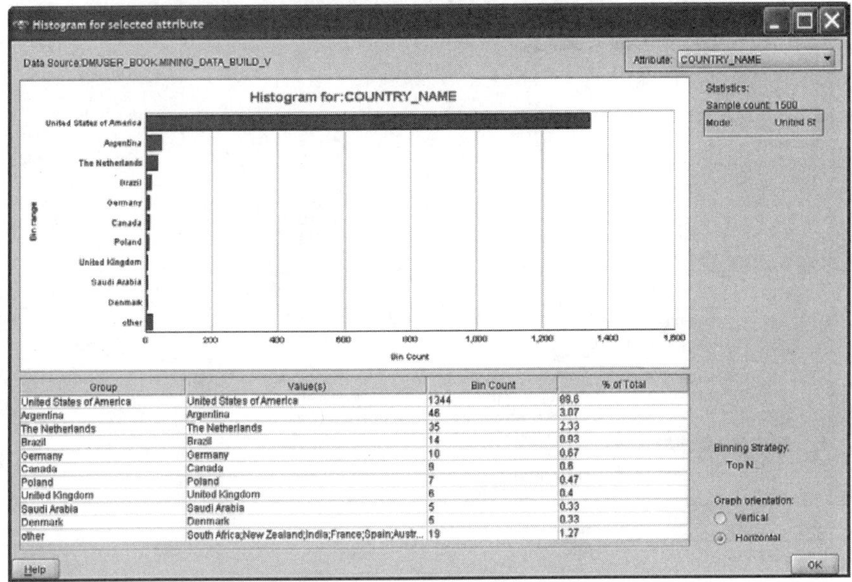

Figure 1.10: *Histogram for COUNTRY_NAME.*

Concentrating on a customer

Suppose we want to concentrate on our customers in the United States. We can filter the data so that only people living in the United States are included in our data mining activity. Right click MINING_ DATA_BUILD_V, choose Transform, then Filter Single Record. You could also click Data on the upper toolbar to reach the Filter Single-Record Transformation Wizard.

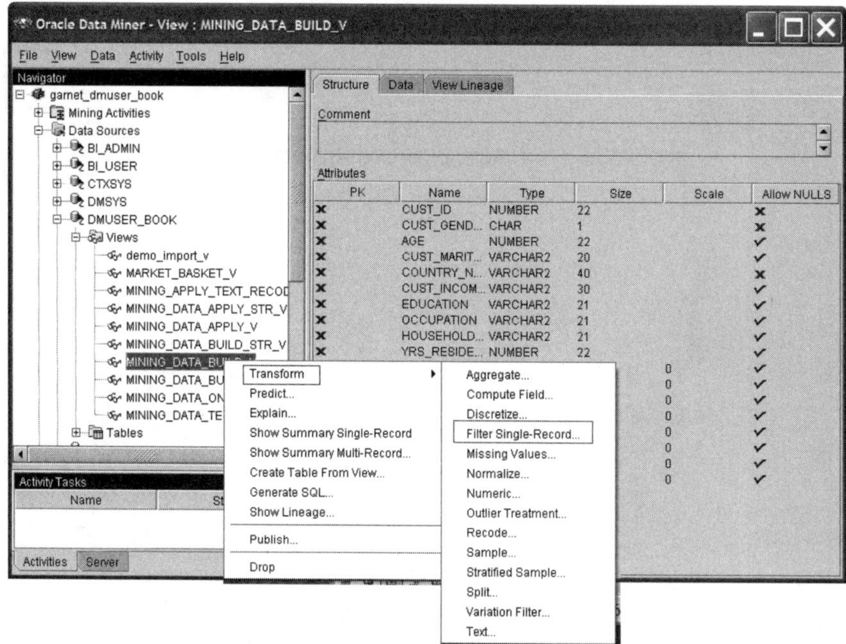

Figure 1.11: *Transformation Filter Wizard.*

After the introductory screen, click Next to go on to Step 1 of 3. Select the MINING_ DATA_BUILD_V view and click Next. Name the new view in Step 2 MINING_DATA_BUILD_V_US.

For the final step, click on the small box next to Filter to open the Expression Editor.

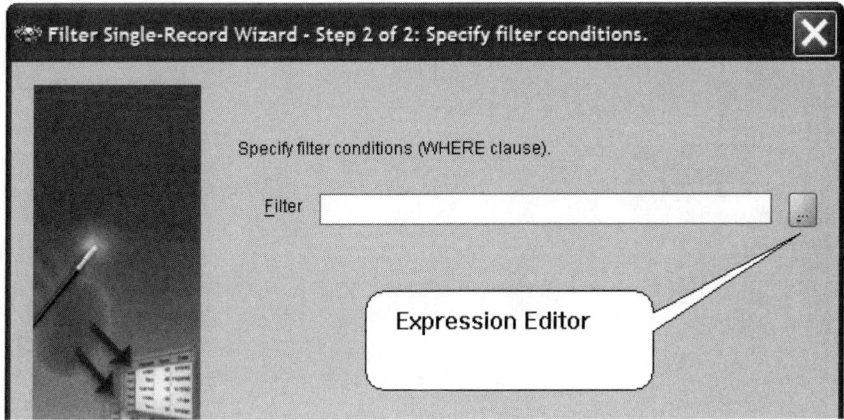

Figure 1.12: *Specify Filter Conditions.*

Use the editor to select COUNTRY_NAME, click the equal sign (=), and then type in 'United States of America'.

The message Validation successful should be displayed when you click Validate, and the expression builder shows:

```
"MINING_DATA_BUILD_V"."COUNTRY_NAME" = 'United States of America'.
```

Click OK. You may preview the results and then choose to generate a stored procedure by clicking Preview Transform on the Finish page. Click Finish to complete the transformation view containing only US customers.

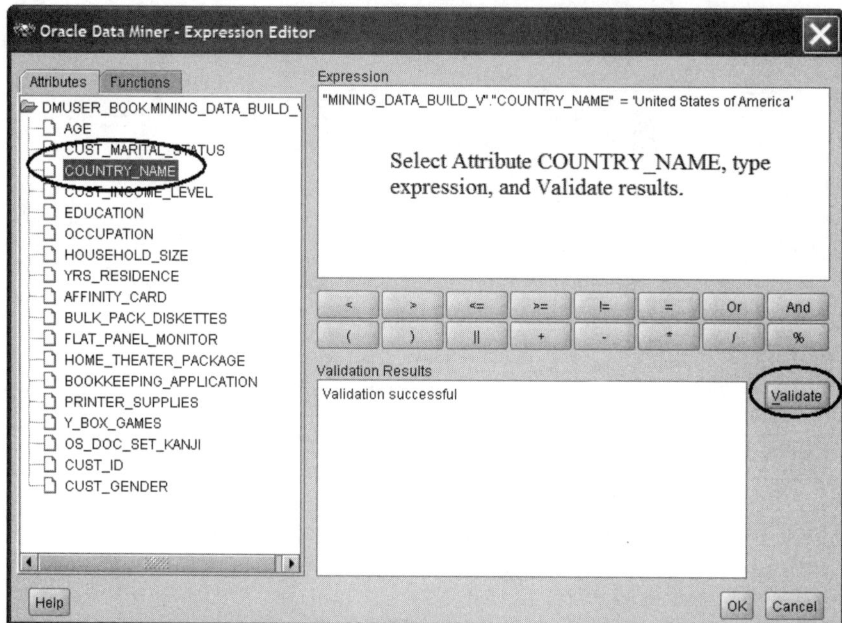

Figure 1.13: *Specify Filter Conditions.*

The following code was generated by the Wizard to create a new view for customers residing in the United States of America.

```
CREATE VIEW "DMUSER_BOOK"."MINING_DATA_BUILD_US_FILTER" AS
SELECT * FROM "DMUSER_BOOK"."MINING_DATA_BUILD_V" WHERE
"MINING_DATA_BUILD_V"."COUNTRY_NAME"  = 'United States of America'

COMMENT ON TABLE "DMUSER_BOOK".MINING_DATA_BUILD_US_FILTER IS
'Created by Filter Single-Record Wizard. Data source is Schema:
DMUSER_BOOK, Table: MINING_DATA_BUILD_V.'
```

Building a Classification Model

We have now completed defining the case table and are ready to begin building our model. Oracle Data Mining provides four algorithms for solving classification problems:

- Adaptive Bayes Network
- Decision Tree

- Naïve Bayes
- Support Vector Machine

Each classification data mining activity has distinct advantages depending on the data and the business solution. These will be described in more detail in the next chapter.

To start the classification problem, we will begin by using the Build Mining Activity to build a Naïve Bayes model. The Naïve Bayes algorithm has the advantage of being quick to run.

The Mining Activity Build wizard is launched from the Activity pull-down menu. Select Build to activate the wizard and click Next on the Welcome page. Choose the Classification function type, Naïve Bayes algorithm, and click Next.

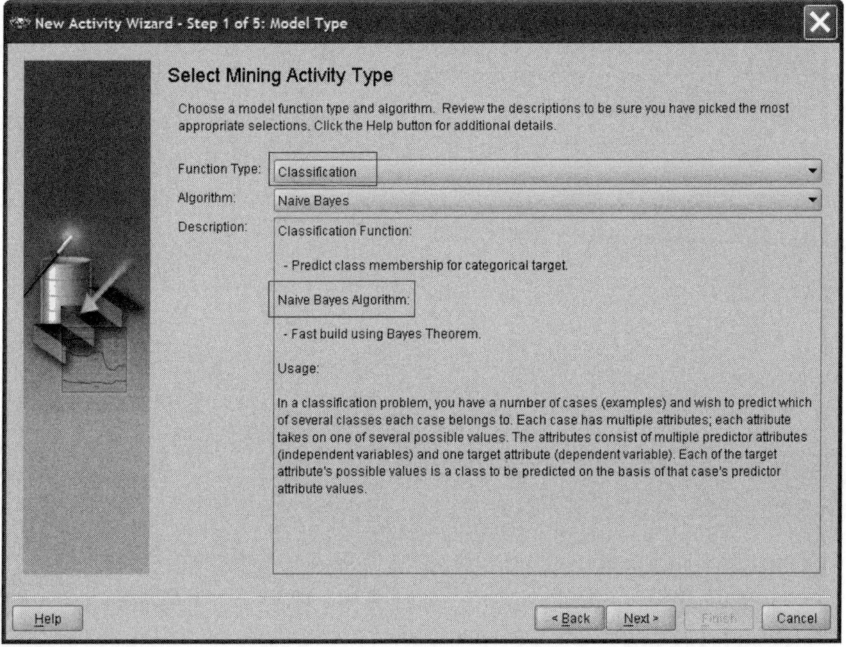

Figure 1.14: *Select Classification Algorithm.*

In Step 2 of the New Activity Wizard, select MINING_DATA_BUILD_V_US as the case table or view, choose Single Key CUST_ID as the unique identifier, and select all columns to include in the analysis. Note that clicking Sampling Settings opens a new window that allows you to change how the data is sampled. For this exercise we will keep the default Random sampling, which means that the subset will have approximately the same distribution of values for the target attribute as in the original data.

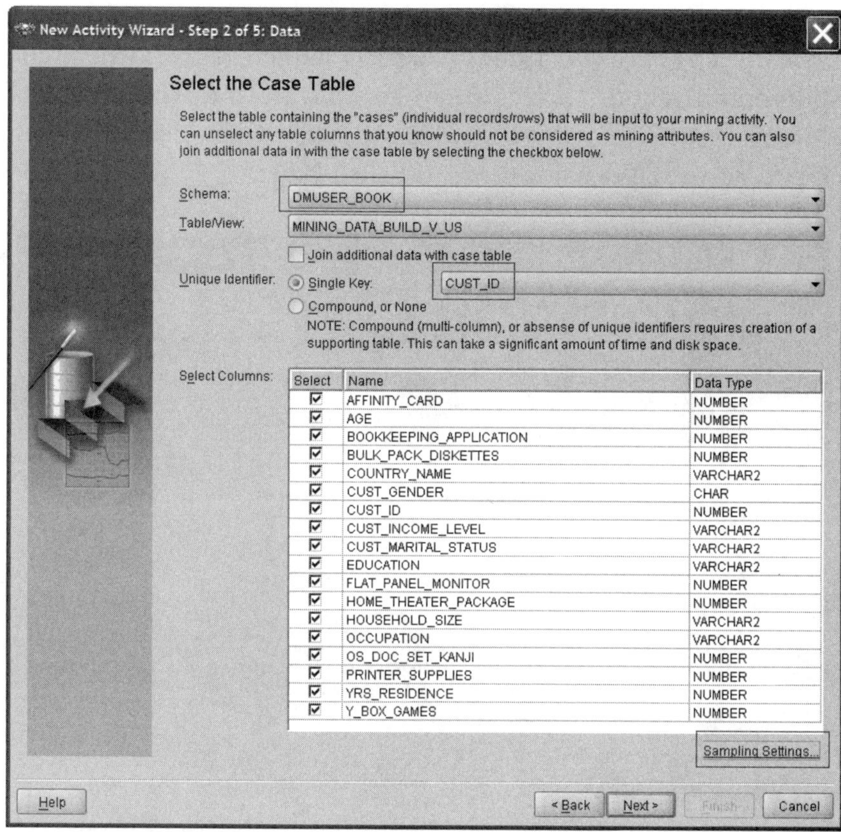

Figure 1.15: *Select Unique Identifier.*

In classification problems, a target is identified and in this case we are using the attribute AFFINITY_CARD to distinguish highly valued customers where 1 = High-value and 0 = Low-value. On step 3 of the New Activity Wizard, choose AFFINITY_CARD as the Target column. Selecting AFFINITY_CARD as the target identifies the customers predicted to be offered such a card. Note that COUNTRY_NAME and PRINTER_SUPPLIES were not automatically selected as attribute variables. Neither of these attributes will contribute to the classification model because there is only one country in this view, the United States, and all consumers order printer supplies. You can check this by clicking the Data Summary link and seeing that the average, max, and min columns for PRINTER_SUPPLIES are average =1, max = 1 and min = 1 with 0 variance.

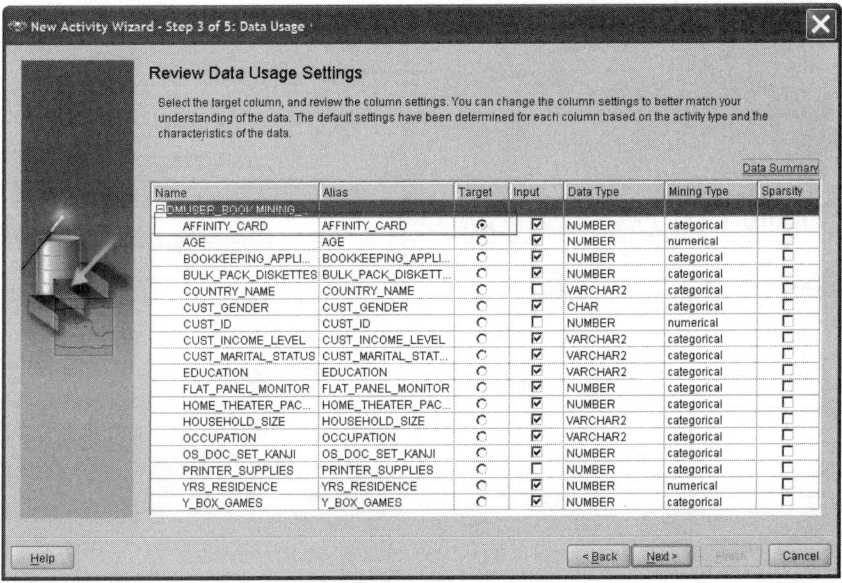

Figure 1.16: *Select Target Attribute.*

In step 4 of the New Activity Wizard, select 1 as the preferred target value which identifies the cases we are targeting, where our best customers have AFFINITY_CARD = 1.

Naming Data Mining Activities

For step 5, Data Miner provides a name for the data mining activity, but you will probably want to change this to a name that explains the activity, such as ALL_US_NB1 for all US customers, and Naïve Bayes activity = 1.

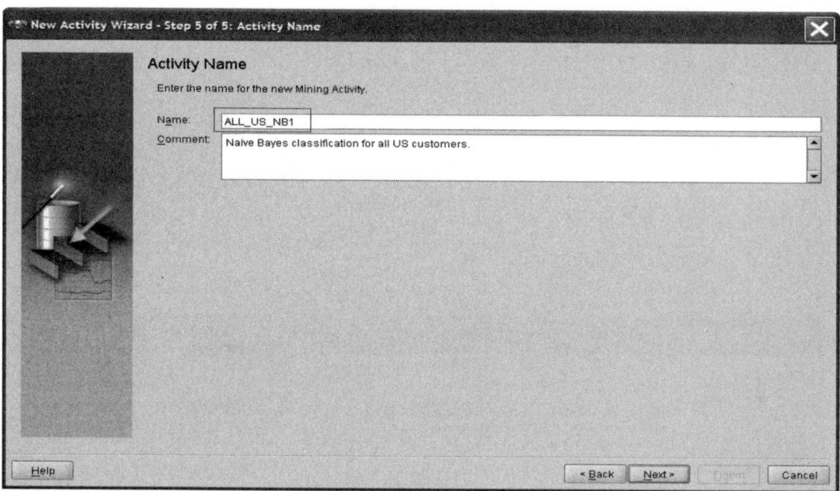

Figure 1.17: *Type Name of New Activity.*

On the final page, the New Activity Wizard is complete and the Data Mining Activity is set to run upon finish. Click Advanced Settings to display and possibly modify the default settings.

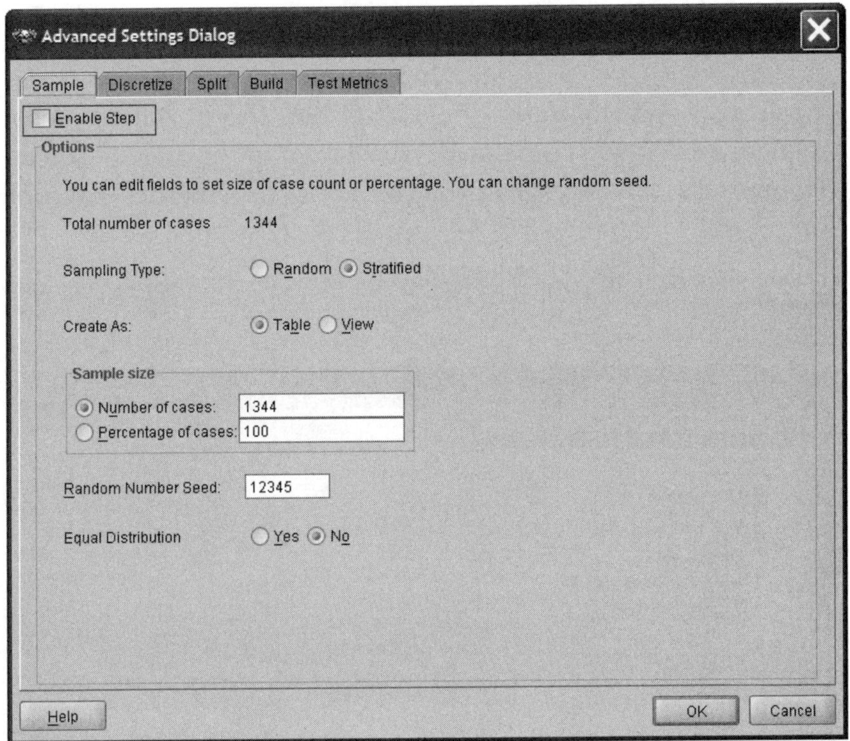

Figure 1.18: *View of Sampling Defaults.*

The Advanced Settings Dialog window shows five tabs: Sample, Discretize, Split, Build, and Test Metrics. The wizard has determined that sampling is not needed for this small dataset, and you will want to leave the Enable Step box unchecked. For now, accept the defaults, click OK or Cancel in the Advanced Settings Dialog window, and finish the model.

Now that we have configured the Naïve Bayes build settings, we are ready to run the Data Mining Activity and then determine how well the model fits, i.e. predicts the target. The next sections explore the Mining Activity steps, showing the completion of every phase necessary for building the classification model.

Running a Data Mining Activity

While the Activity runs, the status bar shows which steps in sequence are being completed. As shown in the activity screen in Figure 1.19, all steps from discretize to test metrics have been successfully completed. In our U.S. customer dataset, Data Miner skipped the sampling activity due to the small size of the dataset.

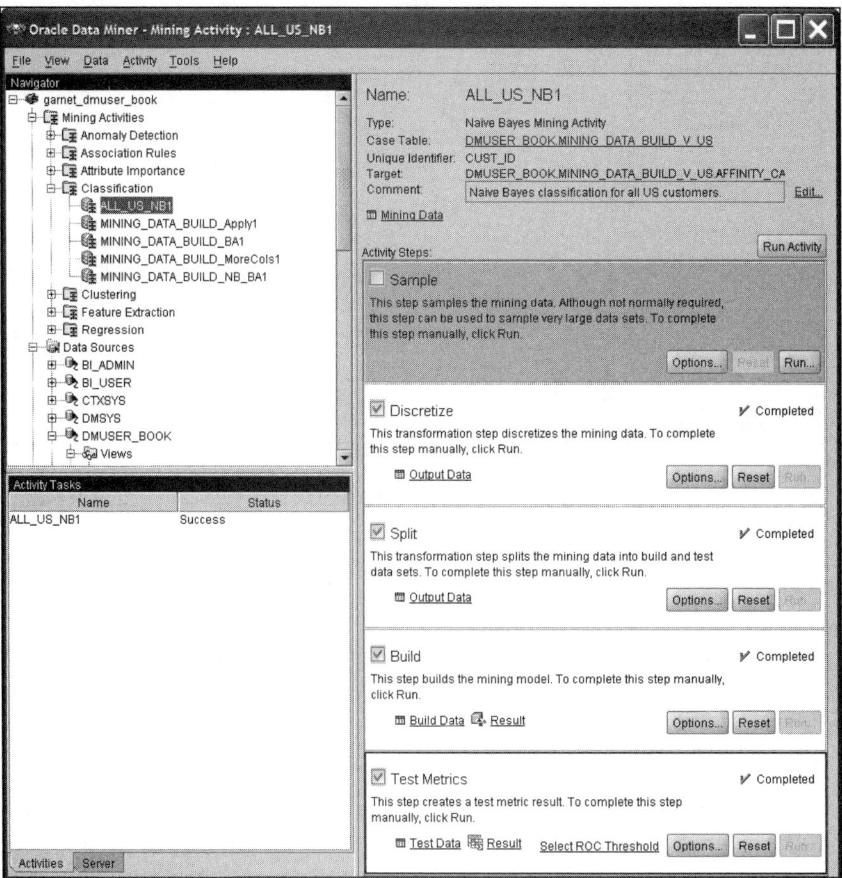

Figure 1.19: *Data Mining Activity.*

The Activity Wizard takes appropriate steps to ensure that numerical data and categorical data are divided into bins or discretized. The dataset is then separated into build and test sets by random selection of cases using the Split Transformation.

Finally, a classifier is constructed using the build dataset, and applied to the test set. Test metrics are summarized and written in the result section.

If one of the steps fails, an error message is displayed. You can re-run any of the Mining Activity Steps after reconfiguring the options, resetting the step, and clicking Run.

Viewing your Results

Here is a recap of our accomplishments up to this point. We explored the MINING_DATA_BUILD_V dataset by examining the structure, data and lineage of the view. Histograms revealed distributions of all attributes, showing statistics and graphical groupings of binned data. We sampled and reduced the dataset to customers residing in the United States. The Activity Wizard split the case dataset into training, or build, and test datasets. A Naïve Bayes classification model was built and tested. Now it is time to examine the results. Because the dataset is small and the training data was randomly selected, these results may be slightly different if you ran this analysis yourself.

Click Result in the test metric step to see the Result Viewer as shown in Figure 1.20. The Result Viewer has six tabs:

- Predictive Confidence
- Accuracy
- ROC
- Lift

- Test Settings
- Task

The first tab in the results window indicates that the Predictive Confidence is Good in comparison to the naïve model.

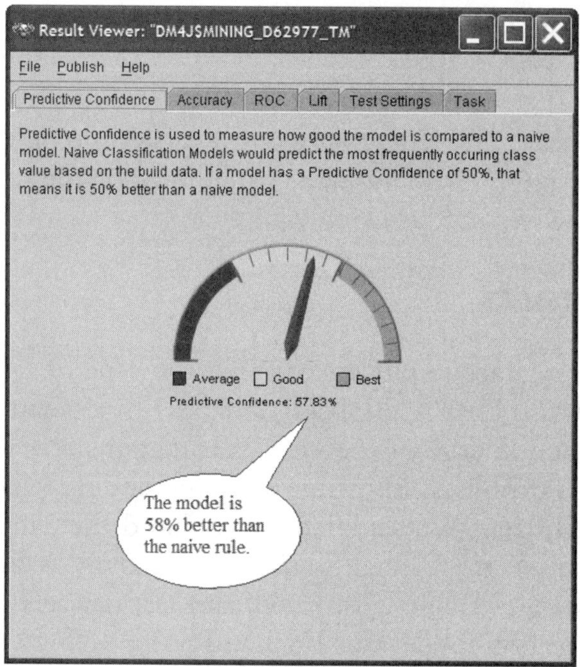

Figure 1.20: *Predictive Confidence.*

What does this mean? We ran the Naïve Model, did we not? In fact, we ran the Naïve Bayes classification model. The naïve model is a very simple method for classifying customers by classifying the record as a member of the majority class. The naïve rule is important as it is commonly used as a baseline for evaluating the performance of classification models. In our dataset MINING_DATA_BUILD_V_US, the majority of cases (74.18%) have AFFINITY_CARD = 0.

Ignoring all the predictor information that we have, the naïve rule would classify all customers as not having an affinity card. The predictive confidence of 57.83% indicates that the Naïve Bayes model we built is about 58% better than the naïve rule.

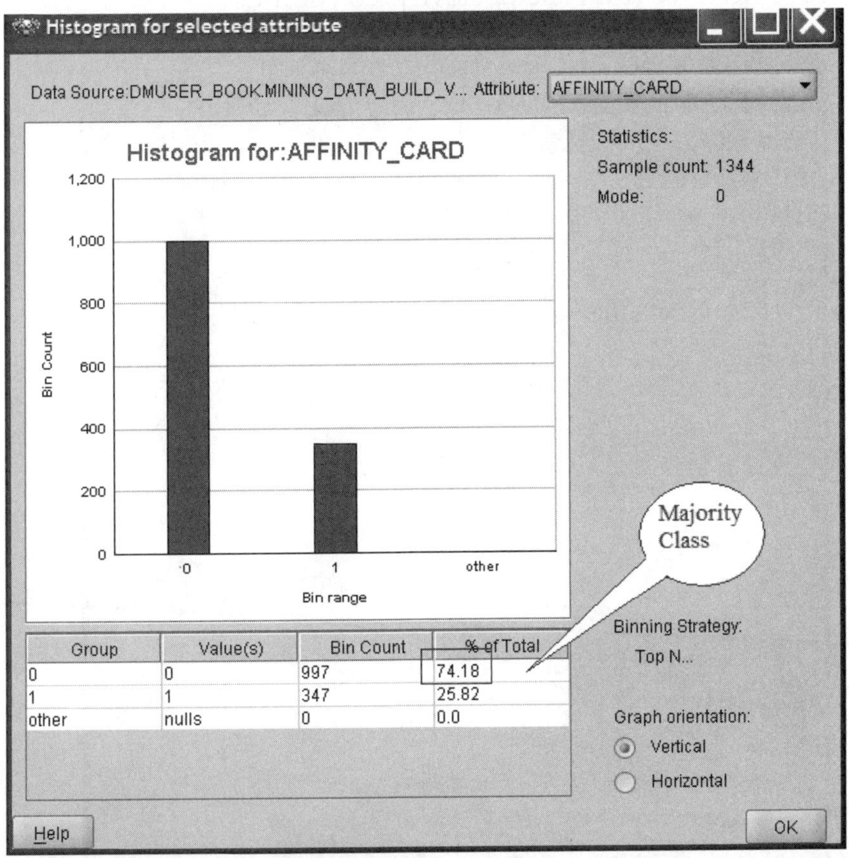

Group	Value(s)	Bin Count	% of Total
0	0	997	74.18
1	1	347	25.82
other	nulls	0	0.0

Figure 1.21: *Histogram for AFFINITY_CARD.*

The Accuracy tab takes us to the classification matrix, also called the confusion matrix, where the model is applied to the hold-out test sample. Click the More Detail button to view the confusion matrix. The columns are the predictions made by the classification model and the rows are the actual data. The overall accuracy of the model is 77%, with 312 cases correctly classified as No-Affinity Card because they did not have one, and 26 misclassified as not having one. Similarly, 105 cases were accurately classified as having a card, and 127 were misclassified as having one. The cases that the model misclassified are the false-negative and false-positive predictions.

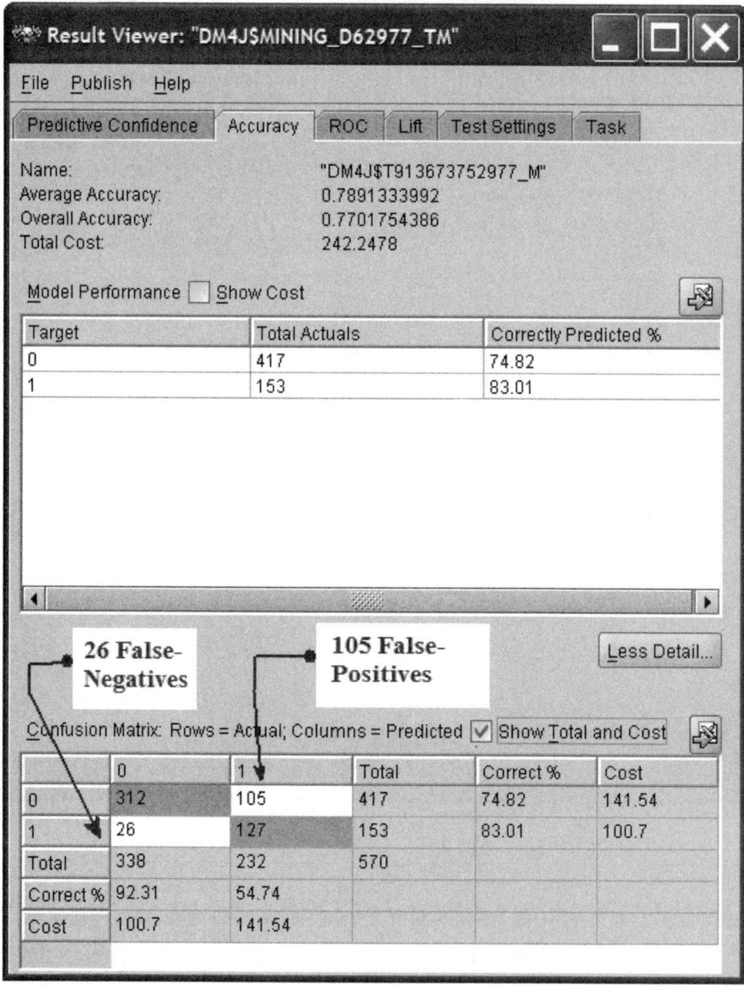

	0	1	Total	Correct %	Cost
0	312	105	417	74.82	141.54
1	26	127	153	83.01	100.7
Total	338	232	570		
Correct %	92.31	54.74			
Cost	100.7	141.54			

Figure 1.22: *Model Accuracy.*

Oracle Data Mining Lift Curve

The Lift tab demonstrates two graphical interpretations of the results, the cumulative lift and cumulative positive cases chart. The lift tab is important because it measures the efficiency of the model. The lift curve, also called a gains curve or gains chart, is a popular technique in direct marketing.

We want our classification model to sift through the records and sort them according to which customers are more likely to respond to our mailing.

The lift curve will help us discover how to effectively skim the cream off our mailing list so we pick the smallest number of cases with the greatest probability of answering our mailing campaign.

Data Miner applies the model to the test data, sorts the predicted results by probability, divides the ranked list into 10 equal parts or quantiles, and counts the actual positive values in each quantile.

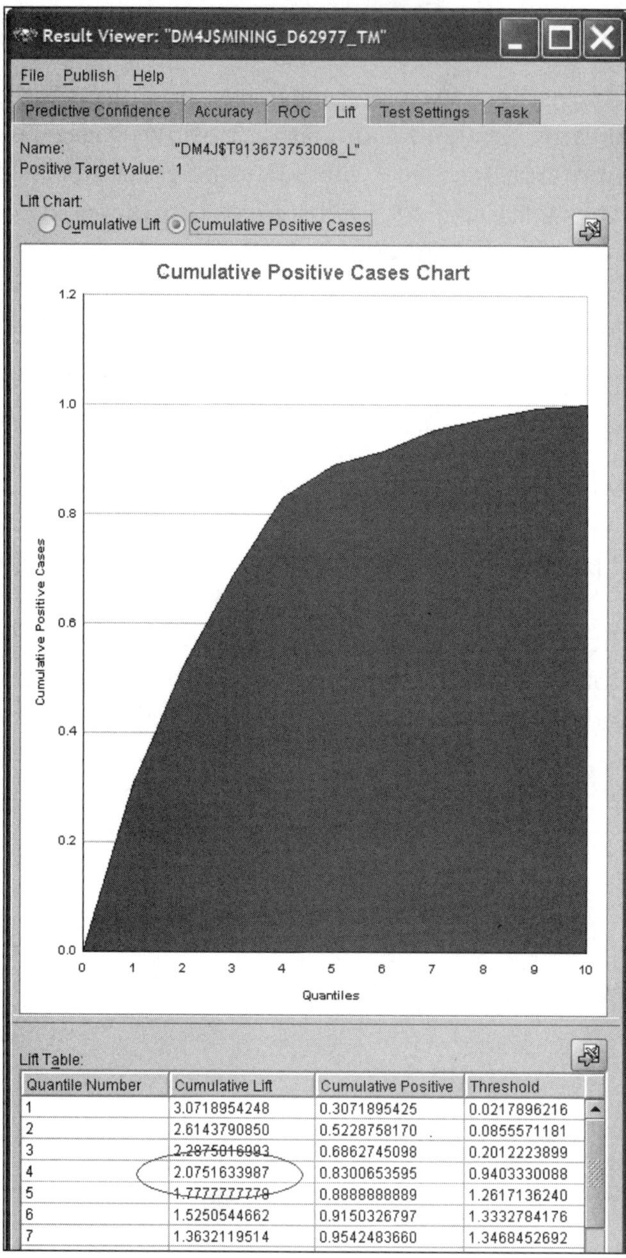

Quantile Number	Cumulative Lift	Cumulative Positive	Threshold
1	3.0718954248	0.3071895425	0.0217896216
2	2.6143790850	0.5228758170	0.0855571181
3	2.2875816993	0.6862745098	0.2012223899
4	2.0751633987	0.8300653595	0.9403330088
5	1.7777777778	0.8888888889	1.2617136240
6	1.5250544662	0.9150326797	1.3332784176
7	1.3632119514	0.9542483660	1.3468452692

Figure 1.23: *Model Lift.*

The test results indicate that if we take the top 40%, or quantile number four, we will have at least twice the response expected from random sampling. A good classifier will give us a high lift to help maximize the number of responders to our ad campaign.

The next section explores what if scenarios using the Receiver Operating Characteristic (ROC) metric. Oracle Data Miner provides an interactive tool that allows us to change the classification model. We can experiment with model settings to change the confusion matrix. We can alter the false negatives, and observe the effects of these changes on the positive predictions. An example of using the ROC to modify the classification model is described in the next section.

The ODM ROC Curve

A similar curve to the lift chart is the Receiver Operating Characteristic or ROC curve. The ROC curve uses the same metric on the y-axis as the lift curve, versus the number of true negatives correctly classified, for different cutoff levels.

The default cutoff level is 0.5, meaning that if the probability assigned to a particular case is greater than 0.5, a positive prediction is made. However, we may be more interested in customers who should be offered an affinity card than those who do not.

We may have a budget constraint so we can only print 150 brochures. The false negatives in our model amount to 77 cases. The red vertical line is set at 0.5 probability threshold. The false negative value can be reduced as much as possible with the requirement that we keep the total number of positive predictions under 150.

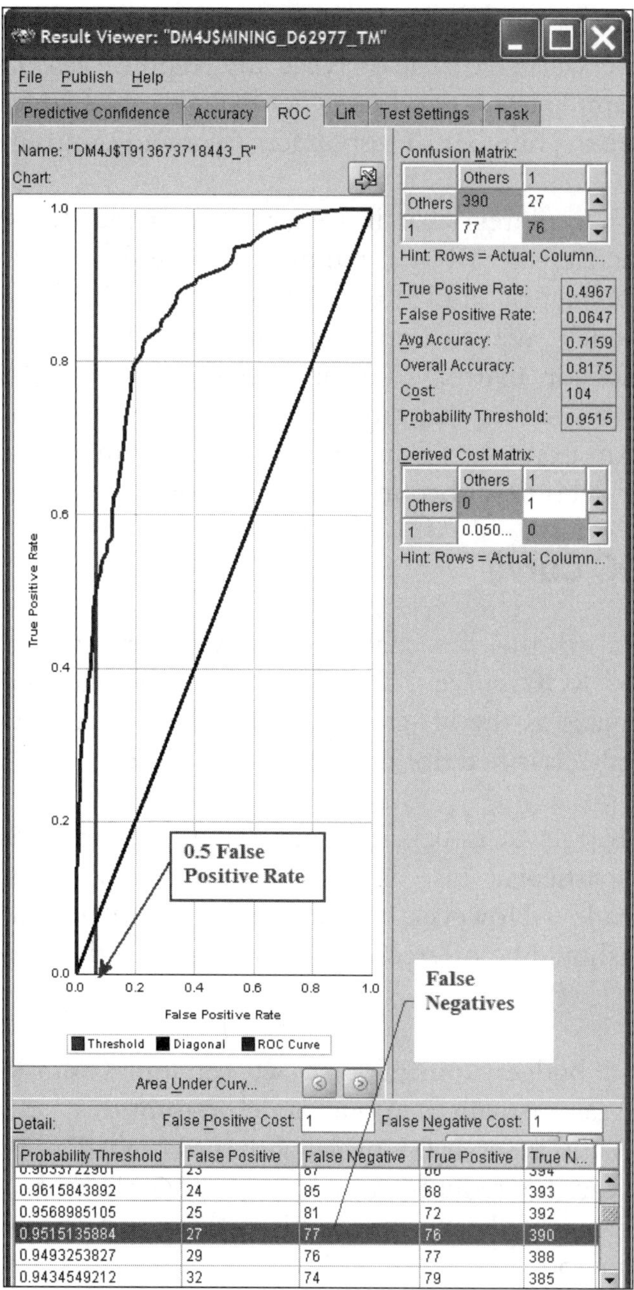

Figure 1.24: *ROC of the Model.*

By moving the vertical line to the right, the values are changed in the confusion matrix.

Changing the probability threshold to 0.886 reduces the false negatives from 77 to 58, and keeps the total number of positives (52 + 95 = 147) to less than 150. Now that we have modified the ROC chart, we can use these metrics when we apply the model to our dataset.

Applying changes to a Model

To change the classification model, we can follow these steps:

1. Return to the Mining Activity display for ALL_US_NB1 and click on the ROC Threshold:0.95151359 link in the Test Metrics block.
2. Move the vertical line to 0.88639 or click this value under Probability Threshold, then click OK.
3. You will see that the ROC Threshold has the new value. You do not need to re-run the test step for this new threshold to be used when you apply the model.

Figure 1.25: *ROC Threshold.*

Attribute Importance in the Naïve Bayes Model

Data Miner has an Attribute Importance feature that ranks the attributes by significance in determining the target value. Attribute Importance can be used to reduce the size of a classification problem by eliminating some attributes, and consequently increase speed and accuracy when building models.

We will use Data Miner's Attribute Importance analysis to find the highest ranking attributes and use these to build another Naïve Bayes classification model.

Pick Attribute Importance under Activity Build and choose MINING_DATA_BUILD_US as the case table. Use Customer ID as the unique identifier, and keep the default columns that the activity chooses to build the model. Finish and run the Activity. Upon completion, we can view the ranking results for customer buying habits, as shown in Figure 1.26.

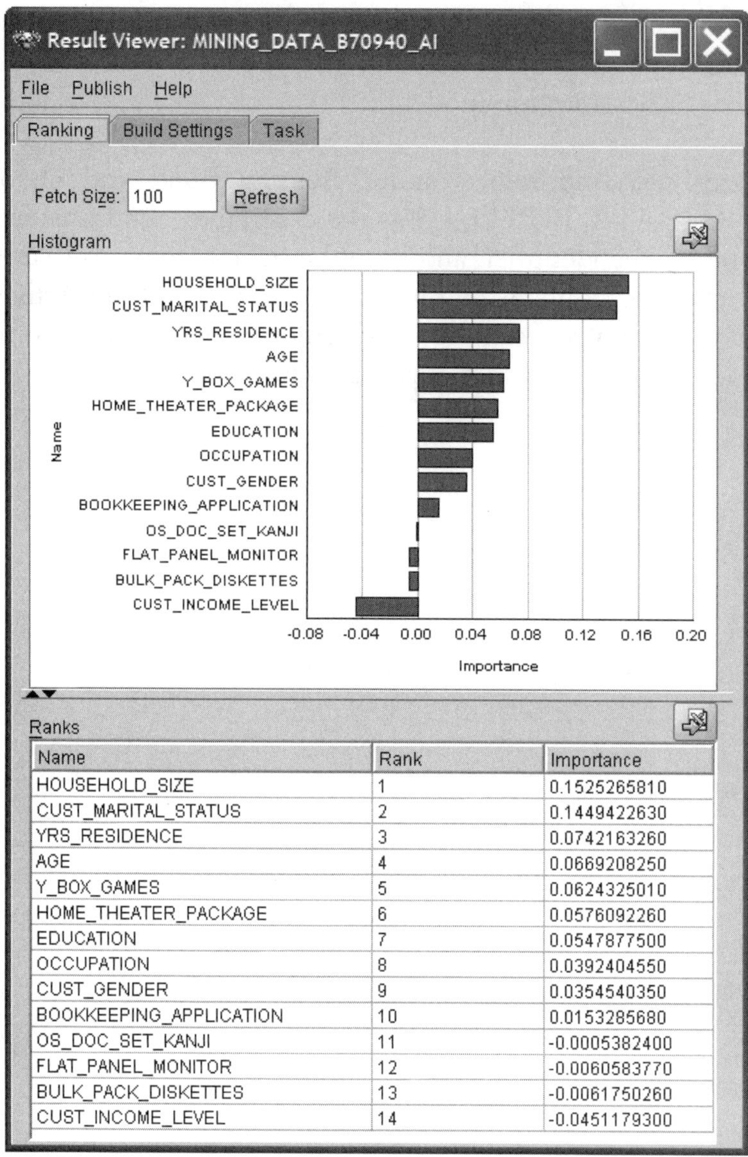

Name	Rank	Importance
HOUSEHOLD_SIZE	1	0.1525265810
CUST_MARITAL_STATUS	2	0.1449422630
YRS_RESIDENCE	3	0.0742163260
AGE	4	0.0669208250
Y_BOX_GAMES	5	0.0624325010
HOME_THEATER_PACKAGE	6	0.0576092260
EDUCATION	7	0.0547877500
OCCUPATION	8	0.0392404550
CUST_GENDER	9	0.0354540350
BOOKKEEPING_APPLICATION	10	0.0153285680
OS_DOC_SET_KANJI	11	-0.0005382400
FLAT_PANEL_MONITOR	12	-0.0060583770
BULK_PACK_DISKETTES	13	-0.0061750260
CUST_INCOME_LEVEL	14	-0.0451179300

Figure 1.26: *Attribute Ranking Customer Buying Habits.*

You see that the Attribute Importance activity ranked HOUSEHOLD_SIZE as the most important attribute, followed by marital status and so on. Now we will use this information in a new Naïve Bayes model.

Building Naïve Bayes Model with Fewer Attributes

Under the Activity menu pick Build, then Classification as the function type, and Naïve Bayes as the algorithm.

1. Choose MINING_DATA_BUILD_V_US for the case table, and customer ID (CUST_ID) as the unique identifier. De-select BULK_PACK_DISKETTES, COUNTRY_NAME, CUST_INCOME_LEVEL, FLAT_PANEL_MONITOR, OS_DOC_SET_KANJI, and PRINTER_SUPPLIES from the Select Columns box. The top ten ranked attributes from the Attribute Importance algorithm remain in the model.
2. Click next and check AFFINITY_CARD for the target column. Keep Preferred Target Value = 1, and name the activity MINING_DATA_BUILD_US_NB2.
3. When you click Finish, the Activity Wizard will show the progress of sampling, discretizing, splitting, building, and testing the new model. Click on Result, Accuracy and More Detail to view the confusion matrix.

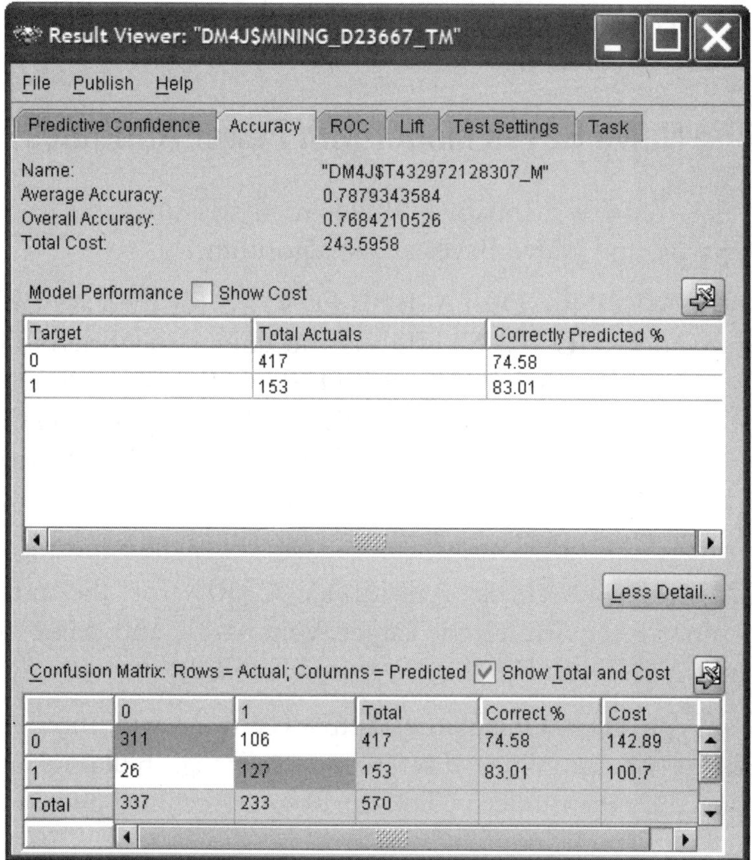

Figure 1.27: *Model Accuracy Naïve Bayes.*

Table 1.1 shows the predictive accuracy, average accuracy, overall accuracy, and total cost between the two models. These differences appear to be negligible, showing that you can drop one third of the data columns and not lose accuracy in the model, possibly saving time and money.

	PREDICTIVE ACCURACY	AVERAGE ACCURACY	OVERALL ACCURACY	COST
Model with 14 attributes	57.8%	78.9%	77.0%	242
Model with 10 attributes	57.6	78.8%	76.8%	244

Table 1.1: *Number of Attributes effect on Naïve Bayes Model Accuracy*

Applying the Model

Now we will apply the model to new data so that we can prepare our mailing list. This is also known as scoring the data. When a model is applied to new data, the data must be prepared and transformed in exactly the same way that the original source data was prepared prior to model building. Remember that we built the naïve classification model on a subset of the MINING_DATA_BUILD_V, which were all the United States of America customers. Now, the model will be applied to all other customers.

Using the Create View Wizard

We want to create a new view, so in the main toolbar, click on Data, then Create View to start the Create View Builder. Expand the data source list under your connection and double click on the MINING_DATA_BUILD_V view. The column names will appear in the window; click on the top-most box to select all the attributes.

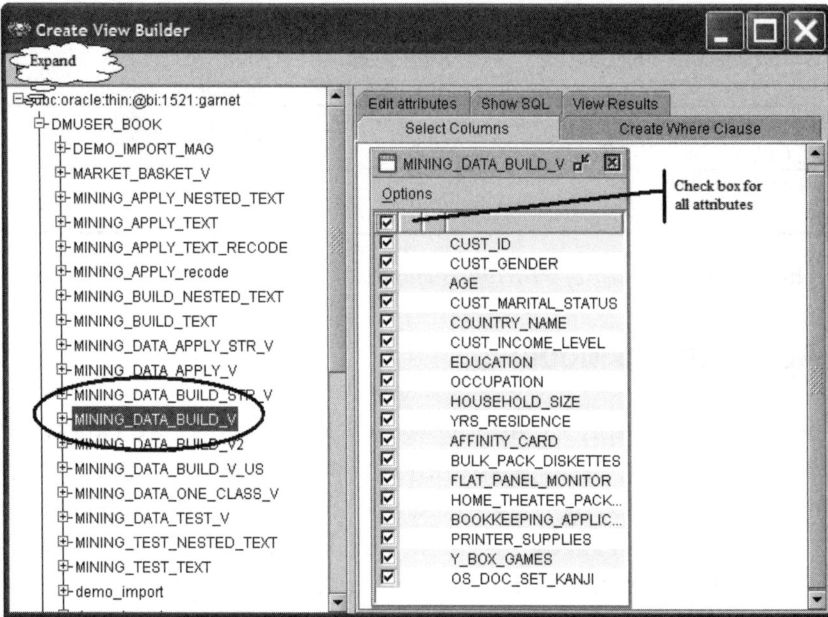

Figure 1.28: *Create View Wizard.*

Under the Create Where Clause, choose COUNTRY_NAME and Doesn't Contain from the drop-down lists, and type in "America" in the third box.

Click the View Results tab to see what the dataset looks like, and if satisfactory, choose Create View under File. Type in a name for the new view, such as MINING_DATA_BUILD_V_NOUS and click OK.

The following describes the process of applying the model to the MINING_DATA_BUILD_V_NOUS.

Launch the Activity Guide Apply wizard from the Activity menu. Choose the ALL_US_NB1 model under Classification. All the information about data preparation and model metadata will be passed to the Apply Activity from the build model.

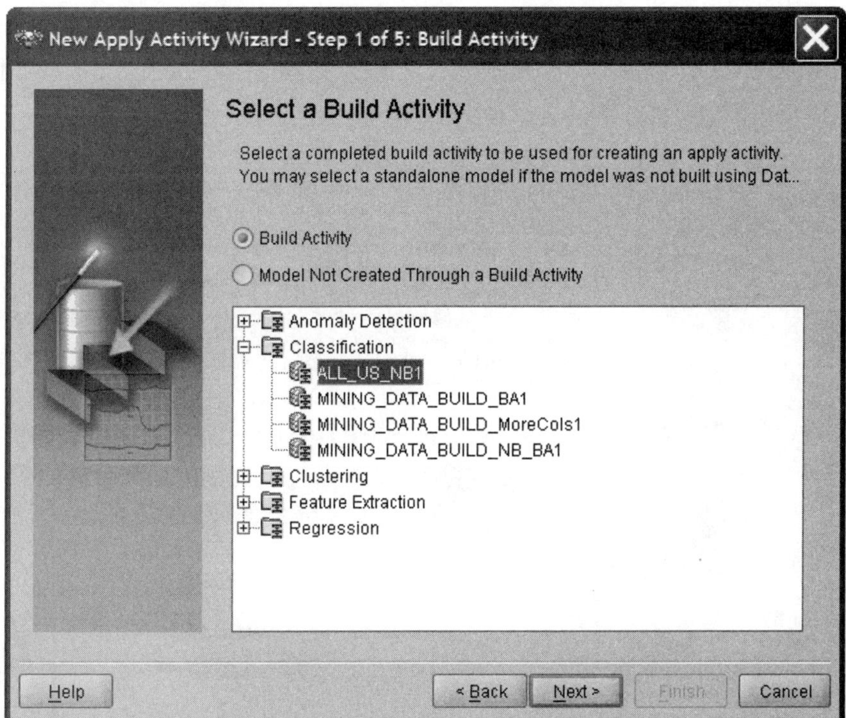

Figure 1.29: *Select a Build Activity.*

Scoring New Data

The next step is to select the apply data source that was created as MINING_DATA_BUILD_V_NOUS in Step 2 of the Apply Data wizard, and click Next.

Now you have the option of selecting additional columns to be included in the table resulting from the Apply operation. The wizard suggests that you include the customer identity attribute so that you can uniquely identify which customers are most likely to have an affinity card.

By default, the Apply Result contains only the case identifier and prediction information. You may want to keep the bare bones set of predictor variables and join this with tables containing the customer contact information later. Select some or all of the attributes in Step 3, and click Next.

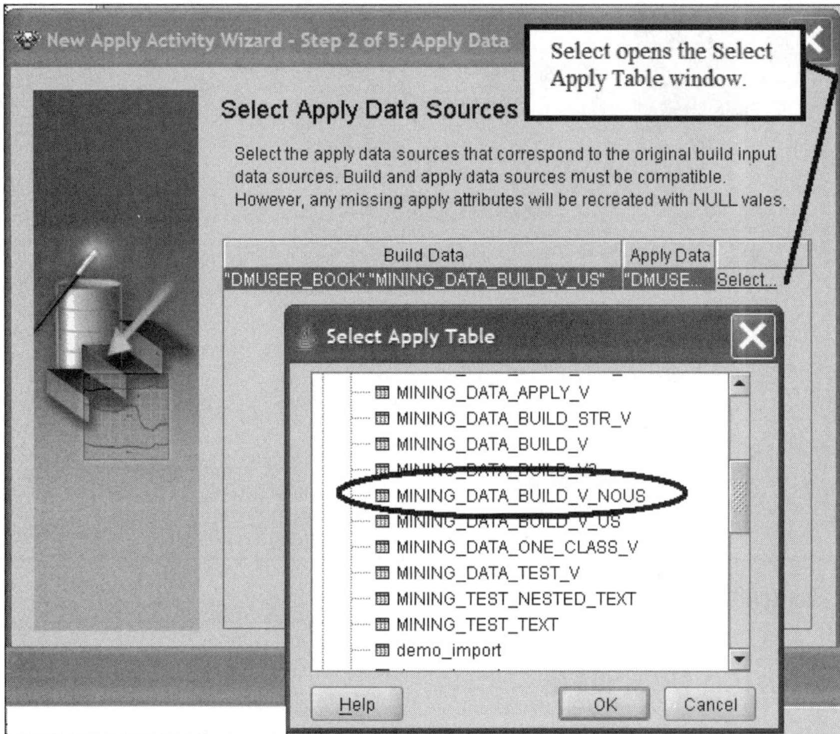

Figure 1.30: *Select Apply Data Source.*

The next step allows you to choose the format for the output table. When the model is applied to a particular customer, a score is generated for each possible target value. A sorted list is generated from the most to least likely value. This list will have only two entries since our target is binary, because our customers either have or do not have an affinity card.

Viewing Top Rankings

The Naïve Bayes, Decision Tree and Adaptive Bayes Network algorithms can be used for both binary, yes/no or 1/0, and multiclass classification problems. Binary targets will have only two values, whereas multiclass targets have more than two values. If your business case had a multiclass target, as in the case of predicting which of 10 stores a customer is most likely to shop, then you might want to see the ranking of the top three choices for each customer, and would click the radio button next to Number of Best Target Values and enter in 3. The output table would have three rows for each individual containing the prediction information for the top three stores.

In the case of which of ten stores the customer is most likely to shop, you may only be interested in a customer's ranking probability for a particular store. Then you would check the radio button next to Specific Target Values and check the box next to the particular store you were interested in. The result would be a table with one row for each customer with the prediction for that store, even though the probability might be extremely low.

Using the Classification Apply Option

The Classification Apply Option has as the default the most probable target value or lowest cost. In our case, the default selection will be kept and you will click Next, opting for an output table with one row per customer. Choose a name, such as ALL_US_APPLY_NON_US, for the Apply Data Mining Activity.

When the Activity has finished running, click Result in the Apply section to view the output table. Since we chose the Most Probable classification option, the table contains the customer or case ID, the predictor variables; prediction, probability, cost and rank, and finally the additional attributes you chose to have in the output table.

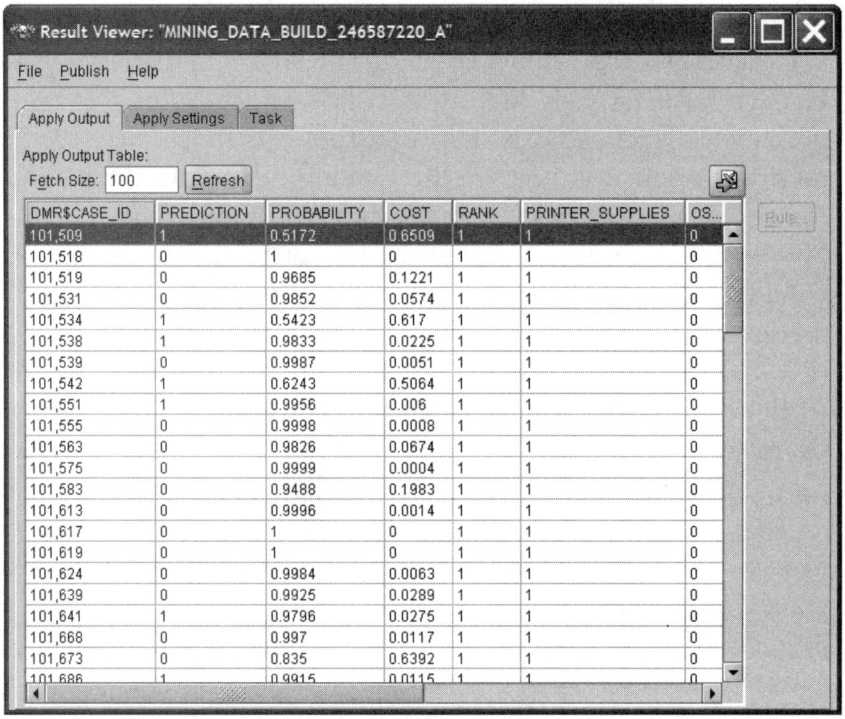

Result Viewer: "MINING_DATA_BUILD_246587220_A"

File Publish Help

Apply Output | Apply Settings | Task

Apply Output Table:

Fetch Size: 100 Refresh

DMR$CASE_ID	PREDICTION	PROBABILITY	COST	RANK	PRINTER_SUPPLIES	OS...
101,509	1	0.5172	0.6509	1	1	0
101,518	0	1	0	1	1	0
101,519	0	0.9685	0.1221	1	1	0
101,531	0	0.9852	0.0574	1	1	0
101,534	1	0.5423	0.617	1	1	0
101,538	1	0.9833	0.0225	1	1	0
101,539	0	0.9987	0.0051	1	1	0
101,542	1	0.6243	0.5064	1	1	0
101,551	1	0.9956	0.006	1	1	0
101,555	0	0.9998	0.0008	1	1	0
101,563	0	0.9826	0.0674	1	1	0
101,575	0	0.9999	0.0004	1	1	0
101,583	0	0.9488	0.1983	1	1	0
101,613	0	0.9996	0.0014	1	1	0
101,617	0	1	0	1	1	0
101,619	0	1	0	1	1	0
101,624	0	0.9984	0.0063	1	1	0
101,639	0	0.9925	0.0289	1	1	0
101,641	1	0.9796	0.0275	1	1	0
101,668	0	0.997	0.0117	1	1	0
101,673	0	0.835	0.6392	1	1	0
101,686	1	0.9915	0.0115	1	1	0

Rule...

Figure 1.31: *Scored Data.*

The prediction is the most likely target value for that case, and the probability is the confidence in that prediction. Cost represents the cost of a wrong prediction, with low cost meaning high probability. The rank will be 1 for all cases since we did not choose a predictor variable with more than two possible outcomes, and consequently do not have more values to predict.

Now, table MINING_DATA_BUILD_246587220_A can be joined with another table containing the customer ID, name, and address information, having prediction = 1.

We have now completed building, testing and applying a model to our customer data. We can go back to the boss having produced a mailing list in our data warehouse that should draw in the most promising customers.

Conclusion

This chapter introduced the Data Mining tool, and went through a complete classification model build using sample data supplied during installation of the tool.

Very useful tools Data Miner tools for sampling datasets were introduced. The chapter demonstrated how to view the data, structure, and lineage of a table or view. Using Show Summary Single-Record we examined attributes and statistics of the dataset, and viewed histograms of the attributes. The Filter Single Record transformation wizard was used to create a new subset of data. The data was modeled using the Naïve Bayes classification algorithm, and the results were reviewed for accuracy. The test metrics were modified and the resultant model was applied to a new dataset created using the Create View Wizard.

We are now ready to take a closer look at data mining classification models to understand how they are used for data mining and predictive analysis. We will start with the Naïve Bayes model and move on to Support Vector Machines algorithms.

Adaptive Bayes Network and Decision Trees

CHAPTER 2

Introduction to Classification

One of the most basic types of data mining is classification. Customers can be loyal or go elsewhere for service. Tax returns can be fraudulent or not. Hospital patients can get better, remain ill, or fare worse. Treatment can succeed or fail. A very common task in data mining is to examine data where the classification is unknown and predict what the classification will be.

Data Mining Classification Models

Oracle Data Miner provides the choice of four different classification models, Naïve Bayes, which was described in Chapter 1, Adaptive Bayes, Decision Tree, and Support Vector Machine. Each approach has distinct advantages over the other, so which one will be the best? The exploratory nature of data mining lends itself to investigating many different techniques and algorithms.

As a general rule, try several different algorithms and examine the differences between the results. Because we are looking for patterns that are most likely unknown to us, we may not even find any useful results at all! The patterns we see may not be meaningful or practical to apply. The usefulness of an algorithm can depend on the size of the dataset, the types of patterns that may exist in the data, meeting the underlying assumptions of the algorithm, the type of data, the goal of the analysis, and many other factors.

Using the Models

In this chapter we will build models with the Adaptive Bayes Network and Decision Tree algorithms. We will use the data import capability to import data into the Oracle database, and describe how to configure the algorithm settings to produce the best results for our dataset, using attribute importance, costs, and priors. As shown in the last chapter, the Naïve Bayes model can be tweaked to perform better given the nature of the data, modifying algorithm settings, or changing results by modifying costs with the receiver operating characteristics (ROC) curve. We also re-designed the Naïve Bayes Model built in Chapter One using a subset of attributes as determined by the Attribute Importance algorithm.

We start with an example of predicting forest cover type using geographical data from the US Forest Service Resource Information System. The dataset available as Forest CoverType under Classification on the UCI KDD Archives site (http://kdd.ics.uci.edu/summary.task.type.html) has 581,012 observations with 54 attributes regarding geological survey characteristics of the land, wilderness area designation, and soil type. The target classifications are 7 types of forest cover:

- 1 = spruce/fir
- 2 = lodgepole pine
- 3 = ponderosa pine
- 4 = cottonwood/willow
- 5 = aspen

- 6 = Douglas-fir
- 7 = Krummholz

Importing a Dataset

We start by importing the data using the Data Miner Import Wizard found under the Data tab. Using the Import Wizard, you can import files with a variety of field delimiters, including comma, hyphen, period, space, tab, vertical bar, white space, and user defined. On step 2 of the Import Wizard, you can choose the field delimiter, field enclosure, preview the data, and use column headings if they are present.

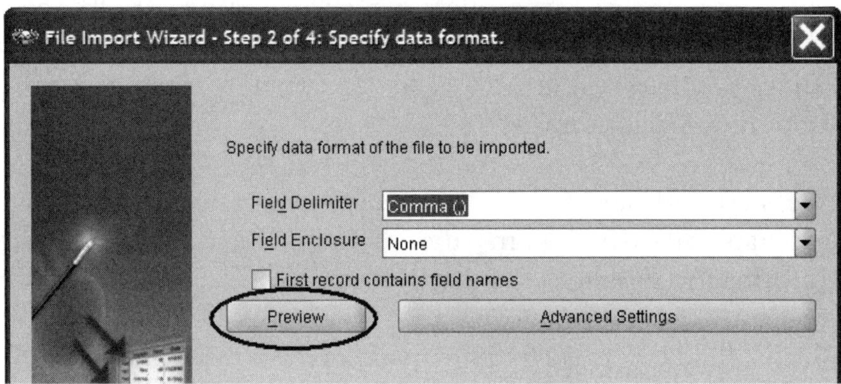

Figure 2.1: *File Import Wizard.*

Advanced Settings give you more options for controlling the data imported into Oracle.

- Discard maximum sets an upper limit on the number of records discarded before the loader terminates.
- Skip count automatically defaults to 1 if the First record contains field names checkbox is checked to prevent loading the field names row into a table.
- Load count limits the number of records to load.

- Max errors is a limit on the number of errors permitted before the load stops.
- Use direct path is checked by default; it enables the greatest load speed.

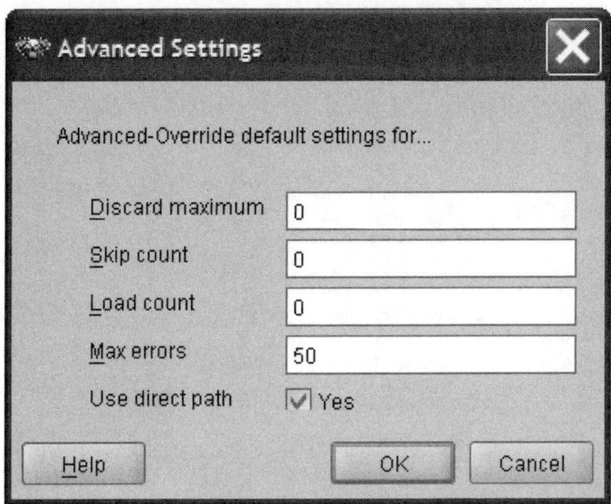

Figure 2.2: *Default Advanced Settings File Import Wizard*

The forest cover dataset is comma delimited, and since there are no column headings, you have the option of changing the column name making sure to enclose the column names with double-quotes (" ") and designating the data type and size. You can preview the data to ensure the settings are appropriate. For simplicity, the forest cover attribute ranging from 1 to 7 was named "TARGET". Specify a new table name, for example COVER_TYPE_IMP, then click Next and Finish.

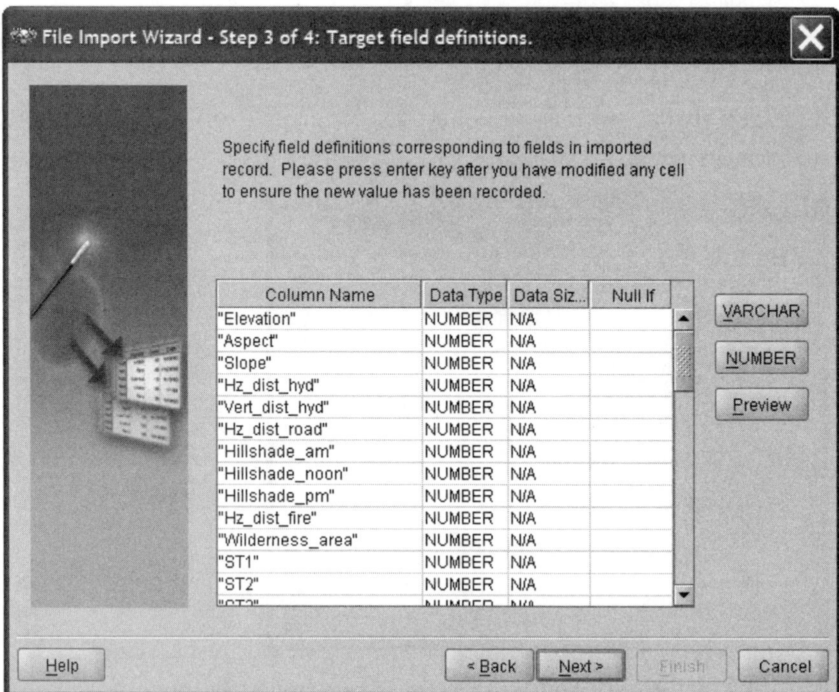

Figure 2.3: *Attribute Data Types.*

Note: The dataset will be imported using SQL*Loader, and for the Import Wizard to work you must set the directory for the SQL*Loader in the Tools menu, under Preferences in the Environment tab.

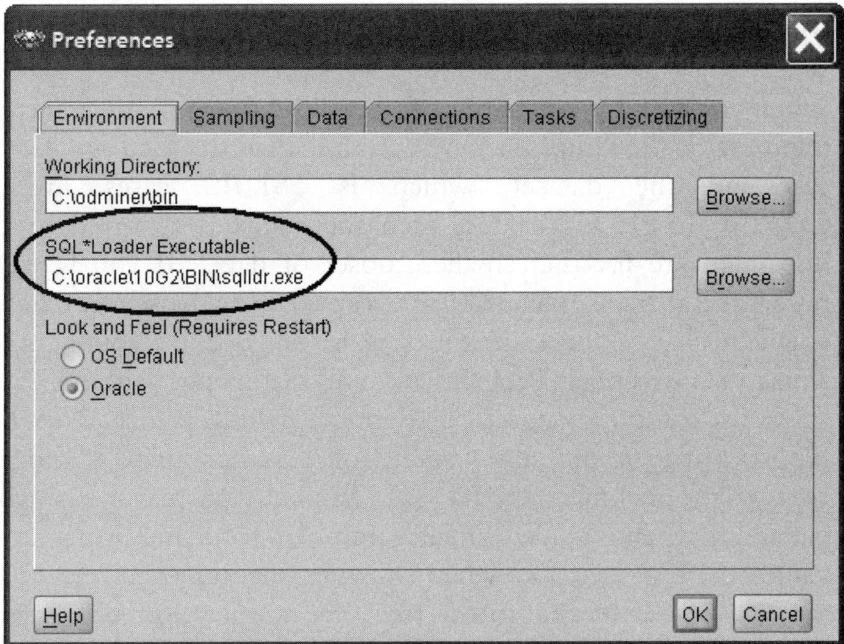

Figure 2.4: *SQLLDR Location.*

Exploring and Reducing the Dataset

Next, it is time to view the dataset we imported. Right click on the table name, COVER_TYPE_IMP, choose Show Summary Single Record, and check the data. Recall from Chapter One that there are two data mining types, categorical and numerical. Data Miner will guess what the data mining type is; however, you should verify that the data is being interpreted correctly. You may need to change the TARGET attribute, which is the type of forest cover for this example, to categorical.

Next examine the statistical nature of the case dataset by viewing the histograms for each attribute.

Viewing Attribute Histograms

When you view the histogram for each of the attributes, keep in mind that if the sample size is set to less than the total number of cases in the dataset, which is 581,012 cases in the COVER_TYPE_IMP table, then the statistics reported in the histogram are for that smaller subset of data. If you want to report the average, max, min, and variance for the whole dataset, you can change the sampling size to 581,012 by going to the Tools menu, under Preferences, and Sampling. Although the statistical computations will take longer to run, you may need to report statistics on all available data rather than a sample. Depending on how the data was sampled, you may find higher variability when you have smaller numbers for some of the target values. For example when viewing the target forest cover attribute, 85% of the forest trees are spruce and pine, while cottonwood/willow trees are only 0.47%.

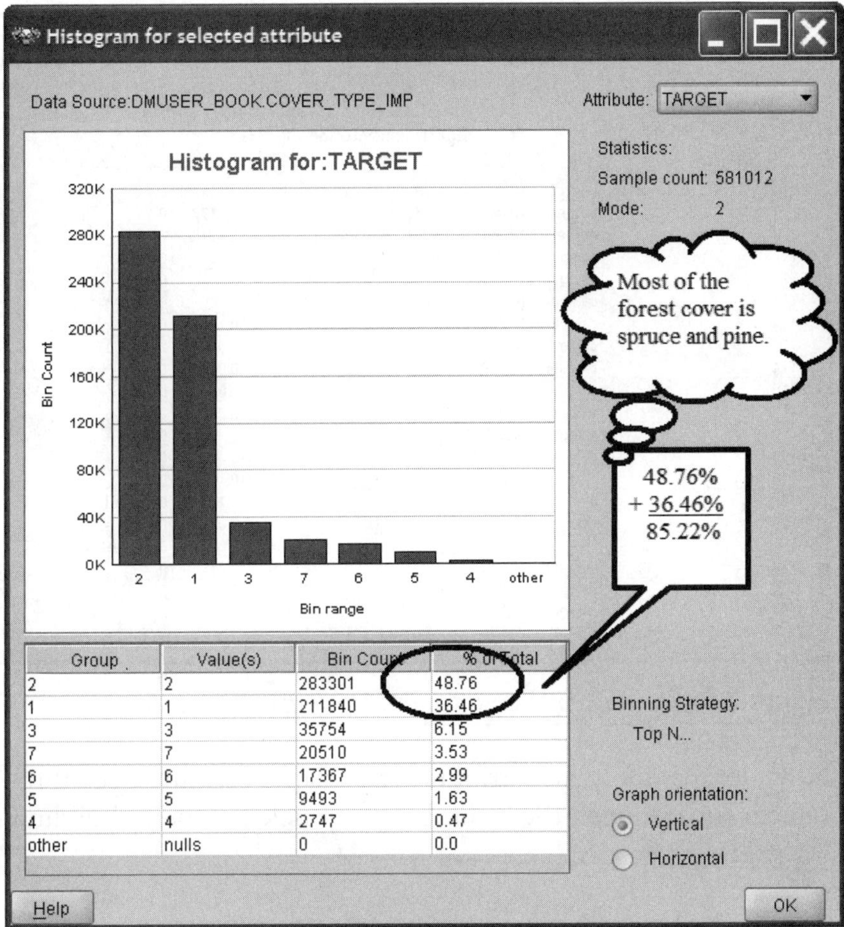

Group	Value(s)	Bin Count	% of Total
2	2	283301	48.76
1	1	211840	36.46
3	3	35754	6.15
7	7	20510	3.53
6	6	17367	2.99
5	5	9493	1.63
4	4	2747	0.47
other	nulls	0	0.0

Figure 2.5: *Histogram for Target Attribute for Forest Cover*

Do we actually need all 55 columns or attributes to build a model? If you look at some of the Soil Type (ST) variables, you will see that for ST's 10, 11, 12, 17, 18, 19, etc. there are not many samples. It is not likely that all attributes will contribute significantly to a predictive model. Some of them may in fact simply add noise and detract from the model's value.

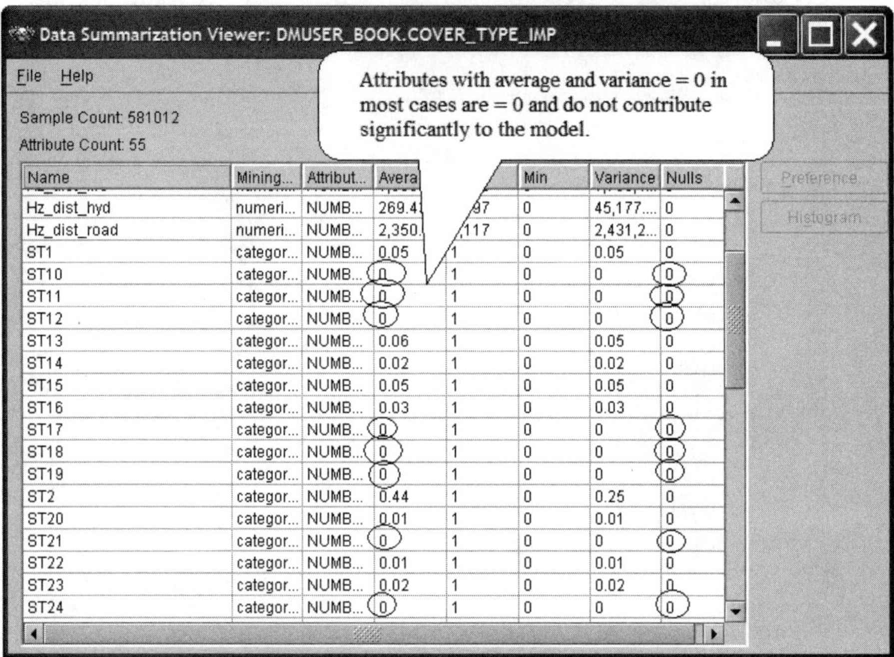

Figure 2.6: *Statistics for Forest Cover Attributes.*

Now let us look at attribute importance as an algorithm to effectively reduce the number of fields when building a classification model.

Attribute Importance

Recall that in Chapter One we used Attribute Importance to rank U.S. customers based on their buying habits. A smaller number of attributes determined by the ranking of important attributes was used to build a Naïve Bayes classification model.

Now, we will run the Attribute Importance algorithm on the forest cover dataset to find the predictor attributes that may have the most effect in our model.

1. Pick Attribute Importance under Activity Build, choose COVER_TYPE_IMP as the case table, and Compound or None for the Unique Identifier.
2. Select TARGET (forest cover) as the target column and make sure that it is set properly as a categorical mining type.
3. Type in a name for the Mining Activity and view the advanced settings before running the activity. We will not change any of the default values for this analysis.
4. Click Finish when you are ready to create the activity. This model may take a while to run, since the dataset is large and there is no unique identifier. You can view the progress of the steps Sample, Discretize and Build as they run.

Interpreting Attribute Importance Results

Upon completion of the Build Activity, we can view the results, as shown in Figure 2.7. The top five attributes are ELEVATION, ST3, HZ_DIST_ROAD, HZ_DIST_FIRE, and WILDERNESS_AREA. We can see that the elevation has the greatest influence on type of forest cover (0.65), with Soil Type 3 a distant second in importance (0.21).

Three man-made features come in next: roads, distance to fire points, and designated wilderness areas. These results can be used to reduce the number of attributes used in a Naïve Bayes analysis, which will be demonstrated in the next section.

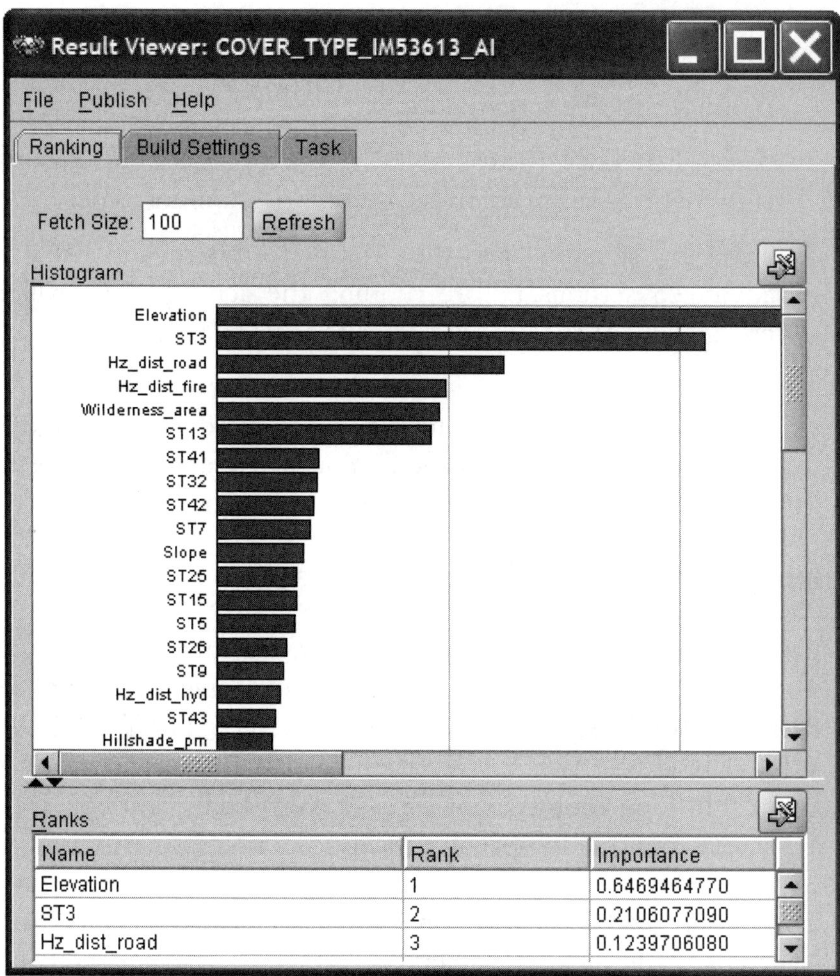

Figure 2.7: *Attribute Ranking Forest Cover Data.*

Comparing Naïve Bayes Models for Forest Cover

We will start with building a Naïve Bayes model using all 55 attributes for the Forest Cover Dataset COVER_TYPE_IMP that was imported earlier.

1. Start the classification Activity Build, and select Naïve Bayes as the algorithm.
2. Designate Compound or None as the unique identifier and leave all columns selected for the model build.
3. Select TARGET as the target column and change the mining type to categorical, if necessary.
4. Select the preferred target of value = 3 for ponderosa pine. We could have picked any value as the preferred target value.
5. Finally, choose an appropriate name, such as COVER_TYPE_NB_55. In this exercise the default settings will suffice, so click Finish to create and run the Activity.

At the successful completion of the Mining Activity, build another Naïve Bayes model using the same case dataset. On Step 2 of the New Activity Wizard, select Compound or None as the Unique Identifier as before.

In the Select Columns section, de-select all but the top 10 attributes identified by the Attribute Importance algorithm. Examining the result set shown in Figure 2.7, the top 10 are ELEVATION, ST3, HZ_DIST_ROAD, HZ_DIST_FIRE, WILDERNESS_AREA, ST13, ST41, ST32, ST42, and ST7. Make sure TARGET is selected for the target attribute which identifies forest cover type and click Continue.

Select 3 as the Preferred Target Value, and choose a name such as COVER_TYPE_NB_10. Keep the default settings as above and click Finish to create and run the new Activity with reduced number of attributes.

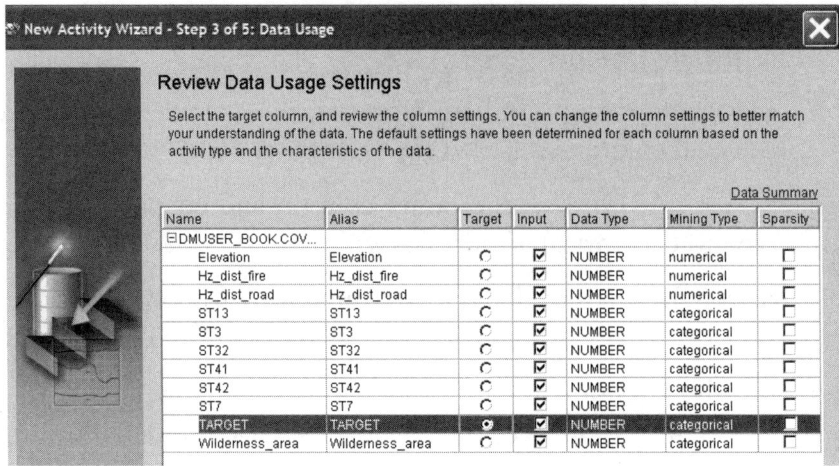

Figure 2.8: *Reduced Attributes Forest Cover Data.*

Now we will compare the results of the test metrics for the two Naïve Bayes classification models. How do we interpret these results? The results will be examined side-by-side.

The test metric results are shown in Figures 2.9 through 2.11. The predictive confidence falls into the Good range for both models; the model with 55 attributes having predictive confidence = 65% compared to 58% for the 10 attribute model.

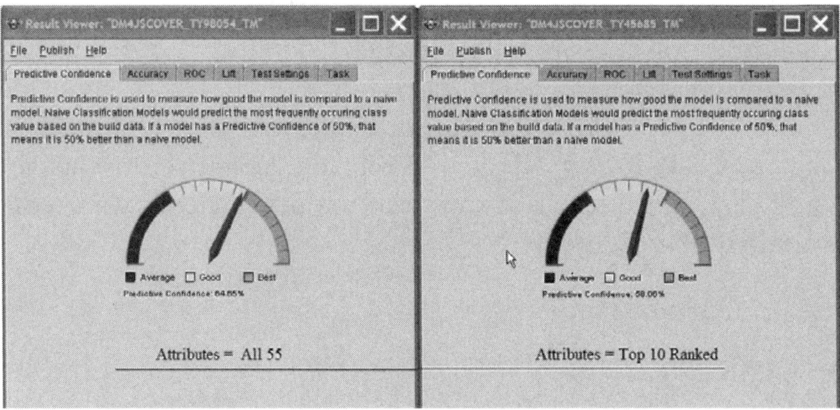

Figure 2.9: *Predictive Confidence for Forest Cover Data.*

Algorithms for classification use the cost matrix during scoring to find the least expensive solution. What are costs and how can costs help us make decisions? Assume we are data analysts for a logging company. Suppose that the company can make a profit of $1,000 on each pine tree and that the cost of cutting down a tree is $4.00. If the tree is actually pine and we predicted pine, then the cost of misclassifying a tree is $0. If our model predicts pine but another type of tree is cut down, then the cost is $4.00. If the model predicts that the tree is not pine and the actual type is pine, then the cost of misclassification is $1,000. If the model predicts that it is not pine and it actually is not, then the cost is $0. If you do not specify a cost matrix then all misclassifications are treated as equally important. The point is to minimize the cost of misclassifying the target attribute.

The costs of making a wrong decision vary for each target value. The percentage costs of an incorrect classification for Target #1 are approximately the same, 17%. The cost of misclassifying Target #5 is higher in the 55 attribute model as compared to the 10 attribute model, 9.1% versus 6.8%, respectively. However the converse is true for Target #6 where the costs are lower in the 55 attribute model and higher in the 10 attribute model, 85,344 versus 113,513.

Total target actuals, percentage of cases correctly predicted, cost, and percent cost are shown in Figure 2.10. The percentages correctly predicted for our preferred target value #3, forest cover type = 3, are 46.9% for all 55 attributes and 31.9% for the top 10 ranked attributes as seen in the Correctly Predicted column.

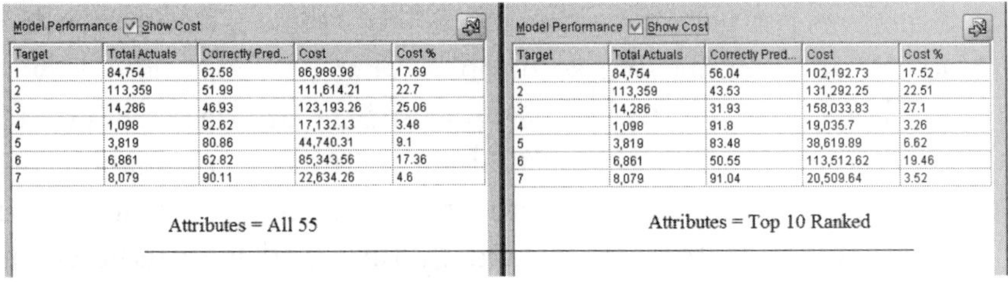

Model Performance ☑ Show Cost

Target	Total Actuals	Correctly Pred...	Cost	Cost %
1	84,754	62.58	86,989.98	17.69
2	113,359	51.99	111,614.21	22.7
3	14,286	46.93	123,193.26	25.06
4	1,098	92.62	17,132.13	3.48
5	3,819	80.86	44,740.31	9.1
6	6,861	62.82	85,343.56	17.36
7	8,079	90.11	22,634.26	4.6

Attributes = All 55

Model Performance ☑ Show Cost

Target	Total Actuals	Correctly Pred...	Cost	Cost %
1	84,754	56.04	102,192.73	17.52
2	113,359	43.53	131,292.25	22.51
3	14,286	31.93	158,033.83	27.1
4	1,098	91.8	19,035.7	3.26
5	3,819	83.48	38,619.89	6.62
6	6,861	50.55	113,512.62	19.46
7	8,079	91.04	20,509.64	3.52

Attributes = Top 10 Ranked

Figure 2.10: *Accuracy of Each Predicted Target Value for Forest Cover Data.*

The confusion matrices are shown in Figure 2.11. The confusion matrix indicates the types of errors that the model is likely to make. Note that there is more of a tendency to wrongly classify cases as Target type #4 in the smaller attribute model. Also, there are fewer errors in the 10 attribute model for Target values #5 and #7. This analysis suggests that if your interest is in Aspens and Krummholz forest cover types, then the smaller attribute model is better than the 55 attribute model.

Confusion Matrix: Rows = Actual; Columns = Predicted ☐ Show Total and Cost

55 Attributes

	1	2	3	4	5	6	7
1	63,0...	15,0...	13	0	3,950	305	12,3...
2	28,7...	58,9...	1,478	13	20,1...	3,822	2,154
3	0	26	6,705	2,418	1,494	3,643	0
4	0	0	38	1,017	0	43	0
5	79	451	50	0	3,088	151	0
6	0	83	1,189	630	649	4,310	0
7	741	29	0	0	29	0	7,280

Confusion Matrix: Rows = Actual; Columns = Predicted ☐ Show Total and Cost

10 Attributes

	1	2	3	4	5	6	7
1	47,4...	15,6...	72	0	6,060	98	15,4...
2	26,8...	49,3...	1,801	53	29,3...	3,462	2,473
3	0	25	4,561	4,690	1,438	3,572	0
4	0	0	46	1,008	0	44	0
5	0	417	54	0	3,188	160	0
6	0	53	1,044	1,490	806	2,468	0
7	687	6	0	0	31	0	7,355

Figure 2.11: *Confusion Matrix for Forest Cover Data.*

Table 2.1 compares the accuracy for each model. Average accuracy assigns the same fraction of error in each class. Different costs are designated for different types of misclassifications. Making a mistake on a class having a large number of cases is not as costly as making a mistake on a less frequent class.

Overall accuracy on the other hand, pays no heed to rare cases, and the model makes the overall error rate as low as possible. A main accuracy measure, the overall accuracy is calculated by adding the number of correct classifications. It is given by:

```
Accuracy =  (n0;1 + n1;0)/n
```

n is the total number of cases in the validation dataset. Looking at the confusion matrix for the 55 attribute model, we get Accuracy = (53037 + 58936 + 6705 + 1017 + 3088 + 4310 + 7280)/232256 = 0.578556.

The predictive confidence is a measure of how much better the model is than a Naïve model, which ignores all predictor information, making classifier predictions based on majority classes.

Although the model accuracy is higher and the cost lower for the model with 55 attributes, perhaps the pay-off of needing less data to construct a viable model makes the model with fewer attributes a very attractive alternative. After all, someone must go into the forest to take the samples and measurements and if the loss of accuracy is acceptable, the time and money spent gathering the data could be considerably less. This kind of analysis can help you make smarter decisions.

	PREDICTIVE CONFIDENCE	AVERAGE ACCURACY	OVERALL ACCURACY	COST
Model with 55 attributes	64.6%	69.7%	57.9%	491647.7
Model with 10 attributes	58.1%	64.0%	50.1%	583196.7

Table 2.1: *Comparing Naïve Bayes Models*

Adaptive Bayes Single Feature Model

Both the Adaptive Bayes Network and the Decision Tree algorithms rank attributes as part of the model building algorithm, so attribute importance is most useful as a preprocessor for Naïve Bayes or Support Vector Machines.

Unlike the Naïve Bayes model, which is something like a black box where we cannot see what is used to create the final results, another advantage to using the Adaptive Bayes Network is that you can generate human-readable rules that can provide insight as to what the model is using to classify cases.

The next section will explore how to build a new classification model using the Adaptive Bayes Network, which uses a built-in Attribute Importance methodology when building the model.

Building the Adaptive Bayes Network Model

This example will start a new Classification Build Activity, selecting the Adaptive Bayes Network for the algorithm. We will use the forest cover dataset for this example.

In Step 2 of the New Activity Wizard, pick COVER_TYPE_IMP as the case table and Compound or None for the Unique Identifier.

You can adjust the sampling settings, as shown in Figure 2.12, to speed calculating statistics on the dataset. There are two sampling strategies, Random and Top N, where Random is the default setting. The sample size is set on the Sampling tab in Data Miner preferences. In most cases, random sampling is the best setting. If the dataset is not performant, meaning that random sampling cannot be done with good speed, then Top N enhances performance by simply picking the first N cases, where N is the sample size.

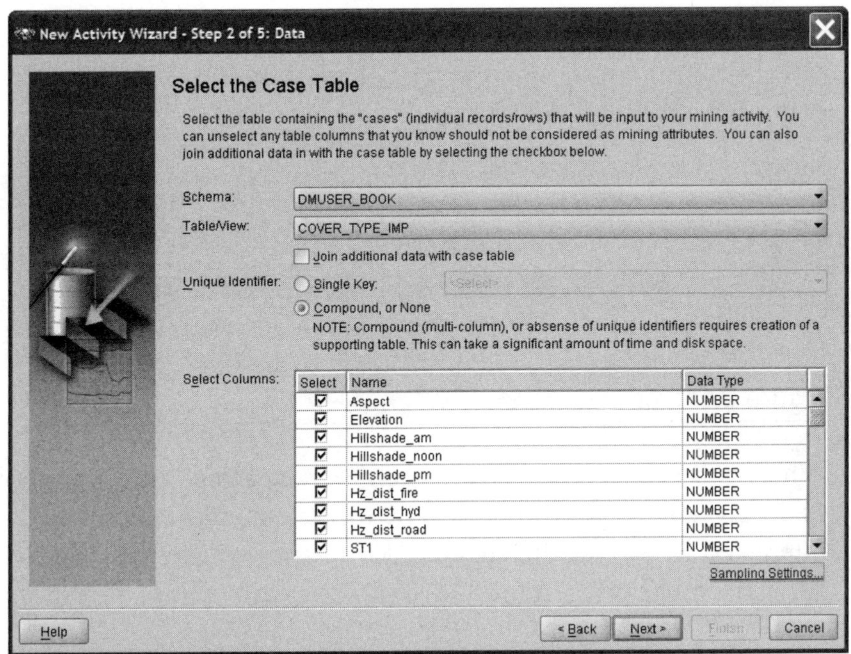

Figure 2.12: *Case Table Selection.*

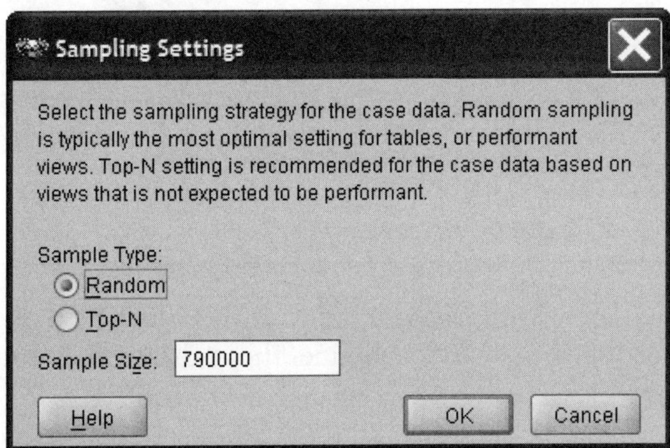

Figure 2.13: *Sampling Settings.*

Select all the columns to be used in the analysis in Step 3 (Data Usage). Next, select TARGET (forest cover) as the target, and review the settings. Make sure that the target attribute is a categorical mining type; otherwise, Data Miner will stop you from going further in the activity.

ST6	ST6			NUMBER	categorical	
ST7	ST7			NUMBER	categorical	
ST8	ST8			NUMBER	categorical	
ST9	ST9			NUMBER	categorical	
Slope	Slope			NUMBER	numerical	
TARGET	TARGET			NUMBER	categorical	
Vert_dist_hyd	Vert_dist_hyd			NUMBER	numerical	
Wilderness_area	Wilderness_area			NUMBER	categorical	

Figure 2.14: *Selecting Categorical Target Attribute.*

When you select the preferred target value, you have the choice of 1 through 7. Pick the type of forest cover that you are most interested in to test the model. You can change this later, so to get started choose Target = 4 (cottonwood/willow) forest cover type.

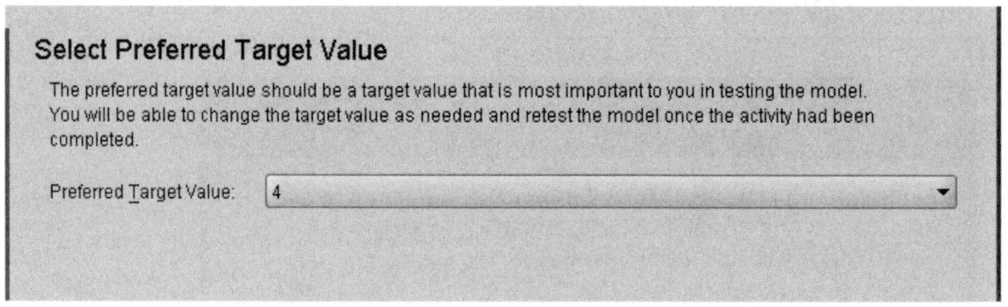

Select Preferred Target Value
The preferred target value should be a target value that is most important to you in testing the model.
You will be able to change the target value as needed and retest the model once the activity had been completed.
Preferred Target Value:
4

Figure 2.15: *Selecting Preferred Target Value.*

After you have named the activity, and on the Final Step page, select Advanced Settings and examine the Advanced Settings Dialog.

Until this point, all steps in the Build Activity are identical to those for Naïve Bayes. To change advanced settings for the Adaptive Bayes Network, click on the Build tab, and then Algorithm Settings under options. You will see a drop down box with three selections for Model Type: Single Feature, Multi

Feature, and Naïve Bayes. Setting the model type to Single Feature (the default) will give you the human-readable rules.

The speed of building the model will be slower or faster depending on the number of predictors chosen for the model, as well as the cardinality of those attributes. You can also limit the build time by entering the number of minutes you want the algorithm to execute. We will keep all the defaults for this example and go ahead and finish the model building activity.

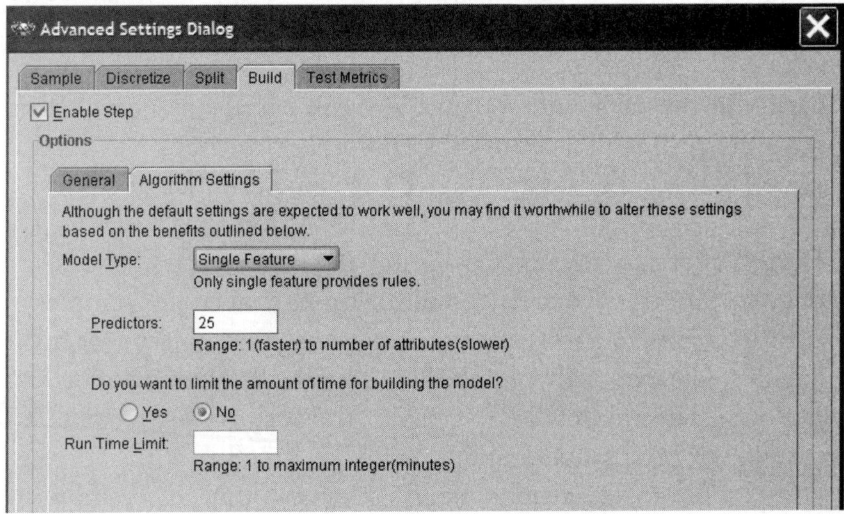

Figure 2.16: *Selecting Single Feature Adaptive Bayes Network.*

Sampling

Before we examine the results of the Adaptive Bayes Network model building activity, we will briefly cover sampling. The COVER_TYPE_IMP case data is a large dataset at 581 thousand records. You can build the model on the entire dataset if you have enough computer resources (i.e. memory, disk space), or you may choose to build the model on a sample of the data.

To speed development of classification models, it is often the case that models are built on smaller subsets of data. The sampling option is found in the advanced settings dialog under the Sample tab. To reduce the dataset, change the sample size by specifying a number of cases, for example 1000, or a percentage of cases.

A random sample chooses cases so that each case has the same chance of being selected. The random number seed defaults to 12345; to replicate the sample you would apply this same value for the seed in subsequent builds.

Dividing the data into separate groups based on the value of an attribute results in a stratified sample. If you check Yes for Equal Distribution, all groups will have the same number of cases.

Data Miner is designed for using data stored in databases and data warehouses, thereby minimizing the need to sample from data to perform robust data mining analytics. However, using a smaller dataset can result in improved performance when building data models and applying the results to new data. The results of the model built with a smaller sample can be comparable to the results using the whole dataset. Additionally, sampling allows you to quickly build an accurate data model for your business organization, as shown in greater detail in Chapter 4 in the section on stratified sampling.

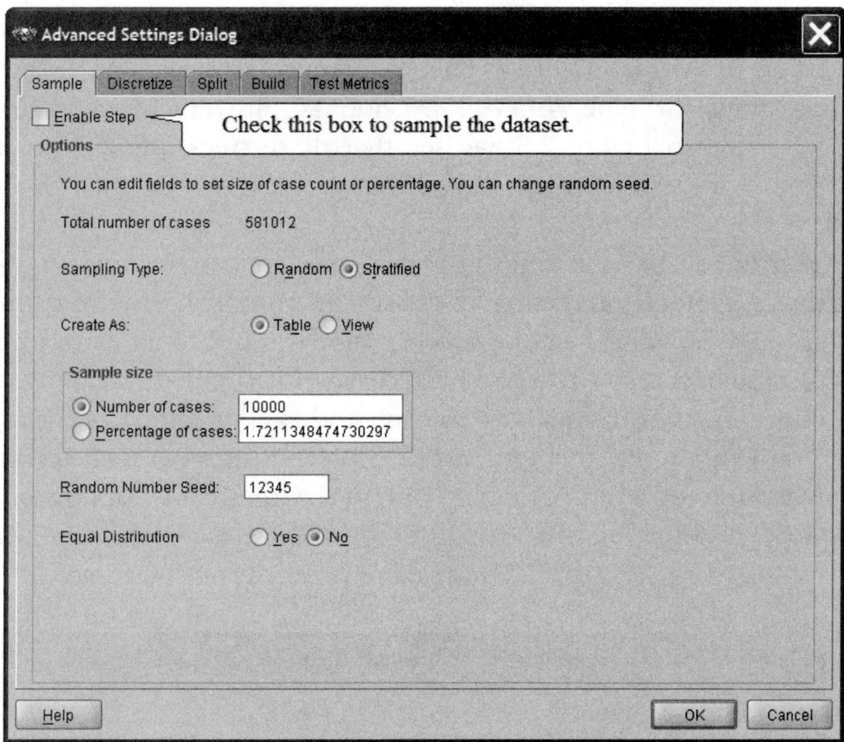

Figure 2.17: *Sampling in Advanced Settings.*

Viewing Adaptive Bayes Network Results

After completion of the Mining Activity, we click on Result under Test Metrics to view the predictive accuracy of the model. Since there were seven possible outcomes of the target attribute, under the Accuracy tab you can see the percentage of correctly classified cases for each value of forest cover.

As shown in Figure 2.18, the best predictions were made for Target value = 5 (aspen), with 93% correctly classified. The model misclassified all cases of ponderosa pine, with Target value = 3.

Generally, this model seems to be good at predicting scarcer types of forest covers. This is because the percent correctly classified for type #4, #5, #6 and #7 are greater than 70%. Referring to Figure 2.5, we see that these trees amount to only 8.62% of the total forest cover types.

The default build settings in Data Miner are used to find a model that is good at predicting all classes by optimizing the Maximum Average Accuracy of the model, which is 60% in this example. Overall accuracy (21%) is the accuracy for predicting a particular target, such as Target = 4 cottonwood/willow forest cover type. You can choose to build a model to maximize overall accuracy when interested in predicting only one target value, but generally you will want one that attempts to classify all the classes. Most models are better when you maximize the average accuracy.

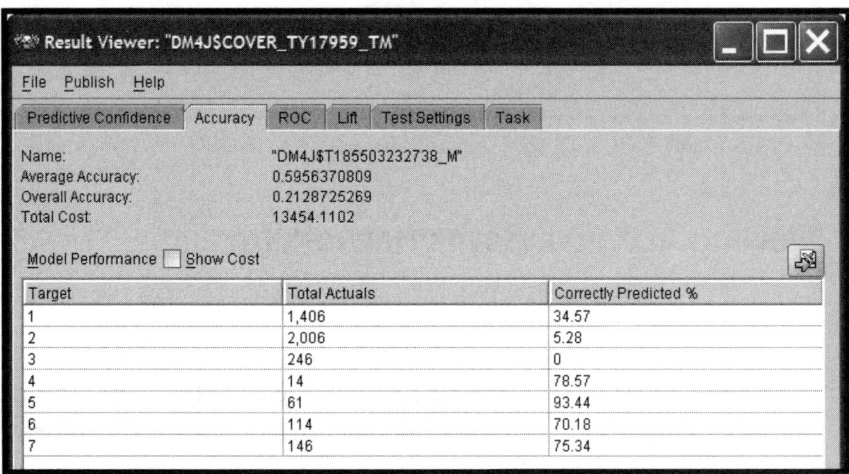

Target	Total Actuals	Correctly Predicted %
1	1,406	34.57
2	2,006	5.28
3	246	0
4	14	78.57
5	61	93.44
6	114	70.18
7	146	75.34

Figure 2.18: *Adaptive Bayes Network Model Accuracy.*

What has the model used to decide which forest cover to predict? To view the human-readable rules, click on Result in the Build step of the Mining Activity, and look under the Rules tab.

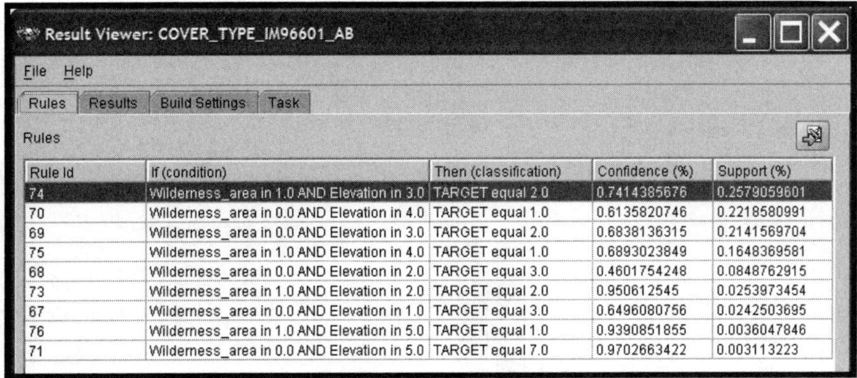

Rule Id	If (condition)	Then (classification)	Confidence (%)	Support (%)
74	Wilderness_area in 1.0 AND Elevation in 3.0	TARGET equal 2.0	0.7414385676	0.2579059601
70	Wilderness_area in 0.0 AND Elevation in 4.0	TARGET equal 1.0	0.6135820746	0.2218580991
69	Wilderness_area in 0.0 AND Elevation in 3.0	TARGET equal 2.0	0.6838136315	0.2141569704
75	Wilderness_area in 1.0 AND Elevation in 4.0	TARGET equal 1.0	0.6893023849	0.1648369581
68	Wilderness_area in 0.0 AND Elevation in 2.0	TARGET equal 3.0	0.4601754248	0.0848762915
73	Wilderness_area in 1.0 AND Elevation in 2.0	TARGET equal 2.0	0.950612545	0.0253973454
67	Wilderness_area in 0.0 AND Elevation in 1.0	TARGET equal 3.0	0.6496080756	0.0242503695
76	Wilderness_area in 1.0 AND Elevation in 5.0	TARGET equal 1.0	0.9390851855	0.0036047846
71	Wilderness_area in 0.0 AND Elevation in 5.0	TARGET equal 7.0	0.9702663422	0.003113223

Figure 2.19: *Adaptive Bayes Network Model Rules.*

Here you see that the model used wilderness area and elevation to classify forest cover. Reading over the rules, you can see common elements for the various types of trees. For example, rule # 70 = IF Wilderness_area in 0.0 AND Elevation in 4.0 then TARGET equal 1.0 and rule # 75 = IF Wilderness_area in 1.0 AND Elevation in 4.0 then TARGET equals 1.0. The wilderness area can be either 1 or 0, and if the elevation is = 4 then the forest cover is = 1.

Interpreting Adaptive Bayes Network Results

The Adaptive Bayes Network model was very good at predicting forest cover = 7 (75% correctly predicted), and you can see from rule #71, which = IF Wilderness_area in 0.0 AND Elevation in 5.0 then TARGET equals 7.0, that this type of tree grows outside the wilderness area at elevation = group 5. To see what elevations are grouped in bin 5, return to the Show Summary Single-Record and examine the histogram for Elevation. Using Equal Width Strategy, group 5 contains elevations from 2858.5 to 3058.4 feet.

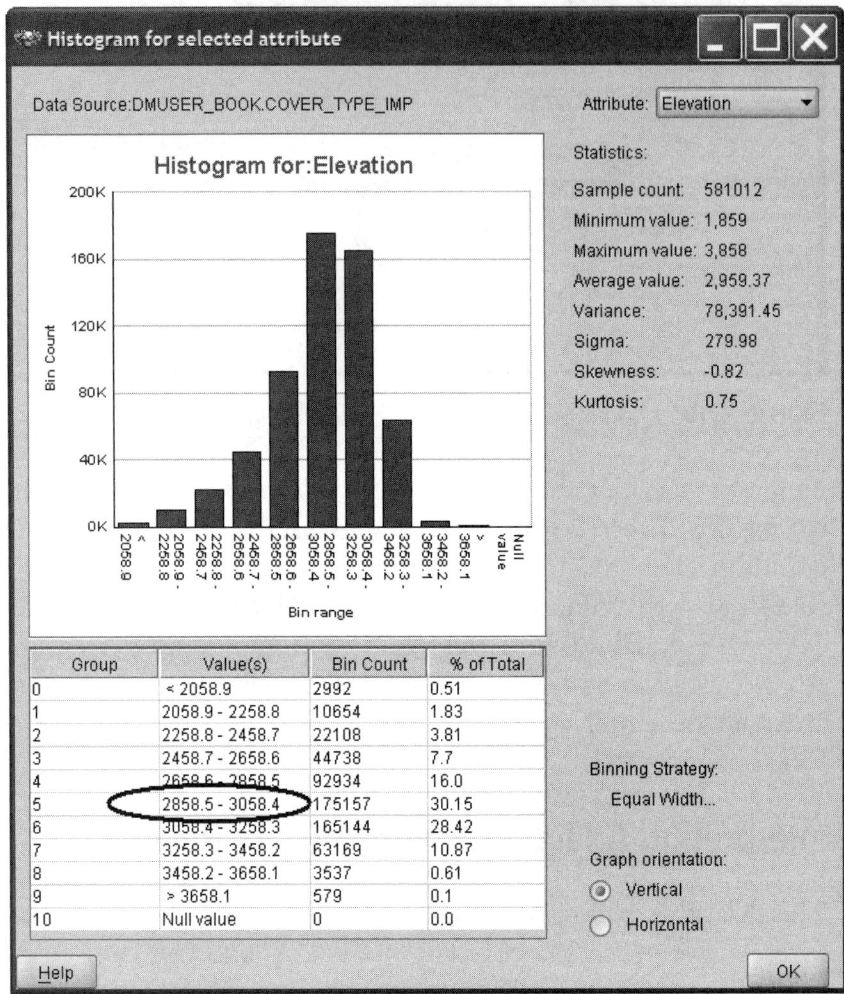

Group	Value(s)	Bin Count	% of Total
0	< 2058.9	2992	0.51
1	2058.9 - 2258.8	10654	1.83
2	2258.8 - 2458.7	22108	3.81
3	2458.7 - 2658.6	44738	7.7
4	2658.6 - 2858.5	92934	16.0
5	2858.5 - 3058.4	175157	30.15
6	3058.4 - 3258.3	165144	28.42
7	3258.3 - 3458.2	63169	10.87
8	3458.2 - 3658.1	3537	0.61
9	> 3658.1	579	0.1
10	Null value	0	0.0

Figure 2.20: *Histogram for Elevation.*

The Support (%) for a rule is the percentage of cases in the build dataset having the predicted target value. For rule #73, which is IF Wilderness_area in 1.0 AND Elevation in 2.0 then TARGET equals 2.0, the percent confidence is high at 95%, but support is low at 2.5%. This indicates that there is a marked improvement in accuracy provided by this rule, but it is true for only a few cases. When a single feature model is applied to another dataset, the output of the apply activity identifies the rule used to predict the classification result for each case.

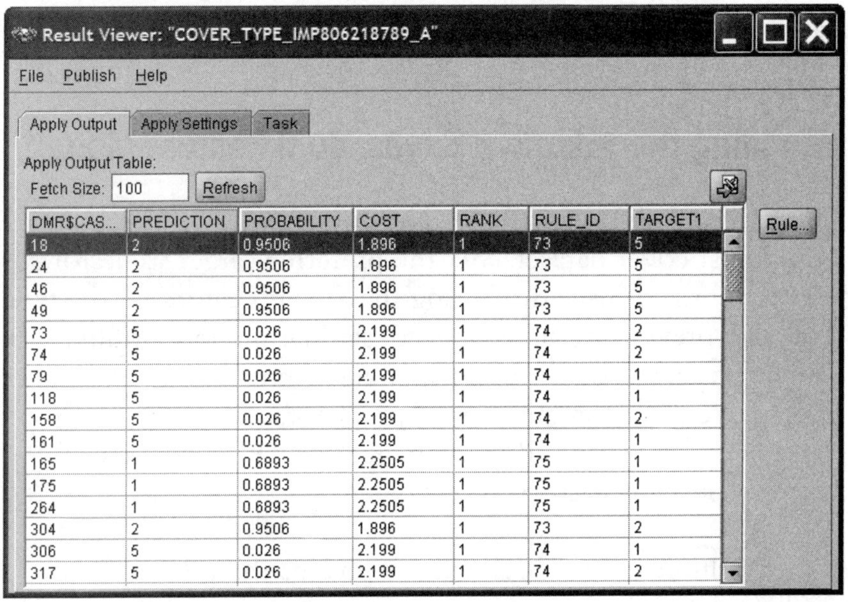

Result Viewer: "COVER_TYPE_IMP806218789_A"

File Publish Help

Apply Output | Apply Settings | Task

Apply Output Table:

Fetch Size: 100 Refresh

Rule...

DMR$CAS...	PREDICTION	PROBABILITY	COST	RANK	RULE_ID	TARGET1
18	2	0.9506	1.896	1	73	5
24	2	0.9506	1.896	1	73	5
46	2	0.9506	1.896	1	73	5
49	2	0.9506	1.896	1	73	5
73	5	0.026	2.199	1	74	2
74	5	0.026	2.199	1	74	2
79	5	0.026	2.199	1	74	1
118	5	0.026	2.199	1	74	1
158	5	0.026	2.199	1	74	2
161	5	0.026	2.199	1	74	1
165	1	0.6893	2.2505	1	75	1
175	1	0.6893	2.2505	1	75	1
264	1	0.6893	2.2505	1	75	1
304	2	0.9506	1.896	1	73	2
306	5	0.026	2.199	1	74	1
317	5	0.026	2.199	1	74	2

Figure 2.21: *Adaptive Bayes Network Model Rules to Applied Dataset.*

The rules for this dataset are quite simple, having only two attributes in the If condition. In large datasets, the rules can become very complex. The optimal number of rows of data depends on the nature of the data, and can be as high as 100,000 or more records. As a general rule of thumb for Adaptive Bayes Network, you should not expect meaningful rules unless the case data has over 20,000 rows.

Consider another example where we are really interested in classifying ponderosa pine (Target value = 3), which this first model completely misclassified. How do we influence the model to detect this type of forest cover? We have the choice of two different methods: building bias into the model with priors and costs, and using a different classification model.

The next step will be to build a new Adaptive Bayes model with a new type of algorithm, the Multi Feature model. This section will also include a demonstration of how to modify the costs to improve the predictive accuracy of the classification model.

Building the Adaptive Bayes Multi Feature Model

First, a new Adaptive Bayes Network model will be built using the forest cover dataset. Set the preferred target value for forest cover = 3 and instead of using the Single Feature model type as we did previously, in advanced settings choose Multi Feature model type under the Build tab, algorithm settings, keeping the default settings for number of predictors. Maximize the Overall Accuracy under the Build tab general setting, and enable the sample option for 20,000 cases.

The Multi Feature model will not give us the rules as before, but will build multiple features to improve the model with each feature, and may result in a more effective model.

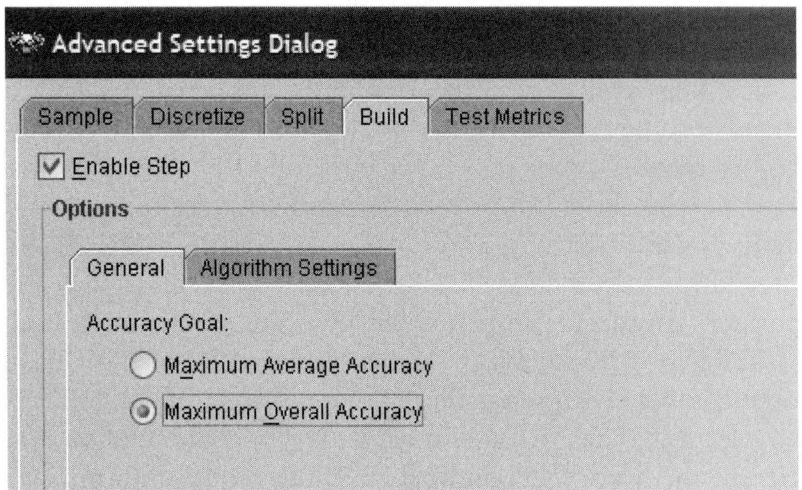

Figure 2.22: *Advanced Build Settings for Adaptive Bayes Network*

By maximizing the Overall Accuracy we hope to increase the percentage of correctly predicted cases for our particular target (ponderosa pine). Recall that the Single Feature Adaptive Bayes Network Model created in the previous section was a poor predictor of ponderosa pine.

The results of our new model improved the overall accuracy from 21% to 45% (as compared to the Single Feature model), and correctly classified 42% of the ponderosa pines (forest cover type = 3). The average accuracy is approximately 60% for both models. Lower cost is an indicator of improved prediction, and the cost of the Multi Feature model is 11804 compared to 13454 in the Single Feature model.

Two characteristics were changed in this example, maximizing the overall accuracy and the type of data mining algorithm. By changing only the algorithm to multi-feature, the overall accuracy is increased to 48% and the average accuracy increases to 60%, but the total cost also increases to 22880.

Accuracy in and of itself should not be your only goal. Decreased costs and substantial savings may be achieved with seemingly low accuracy models.

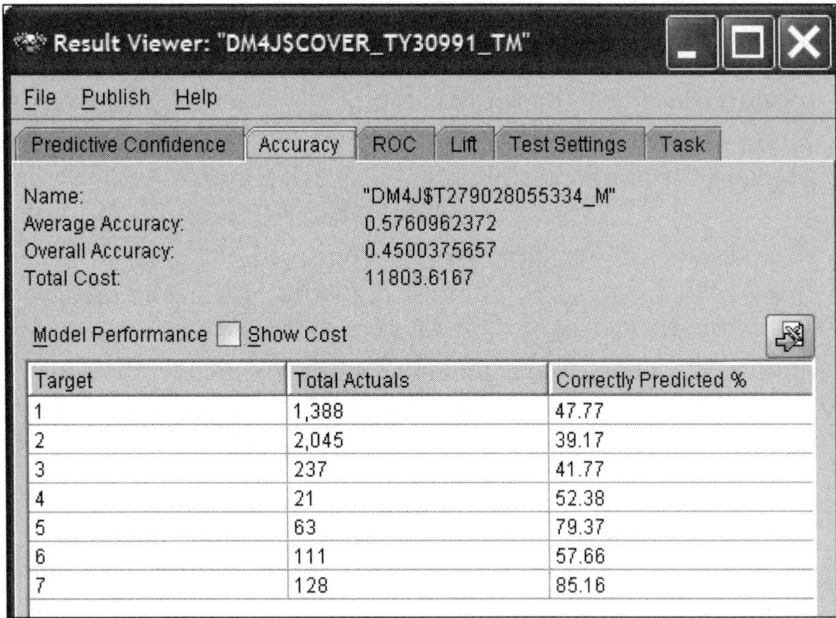

Figure 2.23: *Model Accuracy.*

By changing the type of model used to classify our data, and changing the accuracy goal from "maximum average" to "maximum overall accuracy," we were able to influence the predictive accuracy of our model. As mentioned earlier, manipulating cost and priors are two more ways to nudge the model into producing different results that might be more interesting for a particular business case. The section on Decision Trees will demonstrate how to change priors. The next section steps through the methods involved in changing the cost matrix.

Using the ROC Feature

One of the methods is to introduce *cost bias* into our build model, and the steps for doing this were described in Chapter One. To review, go to the ROC tab in the result viewer of the Mining Activity of the Adaptive Bayes Network model.

The Receiver Operator Characteristics metric shows the change in probability given modification to the Cost Matrix. For example, we want to predict more of the ponderosa pines forest cover and avoid false negative predictions. Under the ROC curve, there are two boxes labeled False Positive and False Negative Cost. Type "3" in the False Negative Cost box, telling the model that a false negative is three times more costly than a false positive error, and click Compute Cost. Note that the vertical red line jumps to the right and in the detail section the line with probability threshold 0.216 is highlighted. The confusion matrix changes to show that there are 22 false negatives, 200 false positives, 215 true positives and 3556 true negatives at this setting.

Oracle Data Miner provides the ROC feature to perform "what-if" scenarios by allowing the analyst to manipulate the cost matrix. We'll show how to actually change costs in the next section.

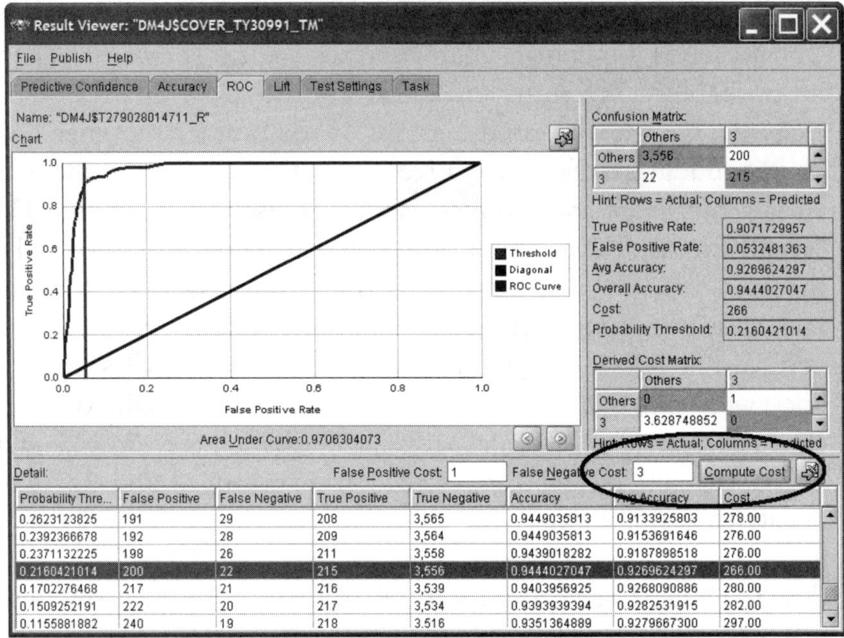

Figure 2.24: *Adaptive Bayes Network Model ROC.*

Introducing Cost Bias to the Classification Model

To modify the model test results, return to the Mining Activity and click on Select ROC threshold in the Test Metrics section. The default costs for False Positive and False Negative are assumed to be equal and are set to 1.00 by default.

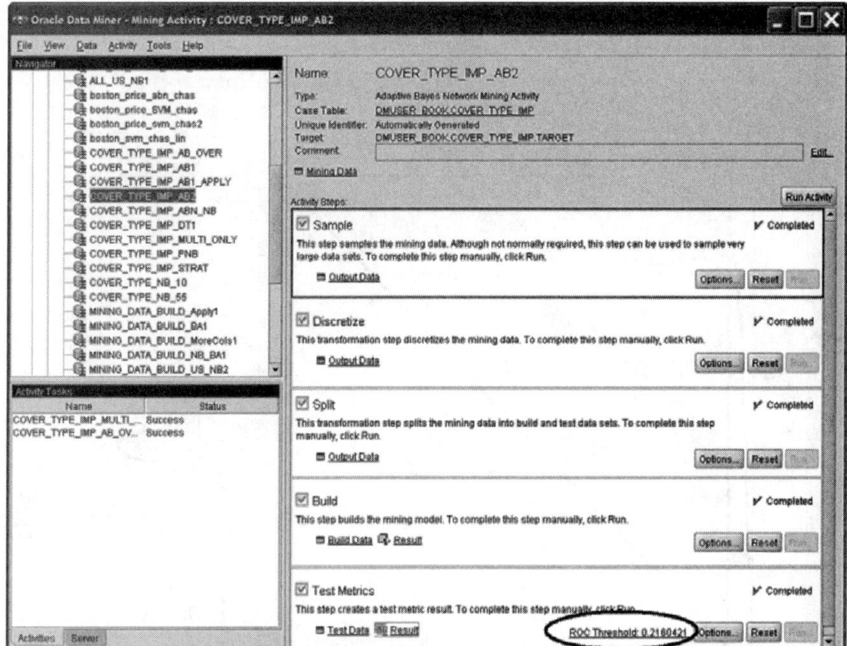

Figure 2.25: *Select the Adaptive Bayes Network Model ROC Threshold.*

Now we change the probability threshold setting from 0.50 to 0.216 and notice that the false negative cost is now 3.63 as shown in Figure 2.26. Click OK to save the settings and now see that the ROC Threshold is changed. The new cost bias will be used when the model is applied to a dataset.

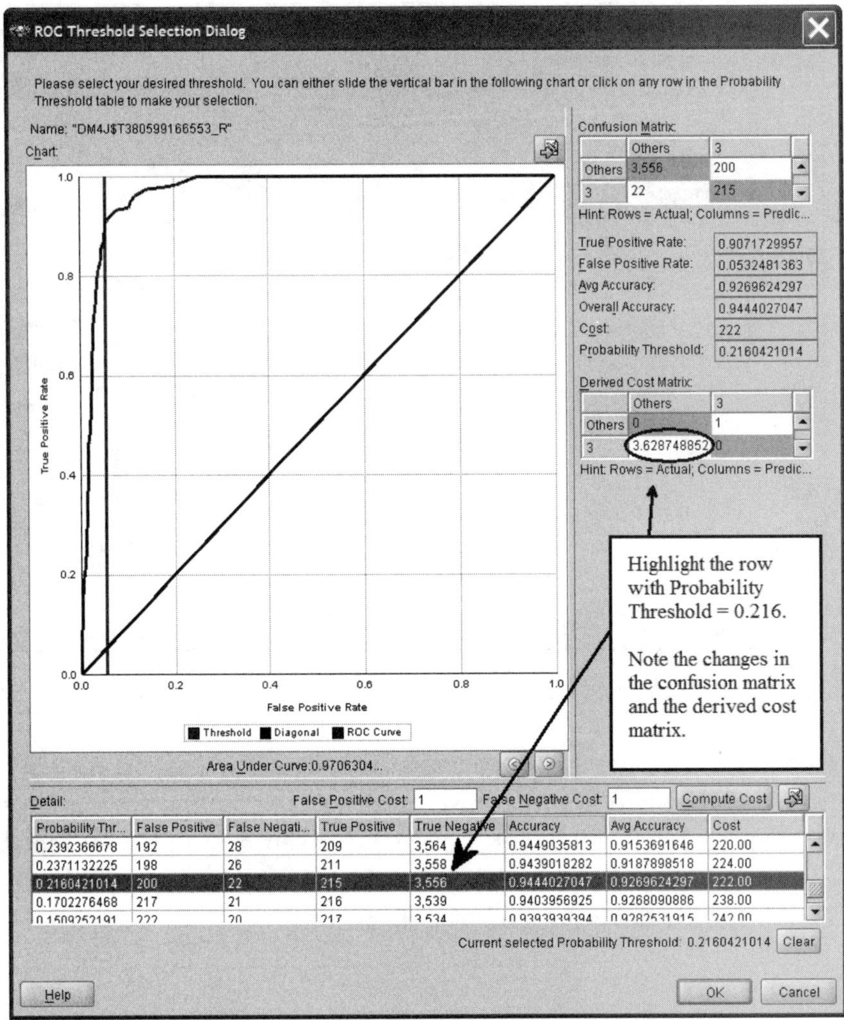

Figure 2.26: *Changing the Adaptive Bayes Network Model ROC.*

We have now built two types of Adaptive Bayes Network models, the Single Feature and the Multi Feature. There is one more type in Data Miner which is the Pruned Naïve Bayes, very similar to the Naïve Bayes that we used in Chapter One, although the results will not be exactly what you would get using the Naïve Bayes Classification model directly. The exploration of the Naïve Bayes Adaptive Bayes model will be left to the reader. The next section will look at Decision Trees, which like the Adaptive Bayes Network Single Feature model gives rules for determining how cases are classified.

Building a Decision Tree

Decision Trees perform well on a wide range of classification problems and result in human-readable rules that are easily understood. The Decision Tree algorithm splits the data in the case data by internally optimizing attributes to use at branching points. As the data is split, a Homogeneity Metric is applied to ensure that the attribute values are predominately one or the other. Branching stops when the algorithm has created 7 (the default) levels of branches in the tree.

What does a Decision Tree look like? Figure 2.25 describes a tree for classifying patients who were admitted into the hospital for preventable reasons. The attributes that determined whether the patient was classified as having either a preventable or appropriate admission were the number of hospital admissions, number of outpatient visits, number of visits to the emergency room (ER), age group the patient belongs to, diagnoses of asthma or chronic heart failure (CHF), and an age-related patient category (ACV).

The rectangular terminal nodes are categorized with a different shade of gray corresponding to a preventable (target = 1) or appropriate (target = 0) hospitalization. The values in the oval nodes give the splitting values on a predictor. The tree is translated into a set of rules for classifying a patient. In the tree shown in Figure 2.25, all but two of the terminal nodes are mostly patients who had at least one preventable admission. For the two terminal nodes for which the target = 0, the rules are:

```
IF (Age Group is 0 to 17, or 45+) AND (Number of admissions <=1.5)
AND (Diagnosis of Asthma = NO) AND (Age Group is 65+) THEN Class = 0
(Appropriate).
```

```
IF (Age Group is 0 to 17, or 45+) AND (Number of admissions <=1.5)
AND (Diagnosis of Asthma = NO) AND (Age Group is 0 to 17 OR 45 to
64) AND (Diagnosis of CHF is NO) and (ACV is E) THEN Class = 0
(Appropriate).
```

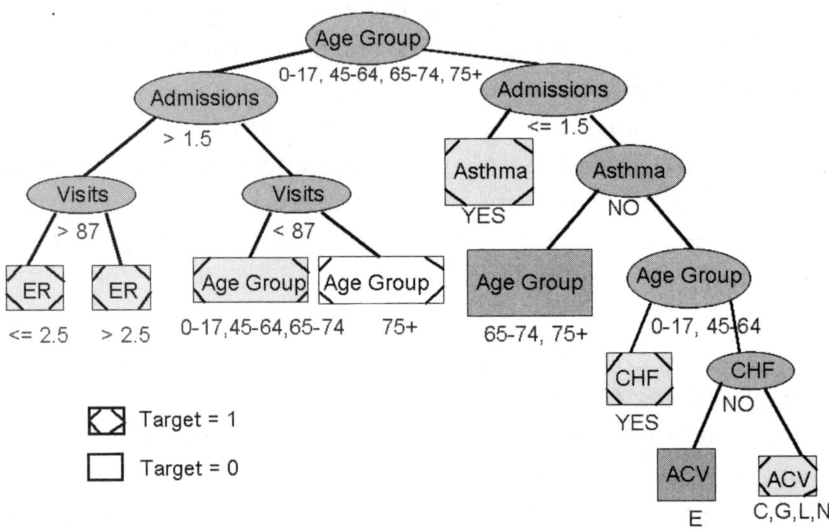

Figure 2.27: *Decision Tree Model.*

Conversely, in the other branch of the tree (shown in Figure 2.26), where the Age Group is 18 to 44, most of the terminal nodes are mostly patients with appropriate admissions. In fact, the only preventable admissions in this tree branch are for patients diagnosed with diabetes. For the terminal node where the target = 1, the rule is:

```
IF (Age Group = 18 to 44) AND (Admission Source is not from the ER)
AND (Diagnosis is Diabetes) THEN Class = 1 (Preventable).
```

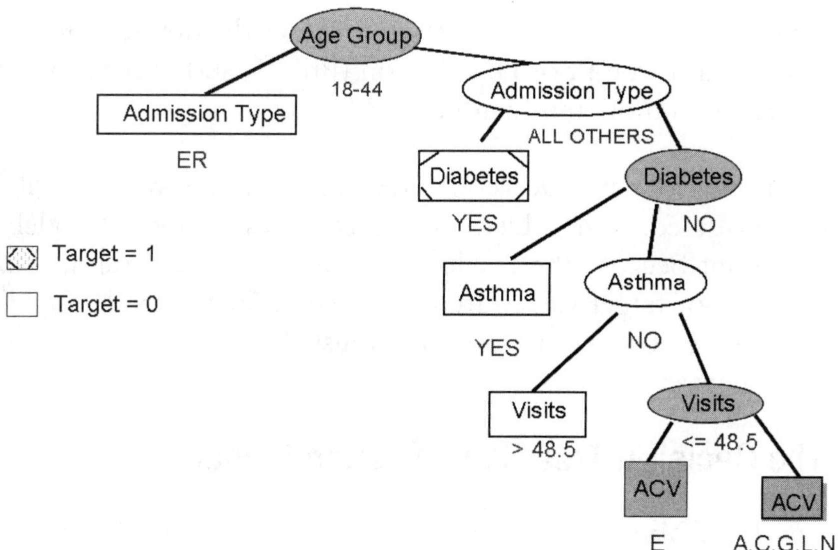

Figure 2.28: *Decision Tree Model Branch.*

In many types of data the target values may comprise only a very small percentage of cases. In hospital data, for example, preventable hospitalizations are somewhat rare events, and account for a very small percentage of admissions.

Likewise of all the users hitting a website, only a small number are initiated by hackers with malicious intent. A classification model built on datasets containing only a few known positive cases will not be able to discriminate very effectively between the two classes. The model may in fact predict that no hospital cases are preventable, or no hacker attempts occurred, and it will be 98 to 100% correct! However, we really have not learned anything to help prevent a potentially damaging rare event, and the model is not very effective.

What we want to do is use case data for the model build that has approximately equal numbers of positive and negative cases. However, the algorithm will take this distribution as if it were realistic, so we need to supply the actual distribution of target values, called the Prior Distribution (Priors), so the build process will result in more meaningful models.

Next, use of the Decision Tree classification model will be demonstrated. The Decision Tree Classification model is important because the results are easily interpreted rules. Small numbers of target values are not obscured in the model building process. Priors will be used to adjust the model for the forest cover dataset.

The Decision Tree Classification Model

The Data Miner classification models will use Priors when you specify *stratified sampling* in the Mining Activity advanced settings for sampling. This will be demonstrated using the Decision Tree classification model. Using the forest cover data, a new Build Activity will be constructed for Classification using the Decision Tree algorithm, keeping the default settings as shown. Priors will also be used in the classification build to target ponderosa pines.

The Build Activity is identical to those we created for the Naïve and Adaptive Bayes Network. Under Advanced Settings on the Final Step page, the build settings (Figure 2.27) have options for the homogeneity metric, maximum depth, minimum records in a node, minimum percent of records in a node, minimum records for a split, and minimum percent of records for a split. Keep the default settings as shown.

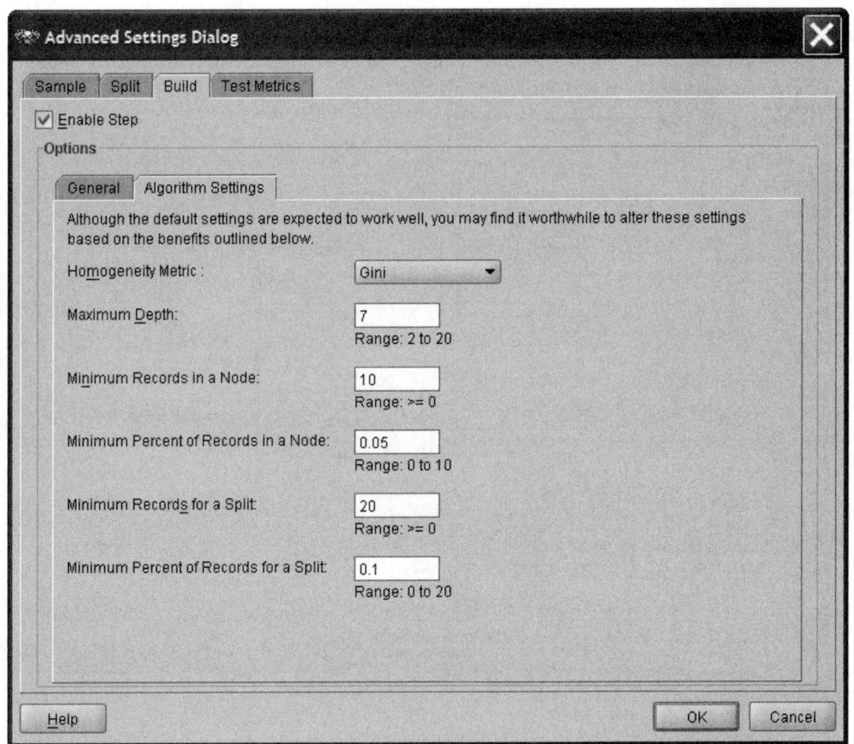

Figure 2.29: *Decision Tree Build Settings.*

Set the sample size at 200,000 cases, using the stratified sampling type. When the build finishes, click on the result in the Test Metrics section.

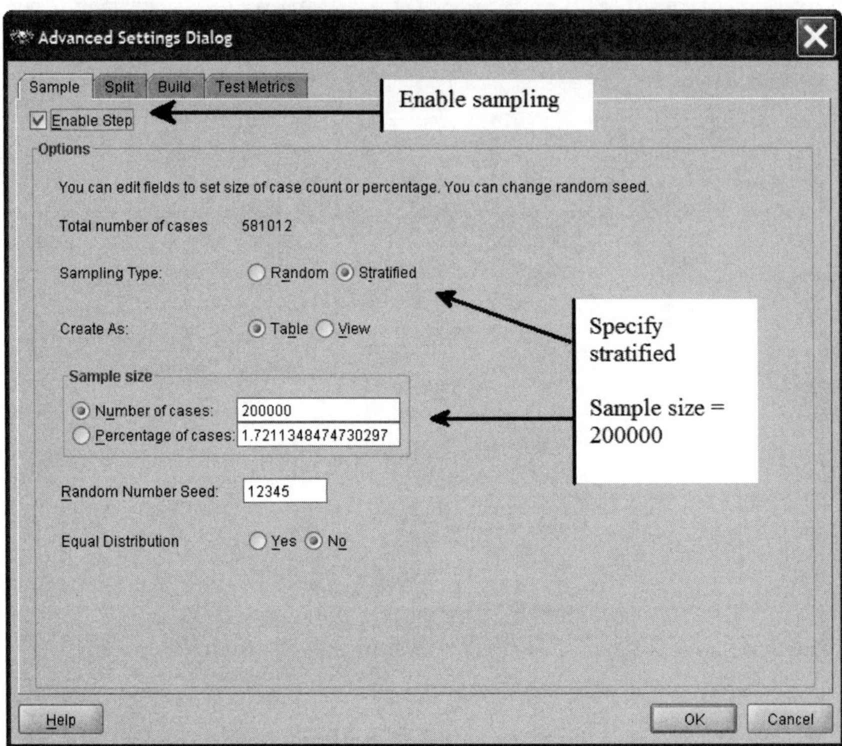

Figure 2.30: *Decision Tree Sampling.*

Here we see that the predictive confidence is good at 38%, the average accuracy is 47%, and the overall accuracy is 71%. However, the accuracy in predicting ponderosa pines (Target = 3) is greatly improved at 86.5% as a result of using Priors in the model build.

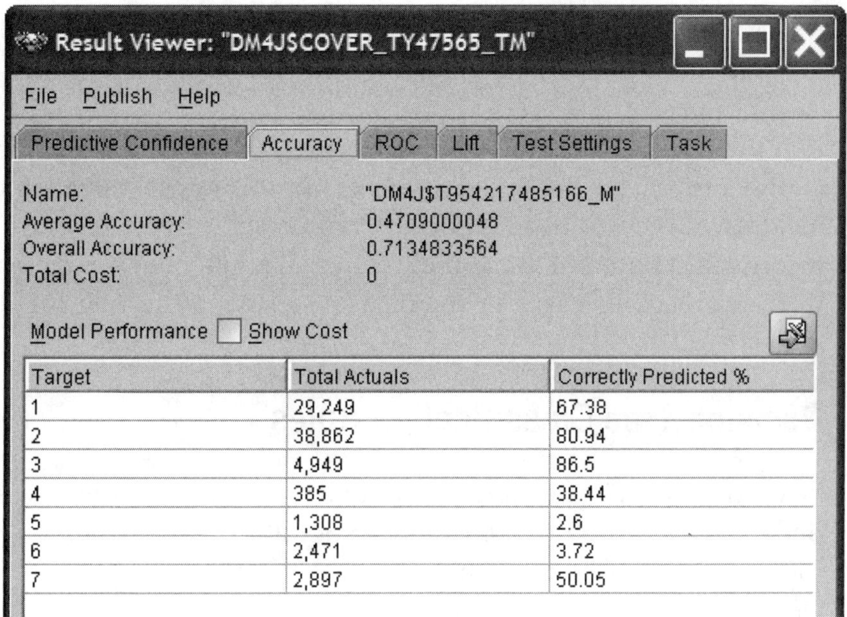

Target	Total Actuals	Correctly Predicted %
1	29,249	67.38
2	38,862	80.94
3	4,949	86.5
4	385	38.44
5	1,308	2.6
6	2,471	3.72
7	2,897	50.05

Figure 2.31: *Decision Tree Model Accuracy.*

If we look at the Results under the Build Activity section, we see the classification tree and the set of rules for classifying forest cover. For example, highlighting the row where the node ID = 59 shows one of the rules for predicting ponderosa pines (Target = 3):

```
IF
Hillshade_am <= 213.5 AND
Elevation <= 2408.5 AND
ST2 is in 0 AND
Hz_dist_hyd <= 15.0 AND
Elevation <= 2513.5 AND
Elevation <= 3044.5
THEN Class = 3.
```

Note that unlike the rules shown for the Adaptive Bayes Network, these rules give precise cut-offs for the attribute values. For example, the splitting values for rule #59 are "Hillshade_am" <= 213.5, "Elevation" <= 2408.5, "ST2" = 0, "Hz_dist_hyd" <= 15.0, "Elevation" <= 2513.5, and "Elevation" <= 3044.5.

Rules can be combined so that the rule can be shortened so that "Elevation" <= 2408.5, eliminating two elevation conditions.

For this rule, there are 207 cases with .17% support and 38% confidence. The predicted value (3) is the target value of the majority of records in that node. Confidence is the percentage of records in the node having the predicted target value. Support is the percentage of cases in the dataset satisfying the rule for that node.

Decision Tree Classification Rules

Decision tree classification is popular because of these easily understandable classification rules. Scroll down to examine the 116 rules available for this model.

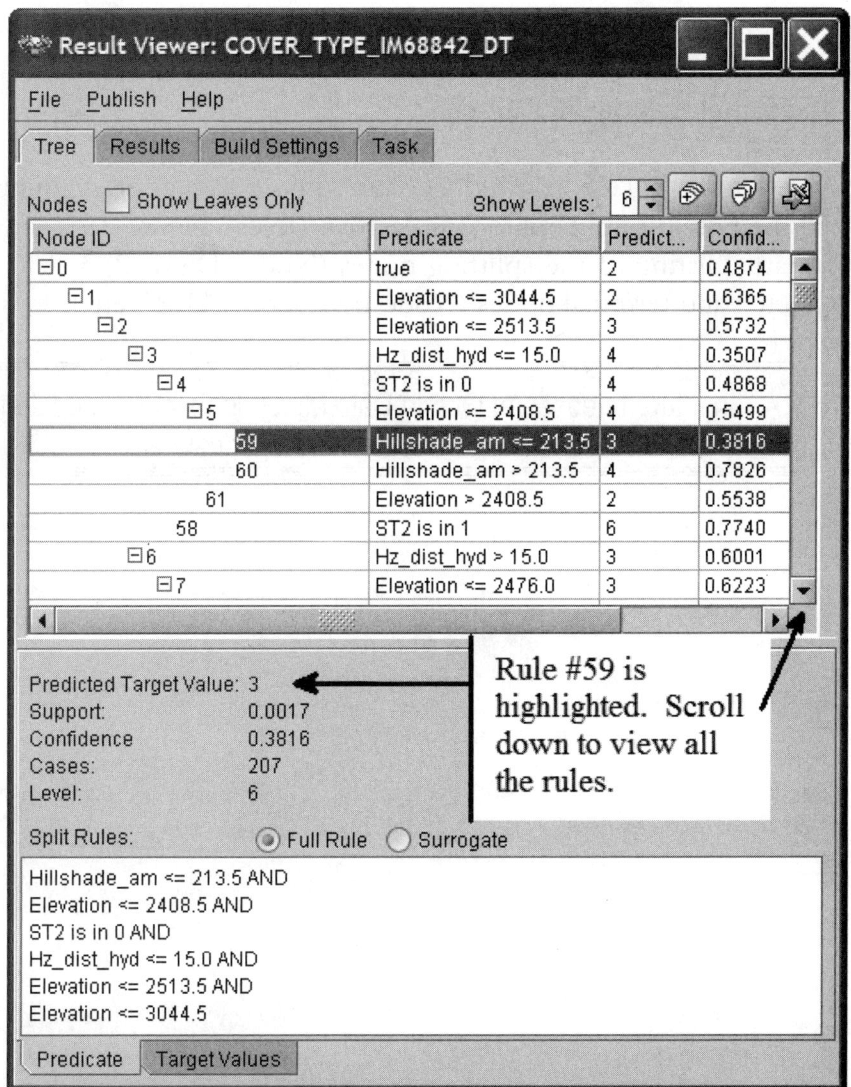

Figure 2.32: *Decision Tree Model Accuracy.*

The classifier selects the attribute Elevation for the first split with a splitting value of 3044.5. The data is now divided into two sets of data, one with Elevation <= 3044.5 and the other with Elevation > 3044.5.

Each of the data in the split is more homogeneous than before the split, although this is difficult to see in this example due to the complexity of the dataset.

The Decision Tree selected the attribute to split after examining all the possible split values for each variable. Figure 2.29 shows a partial listing of the splitting nodes (Node ID's 1, 2, 3, 4, 6, 7, 10 etc.) and terminal nodes (Node ID's 5, 8, 9, 11, 15 etc.).

 In future releases of Oracle Data Miner, look for the addition of a graphical rendition of Decision Tree nodes.

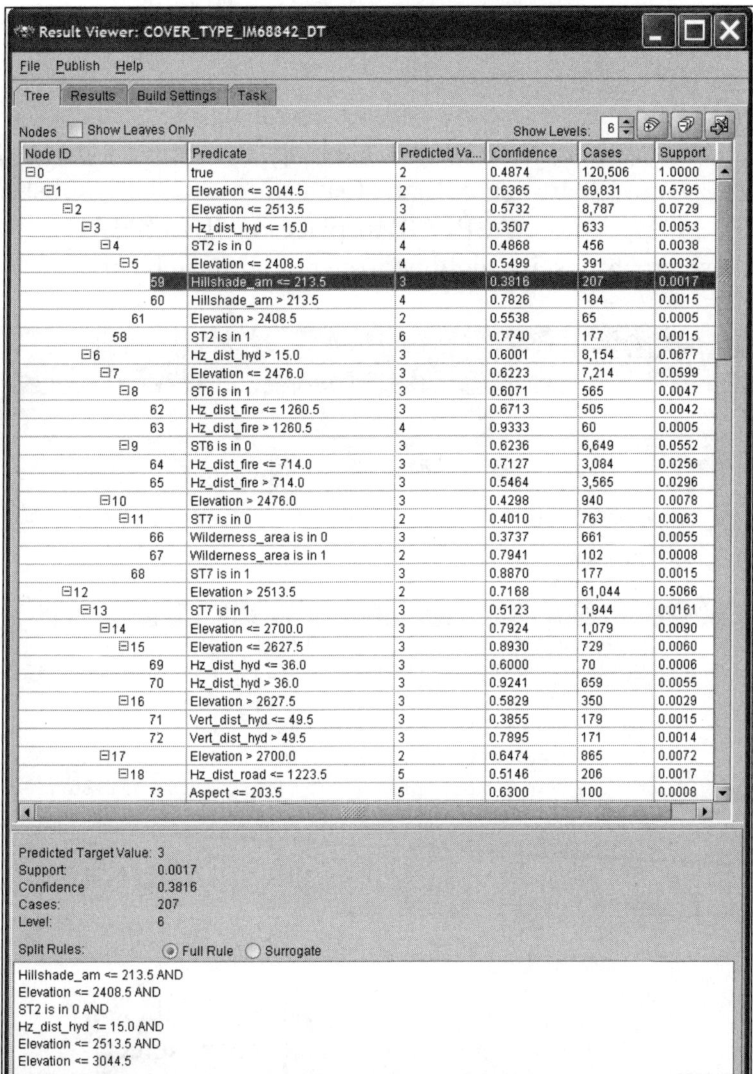

Node ID	Predicate	Predicted Va...	Confidence	Cases	Support
⊟0	true	2	0.4874	120,506	1.0000
⊟1	Elevation <= 3044.5	2	0.6365	69,831	0.5795
⊟2	Elevation <= 2513.5	3	0.5732	8,787	0.0729
⊟3	Hz_dist_hyd <= 15.0	4	0.3507	633	0.0053
⊟4	ST2 is in 0	4	0.4868	456	0.0038
⊟5	Elevation <= 2408.5	4	0.5499	391	0.0032
59	Hillshade_am <= 213.5	3	0.3816	207	0.0017
60	Hillshade_am > 213.5	4	0.7826	184	0.0015
61	Elevation > 2408.5	2	0.5538	65	0.0005
58	ST2 is in 1	6	0.7740	177	0.0015
⊟6	Hz_dist_hyd > 15.0	3	0.6001	8,154	0.0677
⊟7	Elevation <= 2476.0	3	0.6223	7,214	0.0599
⊟8	ST6 is in 1	3	0.6071	565	0.0047
62	Hz_dist_fire <= 1260.5	3	0.6713	505	0.0042
63	Hz_dist_fire > 1260.5	4	0.9333	60	0.0005
⊟9	ST6 is in 0	3	0.6236	6,649	0.0552
64	Hz_dist_fire <= 714.0	3	0.7127	3,084	0.0256
65	Hz_dist_fire > 714.0	3	0.5464	3,565	0.0296
⊟10	Elevation > 2476.0	3	0.4298	940	0.0078
⊟11	ST7 is in 0	2	0.4010	763	0.0063
66	Wilderness_area is in 0	3	0.3737	661	0.0055
67	Wilderness_area is in 1	2	0.7941	102	0.0008
68	ST7 is in 1	3	0.8870	177	0.0015
⊟12	Elevation > 2513.5	2	0.7168	61,044	0.5066
⊟13	ST7 is in 1	3	0.5123	1,944	0.0161
⊟14	Elevation <= 2700.0	3	0.7924	1,079	0.0090
⊟15	Elevation <= 2627.5	3	0.8930	729	0.0060
69	Hz_dist_hyd <= 36.0	3	0.6000	70	0.0006
70	Hz_dist_hyd > 36.0	3	0.9241	659	0.0055
⊟16	Elevation > 2627.5	3	0.5829	350	0.0029
71	Vert_dist_hyd <= 49.5	3	0.3855	179	0.0015
72	Vert_dist_hyd > 49.5	3	0.7895	171	0.0014
⊟17	Elevation > 2700.0	2	0.6474	865	0.0072
⊟18	Hz_dist_road <= 1223.5	5	0.5146	206	0.0017
73	Aspect <= 203.5	5	0.6300	100	0.0008

Figure 2.32: *Decision Tree.*

Check the box "Show Leaves Only" to display only the terminal nodes, or leaves. These are the nodes used to make the prediction when the model is applied to new data. Because the Decision Tree is sensitive to missing values when applied to new data, a surrogate attribute may be assigned if the attribute is missing in the apply data.

By highlighting the leaves, and clicking the radio button for Surrogate, you can see that Data Miner will substitute HILLSHADE_PM, or ASPECT in place of HILLSHADE_AM, since these attributes are highly correlated with each other.

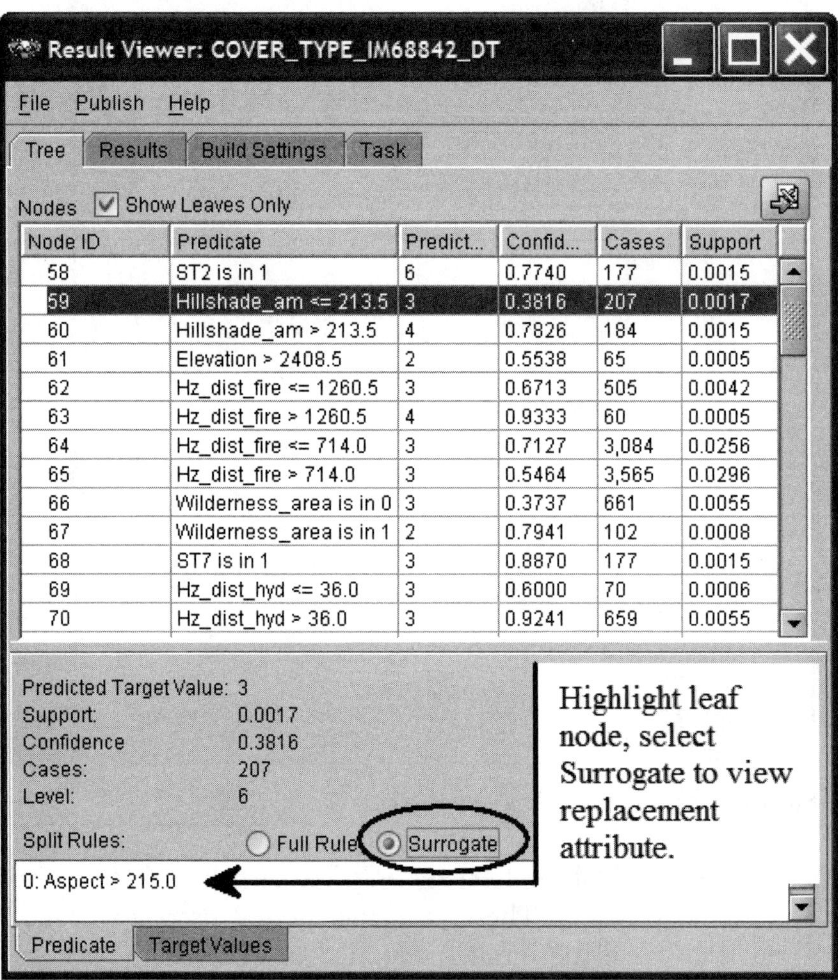

Node ID	Predicate	Predict...	Confid...	Cases	Support
58	ST2 is in 1	6	0.7740	177	0.0015
59	Hillshade_am <= 213.5	3	0.3816	207	0.0017
60	Hillshade_am > 213.5	4	0.7826	184	0.0015
61	Elevation > 2408.5	2	0.5538	65	0.0005
62	Hz_dist_fire <= 1260.5	3	0.6713	505	0.0042
63	Hz_dist_fire > 1260.5	4	0.9333	60	0.0005
64	Hz_dist_fire <= 714.0	3	0.7127	3,084	0.0256
65	Hz_dist_fire > 714.0	3	0.5464	3,565	0.0296
66	Wilderness_area is in 0	3	0.3737	661	0.0055
67	Wilderness_area is in 1	2	0.7941	102	0.0008
68	ST7 is in 1	3	0.8870	177	0.0015
69	Hz_dist_hyd <= 36.0	3	0.6000	70	0.0006
70	Hz_dist_hyd > 36.0	3	0.9241	659	0.0055

Figure 2.33: *Decision Tree Surrogate Attribute.*

Conclusion

In this chapter we built classification models with Data Miner using three popular algorithms: Naïve Bayes; Adaptive Bayes Network; and, Decision Trees. Single and Multi Feature Adaptive Bayes Network classification models were described and built with data downloaded and imported into Oracle data tables. The advantages of using Adaptive Bayes Network single feature model type and Decision Tree classification models are that each results in easily understood rules that can be applied and deployed to new datasets.

The main points of this chapter include techniques for choosing the best classification model to bring out the most accurate predictors for our particular business case. The speed and efficiency of building classification models can be improved by using Attribute Importance to select the attributes that contribute most to the accuracy of the model. Sampling techniques may be used to reduce the number of rows in a dataset, increasing the build speed and improving performance. The predictive accuracy achieved by applying the model to a test dataset can be influenced by optimizing the average or overall accuracy, introducing cost bias, and by using priors in stratified sampling.

We are now ready to move on and explore Support Vector Machines (SVM) in data mining. The SVM algorithms give us additional tools and insights when analyzing complex data sets.

Using Support Vector Machines

CHAPTER

Introduction to Support Vector Machine

Support Vector Machine (SVM) is a suite of algorithms that are used for classification applications. Like the Adaptive Bayes Network and Decision Tree algorithms discussed in Chapter Two, SVM provides coefficients that are useful in understanding the relationships and patterns in the dataset.

The SVM algorithms differ from the previous algorithms by their adaptability for diverse types of data. SVM can be used to solve regression problems, where the predictor values are continuous as opposed to discrete data types. An example will be given of using SVM to predict pollution levels.

Another advantage to using SVM is that it can be used to predict outcomes based on text data, so if you have descriptive data such as clinical notes for hospital patients, customer satisfaction survey results, or other textual information it can be used as part of the classification model.

In this chapter we will show an example using SVM to predict how researchers rated web pages based on content in the web pages themselves. We will show how to use sqlldr and Data Miner to extract and load CLOB data.

Inside Support Vector Machines

The first example will be to use SVM in classifying discrete attributes. The problem will be to predict values such as Yes or No (a binary classification problem), or as in the forest cover problem described in Chapter Two, predicting seven different types of trees depending on altitude and other environmental factors. ODM provides two varients, or kernels, of SVM and they are the Linear and Gaussian kernels.

These linear and non-linear kernels are similar to statistical and artificial machine learning techniques such as neural networks and linear regression, but are much better in terms of prediction accuracy and speed in building the model. Using the linear kernel will give us a list of attributed and attribute values ordered by their coefficients used to build a model, showing which attributes were most important in predicting the target class. The following sections take a closer look.

Importing the Irish Wind Data File

For case data, the daily average wind speeds for 1961 through 1978 at 12 synoptic meteorological stations in the Republic of Ireland will be used. The dataset, available as "wind" (http://lib.stat.cmu.edu/datasets/wind.data) on the StatLib Datasets Archives web site has 6,574 observations with 15 attributes. Each row corresponds to one day of data, with the following attributes: year, month, day, and average wind speed (in knots) at each of these stations: RPT, VAL, ROS, KIL, SHA, BIR, DUB, CLA, MUL; CLO, BEL, and MAL.

We will create a new target class, season, which we will code using months, with months 12, 1, and 2 designated winter, 3 through 5 as spring, 6 through 8 as summer, and 9 through 11 as fall.

Using the import feature of Data Miner, import the csv (comma delimited file), being sure to create a dat type file by renaming the file with the ".dat" extension. Enter new column names in Step 3 of the Import Wizard, name the new table wind_ireland, and finish the wizard to complete the data import.

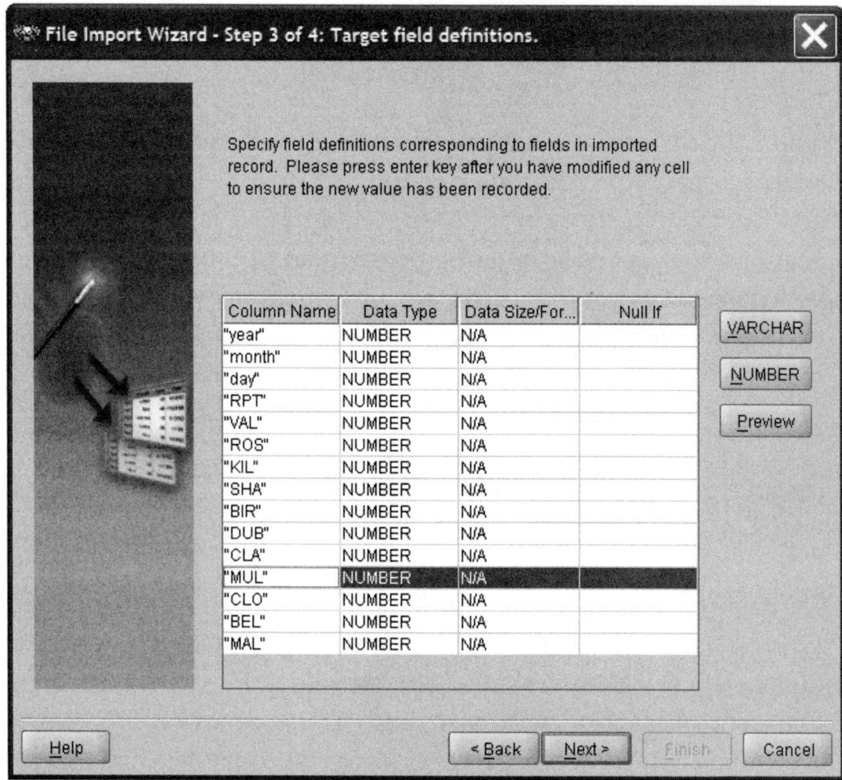

Figure 3.1: *Data Types.*

Computing a New Attribute with Compute Field Transformation Wizard

To create the four seasons, on the Main Menu choose "Data," "Transform," and pick "Compute Field." Choose a new name for the view such as “wind_ireland_V” and type “season” for the new column name. Enter the following statements in the “Expression” box, and click on “Validate” to ensure that the expression is valid.

```
case
 when "wind_ireland"."month"  = 12 or
     "wind_ireland"."month" = 1 or
     "wind_ireland"."month" = 2 then 'winter'
when "wind_ireland"."month" = 3 or
    "wind_ireland"."month" = 4 or
   "wind_ireland"."month" = 5 then 'spring'
when "wind_ireland"."month" = 6 or
    "wind_ireland"."month" = 7 or
    "wind_ireland"."month" = 8 then 'summer'
else
  'fall'
End
```

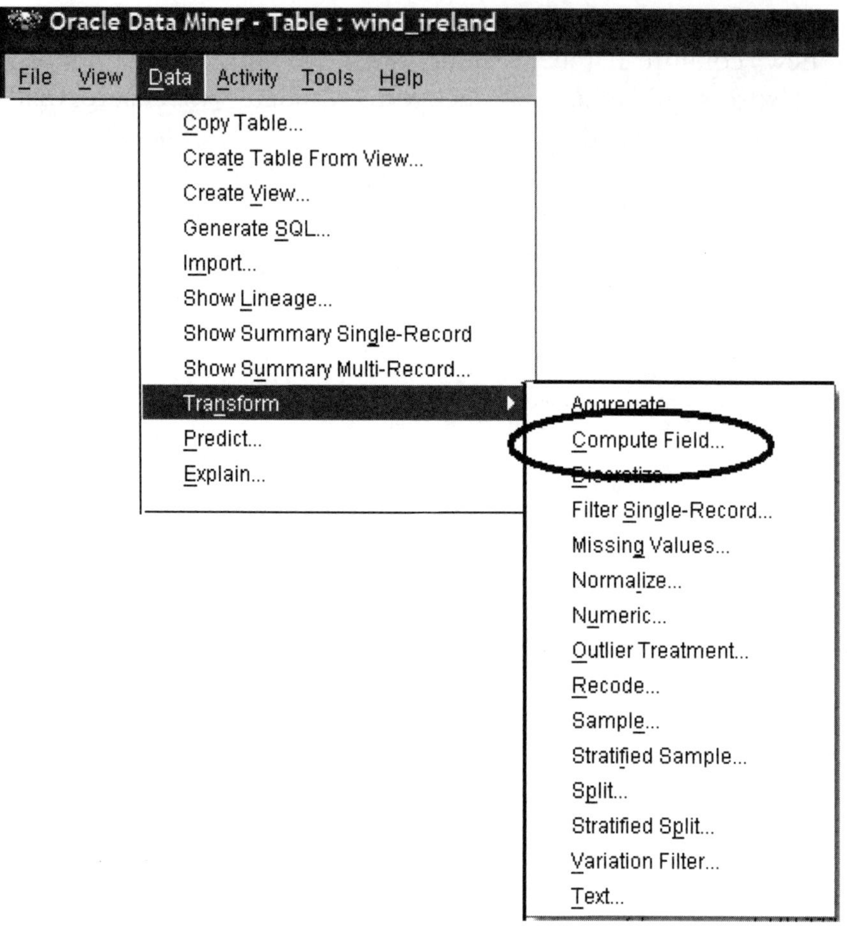

Figure 3.2: *Compute Field Transformation Wizard.*

You can view the SQL code and save the script to a file when you preview the transformation.

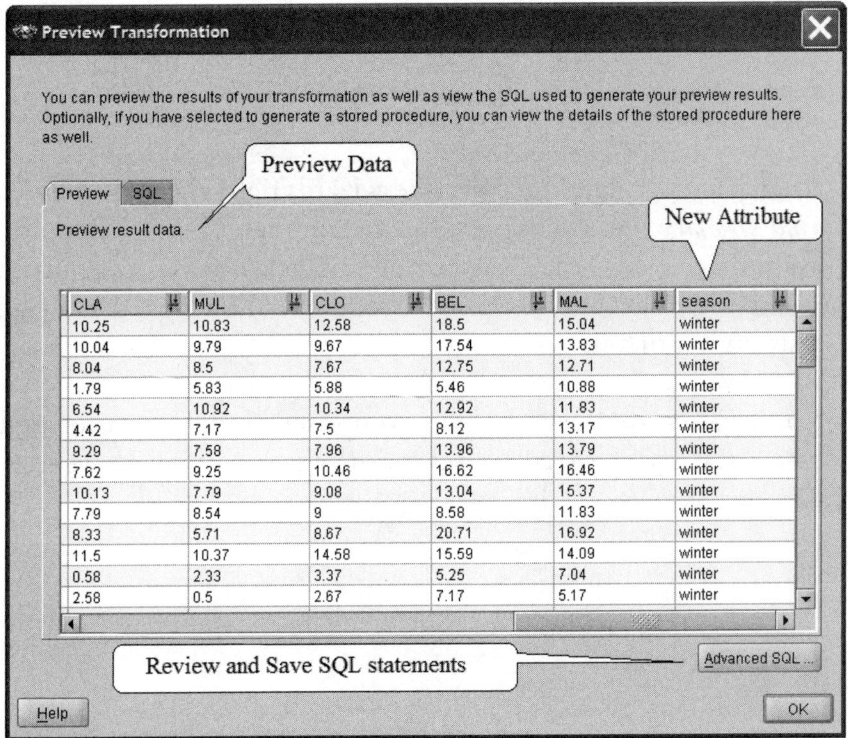

CLA	MUL	CLO	BEL	MAL	season
10.25	10.83	12.58	18.5	15.04	winter
10.04	9.79	9.67	17.54	13.83	winter
8.04	8.5	7.67	12.75	12.71	winter
1.79	5.83	5.88	5.46	10.88	winter
6.54	10.92	10.34	12.92	11.83	winter
4.42	7.17	7.5	8.12	13.17	winter
9.29	7.58	7.96	13.96	13.79	winter
7.62	9.25	10.46	16.62	16.46	winter
10.13	7.79	9.08	13.04	15.37	winter
7.79	8.54	9	8.58	11.83	winter
8.33	5.71	8.67	20.71	16.92	winter
11.5	10.37	14.58	15.59	14.09	winter
0.58	2.33	3.37	5.25	7.04	winter
2.58	0.5	2.67	7.17	5.17	winter

Figure 3.3: *Preview Data and SQL with Compute Field Transformation*

```
CREATE VIEW "DMUSER_BOOK"."wind_ireland_v" AS
SELECT "wind_ireland"."year", "wind_ireland"."month",
"wind_ireland"."day", "wind_ireland"."RPT", "wind_ireland"."VAL",
"wind_ireland"."ROS", "wind_ireland"."KIL", "wind_ireland"."SHA",
"wind_ireland"."BIR", "wind_ireland"."DUB", "wind_ireland"."CLA",
"wind_ireland"."MUL", "wind_ireland"."CLO", "wind_ireland"."BEL",
"wind_ireland"."MAL", case
 when "wind_ireland"."month"  = 12 or
     "wind_ireland"."month" = 1 or
     "wind_ireland"."month" = 2 then 'winter'
when "wind_ireland"."month" = 3 or
    "wind_ireland"."month" = 4 or
   "wind_ireland"."month" = 5 then 'spring'
when "wind_ireland"."month" = 6 or
    "wind_ireland"."month" = 7 or
    "wind_ireland"."month" = 8 then 'summer'
else
  'fall'
End
 AS "season"
 FROM "DMUSER_BOOK"."wind_ireland"
```

```
COMMENT ON TABLE "DMUSER_BOOK"."wind_ireland_v" IS 'Created by
Compute Field Transformation Wizard. Data source is Schema:
DMUSER_BOOK, Table: wind_ireland.'
```

After you complete the compute wizard, right click the new view *wind_ireland_v* and choose Show Summary Single Record to examine the new case data details. Click on the new attribute "season" and check the histogram showing the relative distribution of values.

You can see that each season comprises about a quarter of the case data, so no need to set priors in the Build as we did in Chapter Two.

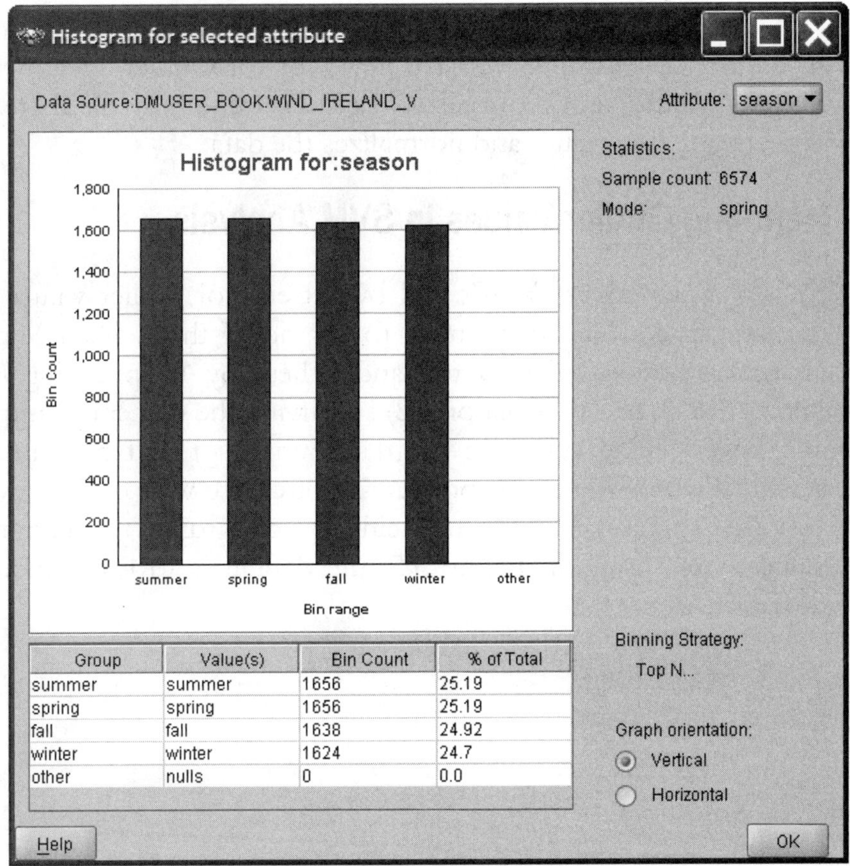

Group	Value(s)	Bin Count	% of Total
summer	summer	1656	25.19
spring	spring	1656	25.19
fall	fall	1638	24.92
winter	winter	1624	24.7
other	nulls	0	0.0

Figure 3.4: *Histogram for SEASON.*

Next, we will build a new model using the Support Vector Machine algorithm.

Building the SVM Model

Now we will create a Build Activity and choose the Support Vector Machine algorithm under the Classification Function. Select "season" as the target class, and pick your favorite season as the preferred target value. All steps in the Activity Wizard are the same as the Naïve Bayes, Adaptive Bayes Network, and

Decision Tree until we come to the Advanced Settings Dialog. In the SVM algorithm, we have new tabs for Outlier Treatment, Missing Values, and Normalize. Let's examine how SVM treats outliers, missing values and normalizes the data.

Handling Outlier Values in SVM Analysis

SVM may be adversely affected by extreme or outlier values in the case data table, so we need to get rid of them. Data Miner gives you options of how to handle these by 1) specifying the number of standard deviations, 2) specifying the percent of upper and lower tailing values in the distribution, or 3) typing in an actual value for the cutoff point. The Replace with option gives you the choice of either replacing or discarding the extreme values. As shown in Figure 3.5, the default is to use standard deviation.

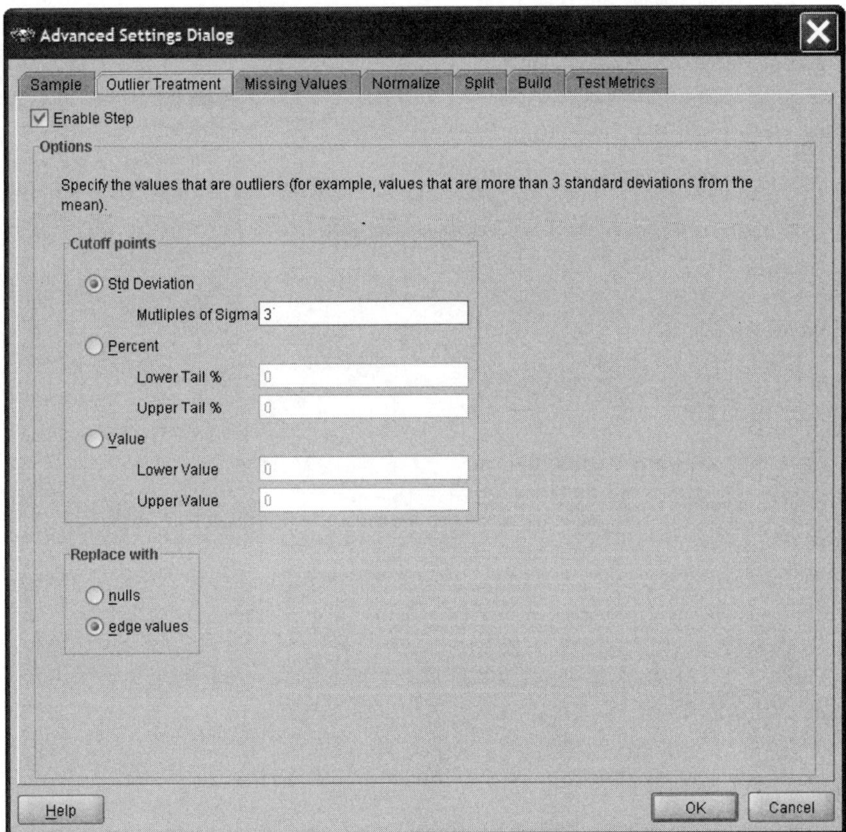

Figure 3.5: *SVM Outlier Treatment Default Settings.*

Missing Values in SVM Analysis

Missing values must also be addressed. Under the Missing Values tab, you can replace numeric types of data with the mean, minimum value, maximum value, a custom value that you type in, or simply drop the attribute if the column is null. For categorical data you can replace the value with the mode, which is the most frequently occurring value, or a custom value that you type in. For numerical data the default is to replace missing values with the mean if the attribute is numerical or mode for categorical fields.

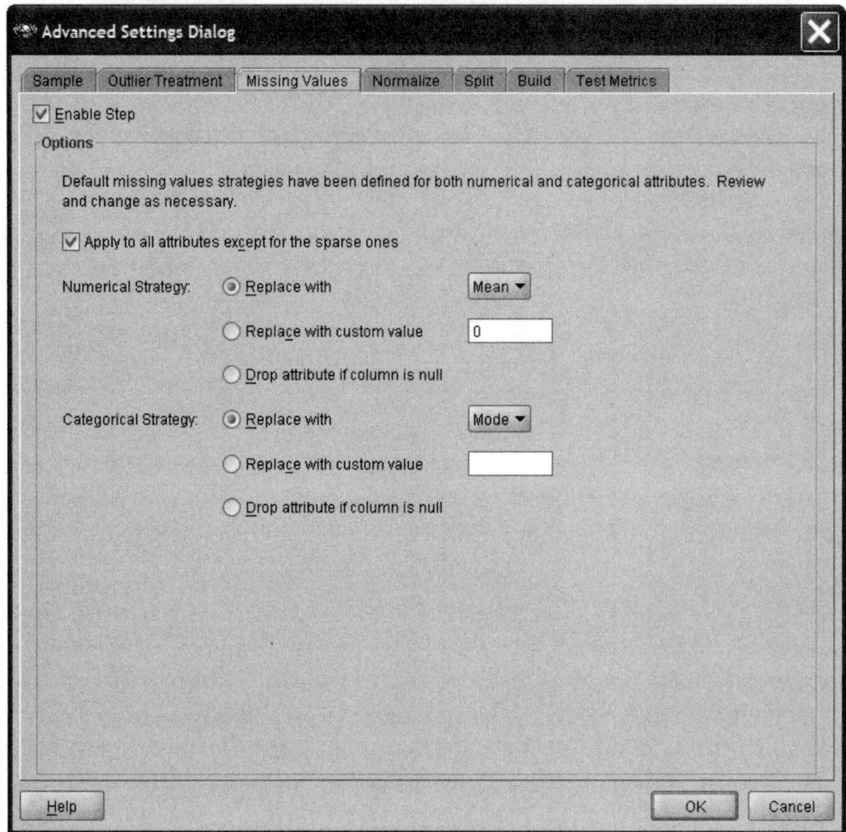

Figure 3.6: *SVM Missing Values Default Settings.*

Sparse Data in SVM Analysis

What is the difference between missing values and sparse data? In the Irish wind data, there is data for every row and every attribute; the data is neither missing nor sparse. But assume you are analyzing data for patients who are hospitalized, and 5 percent of the patients are admitted for complications arising from diabetes. Since diabetic complications such as blindness and limb amputations occur infrequently, the data is considered sparse. Normally you would not impose a missing value on sparse data. As shown in Figure 3.6, the default is to apply a missing value strategy to all attributes except for the sparse ones.

Normalization of SVM Data

Normalization refers to the process of scaling attribute values so that they fall within a small specified range, typically from 0.0 to 1.0. Data normalization controls variance, and in some instances helps speed the process of building the model. Where there is a high degree of variability in the data, normalization prevents attributes with large ranges (wind speed) from outweighing attributes with smaller ranges (seasons of the year). Such deviations in the data may prevent data mining algorithms from discovering patterns in the data, especially when there is limited data or few instances of the target value of interest.

SVM requires that all numerical data is normalized, thereby reducing the variability in the raw data. Min/Max is the default method for normalization, where all values are re-coded in the range of 0 to 1. Z-score is a good choice for normalization if you have chosen to keep outliers in your dataset. The default strategy is to use the min/max scheme.

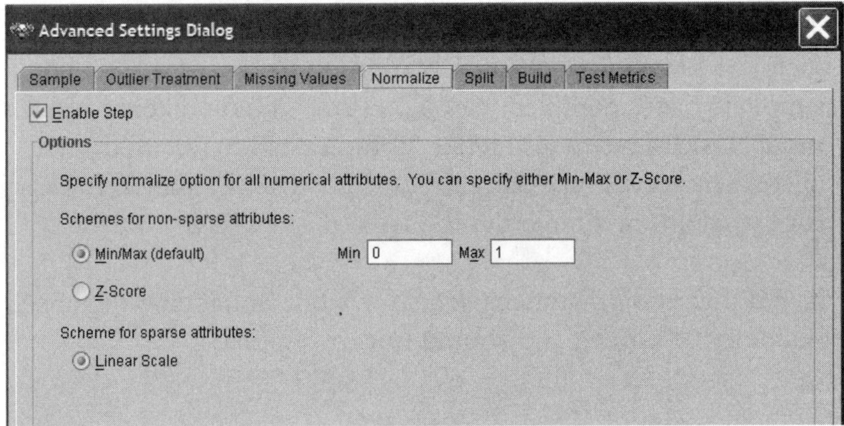

Figure 3.7: *SVM Normalize Default Settings.*

Linear and Gaussian Kernels

In the Build options (see Figure 3.8), ODM can determine the kernel used by the algorithm, or you can specify linear or Gaussian. If linear is used for the kernel, the coefficients for each attribute used to build the model will be rank-ordered and you can see which ones contribute the most in determining the target class. Tolerance value tells the algorithm when to stop building the model; increasing this value to a higher number will build the model faster but may be less accurate.

SVM and Over-fitting

The complexity factor prevents over-fitting. If a model is built that exactly fits the dataset used in its construction, the ability of the model to predict target attributes in this build dataset would be 100%. This sounds great until you try to apply the model to your test dataset, and find that the predictive accuracy is poor. In fact, such a model may only be useful for the build dataset, because errant or extreme values that are not seen anywhere else are operating to prevent the model from being generally applicable to new data.

The SVM algorithm will calculate the most optimal complexity factor to prevent over-fitting by finding the best tradeoff between simplicity and complexity. You may if you like re-build the model and specify a higher complexity factor than the one chosen by SVM, especially if you find that the model is skewing (or favoring) the prediction in favor of one class.

Active Learning maintains accuracy while enhancing the speed of building the model, and should not be disabled.

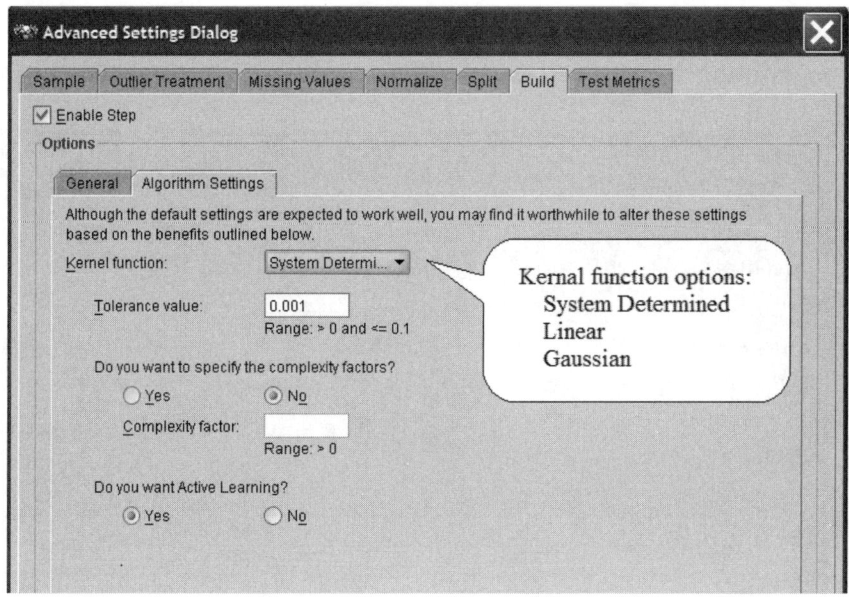

Figure 3.8: *SVM Build Default Settings.*

SVM Results with Gaussian Kernel

For this exercise, we will keep all the defaults in the Advanced Settings dialogue. When the Build and Test Activity Steps are completed for the wind_Ireland_v dataset, click on Result in the Build section. There we see that ODM used the Gaussian kernel function to build the model. Click on Weights and note that all seasons had equal weight. The test results show that the predictive confidence is in the good range at 46.3%.

A look at the accuracy of the model (see Results under Test Metrics) indicates that the spring season had the fewest number of correct predictions, and that many spring days were actually classified as winter. A more accurate model might be constructed by changing the months designated for the different seasons, guided by better knowledge of Irish weather, but the point here is that the model can differentiate seasons simply by examining wind speed data.

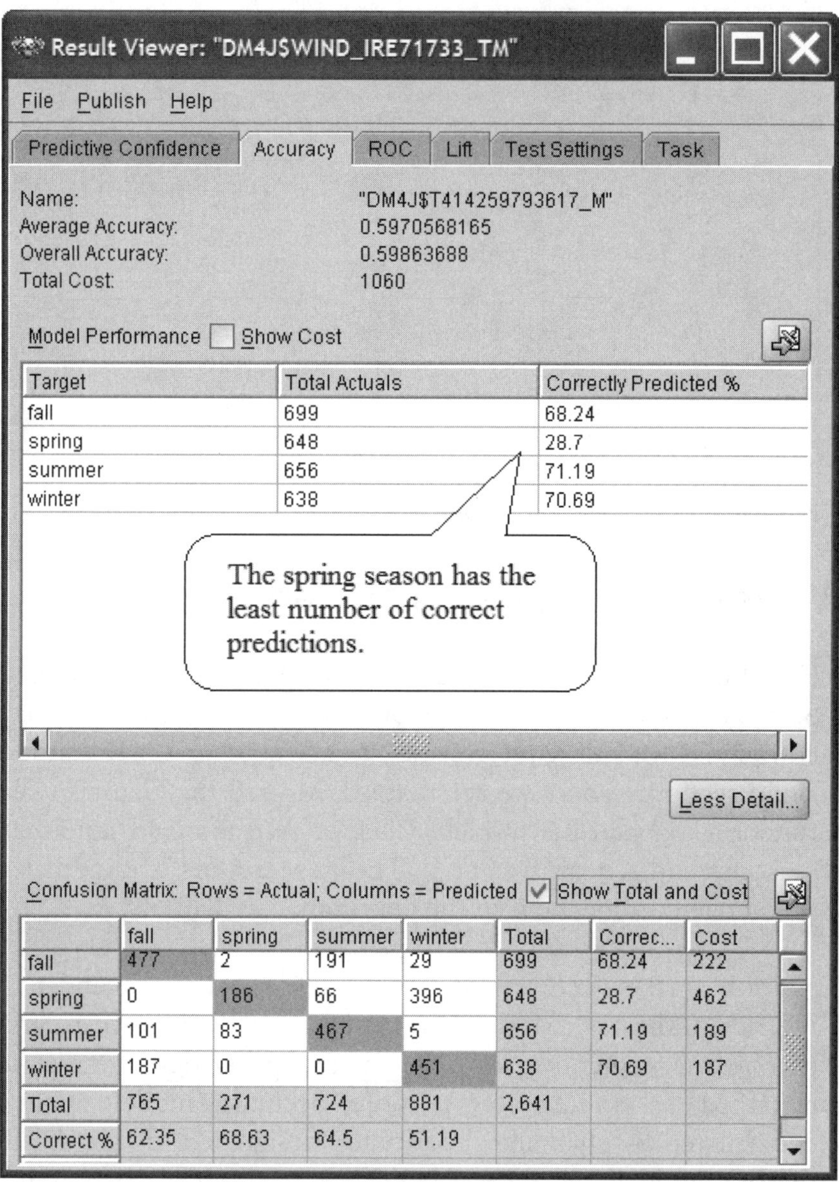

Target	Total Actuals	Correctly Predicted %
fall	699	68.24
spring	648	28.7
summer	656	71.19
winter	638	70.69

	fall	spring	summer	winter	Total	Correc...	Cost
fall	477	2	191	29	699	68.24	222
spring	0	186	66	396	648	28.7	462
summer	101	83	467	5	656	71.19	189
winter	187	0	0	451	638	70.69	187
Total	765	271	724	881	2,641		
Correct %	62.35	68.63	64.5	51.19			

Figure 3.9: *SVM Gaussian Model Accuracy.*

ODM automatically chooses the best kernel to fit the data. The Irish wind data is best fit with the Gaussian kernel; however, you can choose the linear kernel option in Advanced settings under the Build tab. Re-building the model and forcing the SVM model to use the linear kernel results is a very poor model for this dataset, and reduces predictive accuracy to 11.4%. Although using a linear kernel is typically faster, the speed of building the model will be reduced when the data is inherently non-linear.

Another method of examining the differences between the two models is cost. The cost of the linear kernel is 598 as compared to 502 for the Gaussian, illustrating that the linear model is worse when measuring the relative accuracy of the two models. The cost is a value assigned to the number of misclassifications, and cost values for falsely classifying target values (false positives and false negatives) are stored in a cost matrix. If no changes are made to the cost matrix, all misclassifications are treated as equally important.

Examining the coefficients of the attributes is not very revealing for this dataset, except to point out that even though "month" is explicitly built into the definition of "season," it was not as important as wind speeds in predicting the season.

Usually when you derive a new attribute value from one of the existing attributes, you will want to exclude this variable from the model since it is very highly correlated with the target attribute in this example. As shown in Figure 3.10, you can choose a different target class (in this example target class = "summer"). Note that there are different coefficients and rankings of attributes for each season fall, winter, spring and summer, and the values of the coefficients are very small.

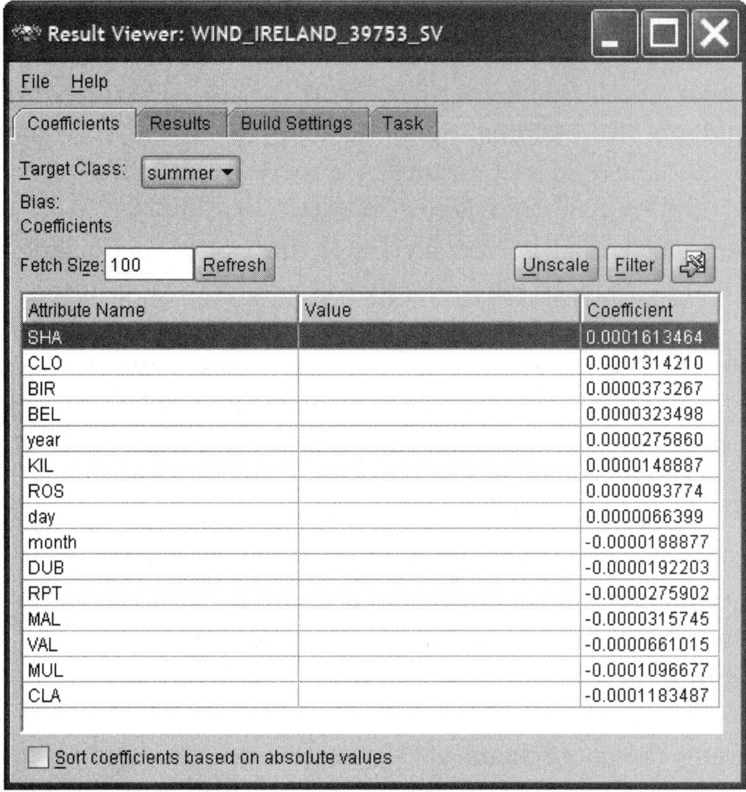

Attribute Name	Value	Coefficient
SHA		0.0001613464
CLO		0.0001314210
BIR		0.0000373267
BEL		0.0000323498
year		0.0000275860
KIL		0.0000148887
ROS		0.0000093774
day		0.0000066399
month		-0.0000188877
DUB		-0.0000192203
RPT		-0.0000275902
MAL		-0.0000315745
VAL		-0.0000661015
MUL		-0.0001096677
CLA		-0.0001183487

Figure 3.10: *Ireland Wind SVM Linear Coefficients.*

Importing Boston House Price Data

To demonstrate another model using the linear kernel of SVM, we'll import the Boston house price dataset from http://lib.stat.cmu.edu/datasets/.

Type the following string into the Google search engine to find more information: **statlib datasets archive**

This data is from the publication Harrison, D. and Rubinfeld, D.L. "Hedonic prices and the demand for clean air," J. Environ. Economics & Management, vol.5, 81-102, 1978.

There are 20 attributes in this example:

```
OBS         unique identifier for each case
TOWN        town where area is located
TOWN#       numeric identifier of the town
TRACT       tract number
LON         longitude
LAT         latitude
CRIM        per capita crime rate by town
ZN          proportion of residential land zoned lots over 25,000
            sq.ft.
INDUS       proportion of non-retail business acres per town
CHAS        Charles River dummy variable (= 1 if tract bounds river;
            0 otherwise)
NOX         nitric oxides concentration (parts per 10 million)
RM          average number of rooms per dwelling
AGE         proportion of owner-occupied units built prior to 1940
DIS         weighted distances to five Boston employment centers
RAD         index of accessibility to radial highways
TAX         full-value property-tax rate per $10,000
PTRATIO     pupil-teacher ratio by town
B           1000(Bk - 0.63)^2, Bk is the proportion of blacks by
            town
LSTAT       % lower status of the population
MEDV        Median value of owner-occupied homes in $1000's
```

Building SVM Classification Models

Now we will build an SVM model. ODM will automatically pick either a linear or Gaussian kernel depending on the linearity of the data. Now we will see which one it chooses.

After importing the data using the Data Miner Import Wizard, initiate a Classification Build Activity using SVM, setting CHAS as the target attribute. The CHAS attribute has two classes, 1 if the tract bounds the Charles River and 0 if not.

Of the total 506 properties in the dataset, only 7% are next to the Charles River. Our classification problem is to find attributes that predict real estate properties near the Charles River. The unique identifier in the case table is OBS. Make sure to change the "OBS." in the original dataset to "OBS" in order to eliminate problems with having a "." in the column headings. The preferred target value is 1, and we will keep all the defaults in the advanced settings.

The results of the SVM classification activity show that the model predictive accuracy is in the best range of 69%, with 80% of the preferred target class 1 correctly classified, and 89% of the class 0 correct.

Since the SVM algorithm chose the Gaussian kernel function, there are no coefficients to examine. We have a model that can predict properties near the river, but we really do not know anything about the model. Now we will re-build the model, forcing the model to use the Linear kernel, and compare the two results.

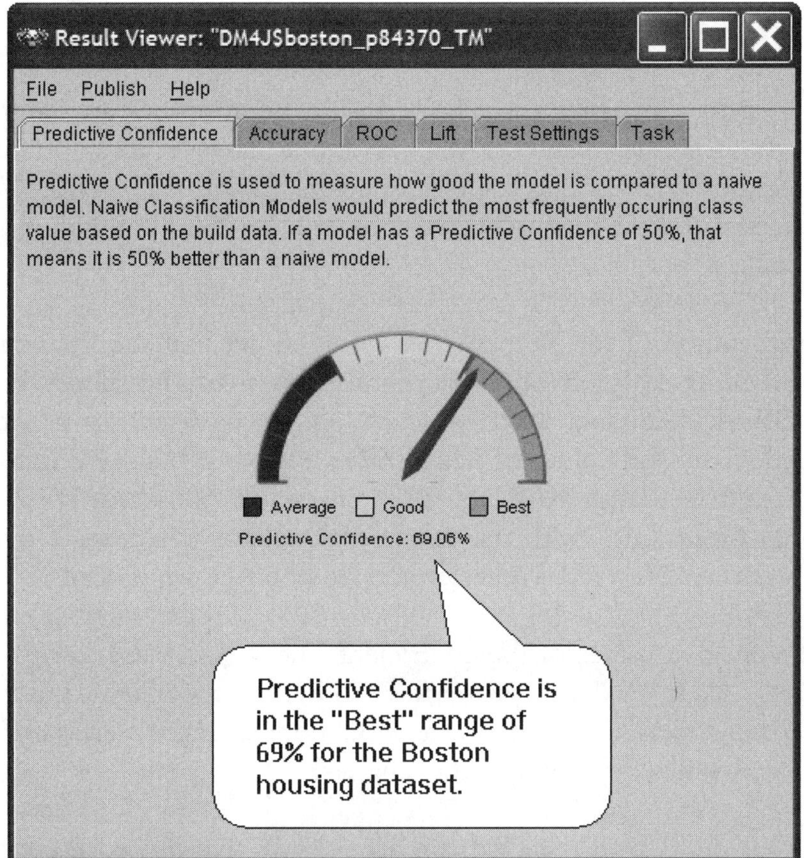

Figure 3.6: *Predictive Confidence.*

First, click on "Activity," and build another SVM classification model as before. This time, however, after completing the New Activity Wizard, choose Advanced Settings, and under the "Build" tab, select "Algorithm" settings and pick "linear" as the kernel function. Keep the default settings for tolerance, complexity factors, and Active Learning. Finally, click "OK" and then "Finish," completing the Build Activity.

Interpreting the SVM Results

It is easy to interpret linear SVM results because they are like the results for the Naïve Bayes, Adaptive Bayes Network, and Decision Tree models as described in Chapter 2. The SVM results also show the ranking of the attributes used in building the model.

Examination of the Test metrics result shows that the Predictive Confidence is good at 57%, slightly less than the model built using the Gaussian kernel. Click on Build Result to see the coefficients and values of the attributes used to build the model. You can see that NOX, a measure of air pollution, was the topmost attribute, with the towns of Dedham, Waltham, Dover, Watertown, Newton, Wellesley and Boston following next.

The positive values of the coefficients mean that these towns are highly likely to have properties bordering the Charles River, whereas towns like Brookline and Belmont with coefficients of -1 are very unlikely to be near the Charles.

A Google Map of the Dedham area shows that indeed there are many residential areas bordering the Charles River.

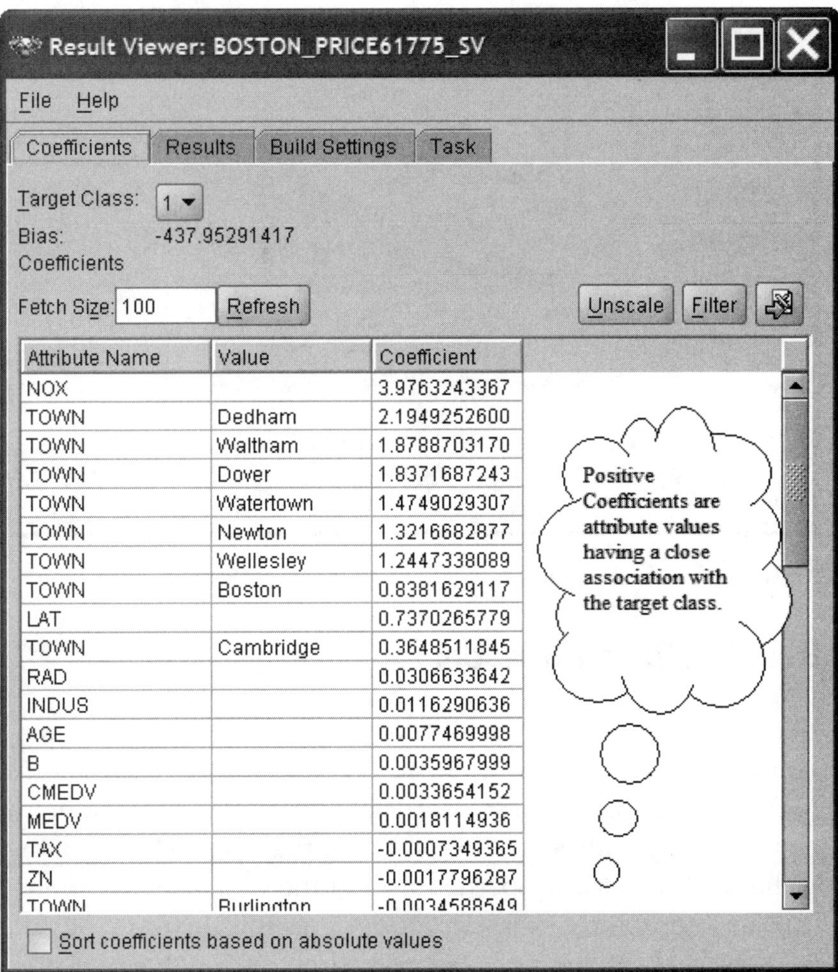

Figure 3.12: *River Properties Coefficients.*

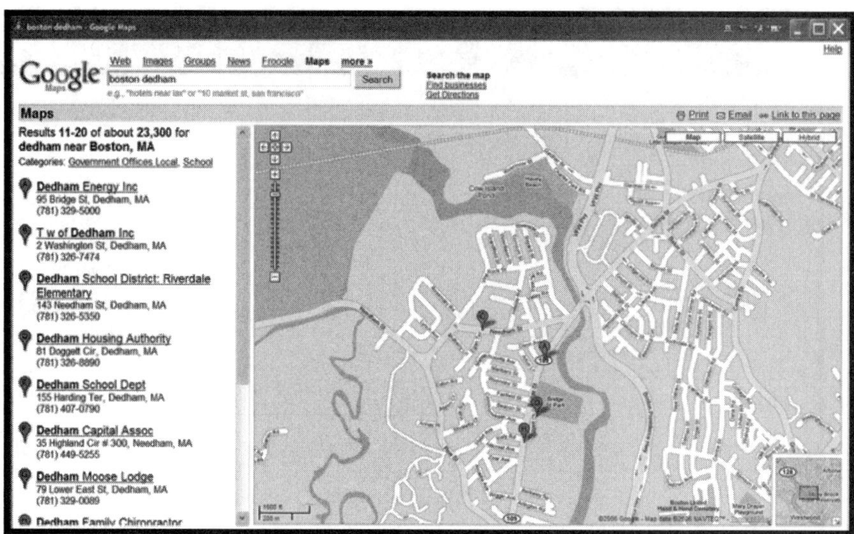

Figure 3.13: *Google Map of Dedham Area near Boston.*

Refining the SVM Model

But wait a minute! What if you were searching the area for housing for yourself or a client? You are concerned about the NOX having the highest coefficient of 3.97. This model does not give any indication of whether the air pollution index is higher or lower for properties around the Charles River, only that it is an important factor. If you look at the Boston case dataset by right-clicking the table name and choosing "Show Summary Single Record," you will find that NOX ranges from 0.38 to 0.87 with mean of 0.55 and variance of 0.01.

NOX is a continuous (as opposed to categorical) variable, meaning that there are an infinite number of possible values between the minimum and maximum. Discrete or categorical variables can possess only exact values, and intermediate values are not possible. Data Miner designates the continuous variables as FLOAT data types, as seen when you click on *data summary* on Step 3 of the Activity Wizard. To examine the effect of NOX on our Charles River target attribute, we have a couple of options. One is to discretize NOX into High, Low, and Medium values. Data Miner has a discretize transformation that will be explored in Chapter 5. For now, the regression capabilities of the SVM algorithm in modeling continuous variables will be examined.

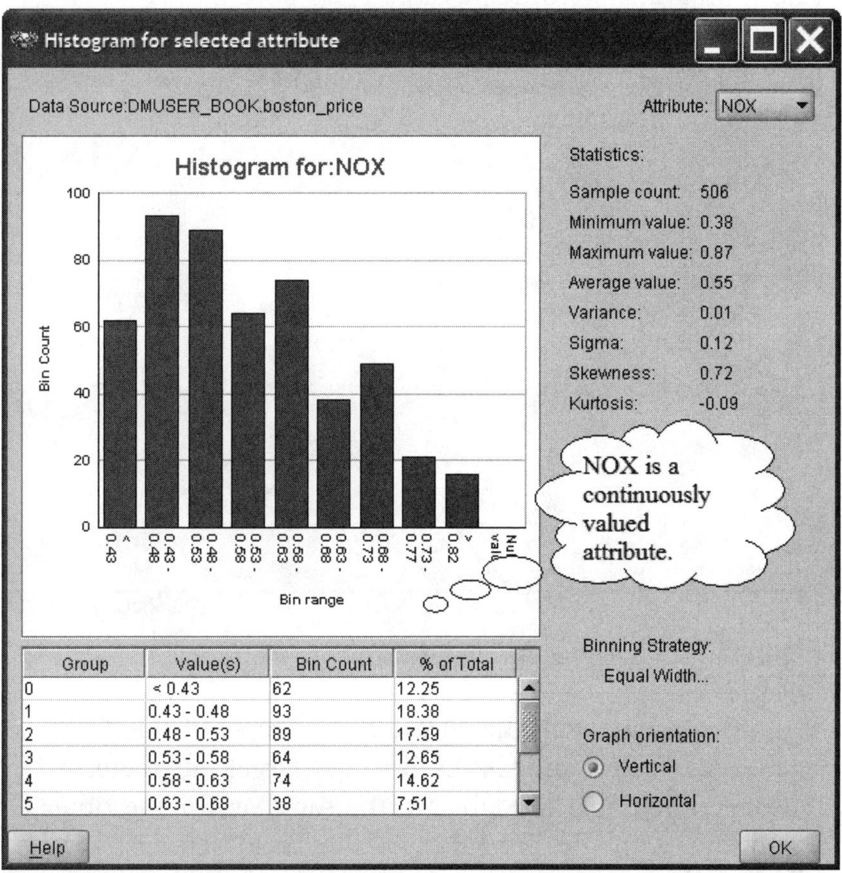

Group	Value(s)	Bin Count	% of Total
0	< 0.43	62	12.25
1	0.43 - 0.48	93	18.38
2	0.48 - 0.53	89	17.59
3	0.53 - 0.58	64	12.65
4	0.58 - 0.63	74	14.62
5	0.63 - 0.68	38	7.51

Figure 3.14: *Histogram of NOX.*

Building a SVM Regression Model

The SVM algorithm is a useful method for predicting the value of a continuous value. To build the regression model, choose "Build" from the Activity tool, and pick Regression as the function type. Note that Support Vector Machine is the only algorithm available for regression.

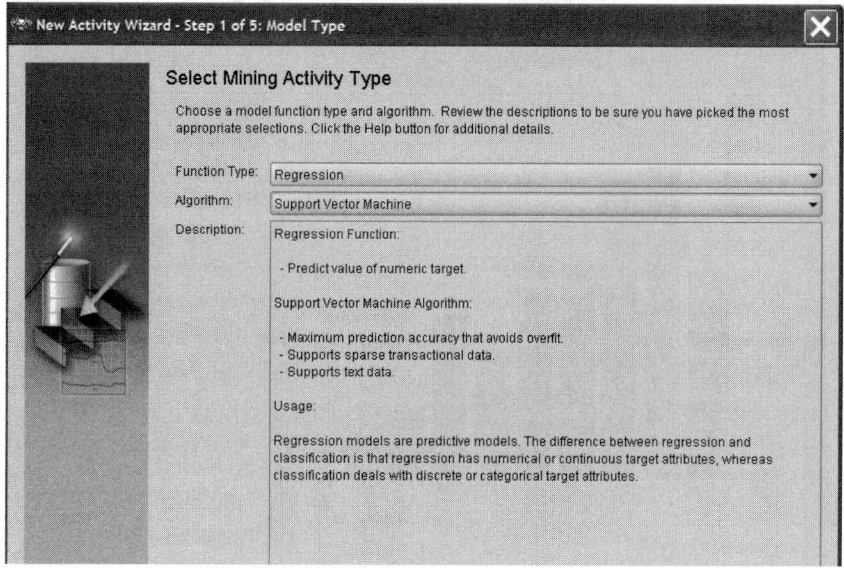

Figure 3.15: *Regression Mining Activity.*

We will continue with the wizard as before, choosing OBS as the unique identifier and NOX as the target attribute. Under Advanced Settings, the tabs are the same as for the other SVM algorithms with the exception of the Build settings. SVM will select and optimize all parameters, such as kernel function, tolerance etc, so we will keep the default settings and go ahead and build the model.

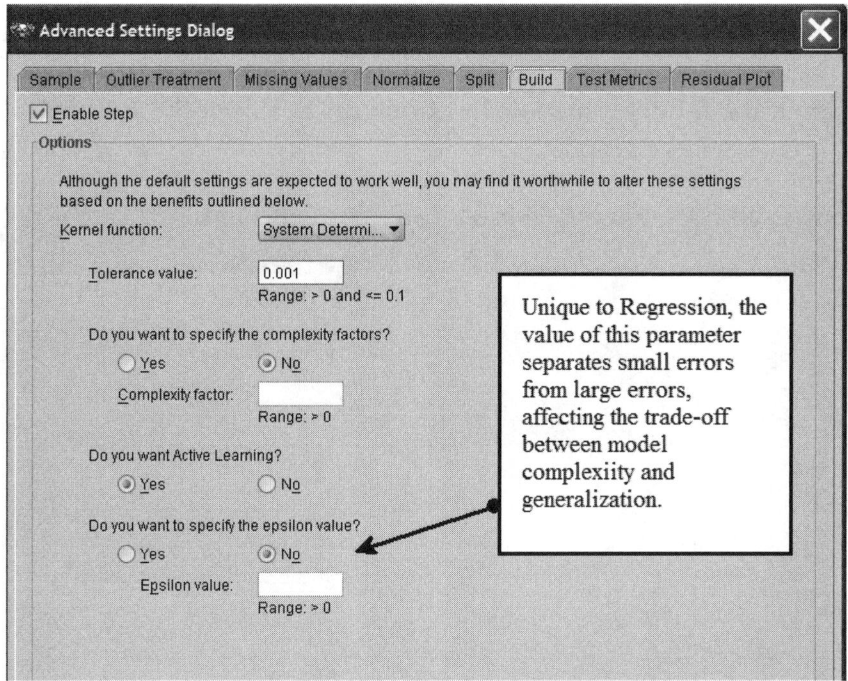

Figure 3.16: *SVM Regression Build Default Settings.*

Regression Model Results

The Build results show that SVM chose the Gaussian kernel for the algorithm, and the predictive confidence of the resulting model is between "good" and "best" at 66%. There are several new measures available in the results of the regression model that indicate the "goodness of fit" of the model.

A good fit explains a high proportion of variability in the data, and is able to predict new cases with high certainty. Data Miner provides both graphical and statistical estimates of goodness of fit with a graphic plot of residuals and calculation of root mean square error. Note that there is a residual plot available in the Build Activity.

Residuals are the differences between the actual and predicted values. If the residuals are randomly distributed around zero, then the model is a good fit. Click on Result in the Residual Plot box to see the graphic.

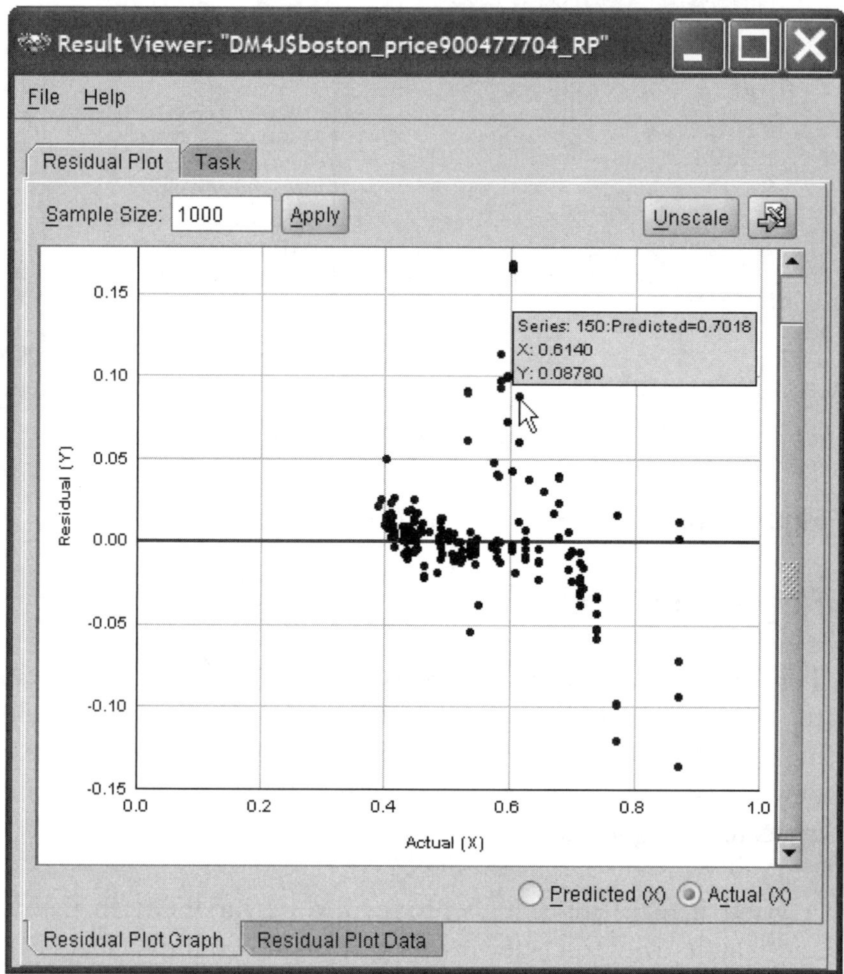

Figure 3.17: *Actual Residual Plot Graph for NOX.*

Dots on the horizontal zero line means that the value was an exact prediction, whereas dots above and below the line show the relative error of the prediction. You can see that the dots are randomly scattered until around NOX = 0.55, where the error of the predictions vary considerably. This indicates that the model is much more accurate for lower values of nitric oxide concentrations than for higher concentrations. You can mouse over a data point to see the actual and predicted values. For point 150 for example, the actual value (x axis) was 0.614 and the model predicted 0.7018. If you were building regression models for air pollution, you might want to build one model for lower levels of NOX and another one for levels exceeding 0.5.

Linear Regression Analysis

Checking the predicted circle at the bottom right of the residual plot will toggle between the actual and predicted plots. The predicted residual plot shows the predicted values on the x-axis and shows which predictions can be trusted the most. As in the actual residual plot, the graph indicates that predicted values over 0.5 are inaccurate. A predicted value of 0.7 may be very close to 0.7, or it could be 0.8 or 0.6.

However, predicted values of 0.6 or less will be very close to 0.6. Clicking on the Residual Plot data tab will show a listing of the actual and predicted values for the test dataset.

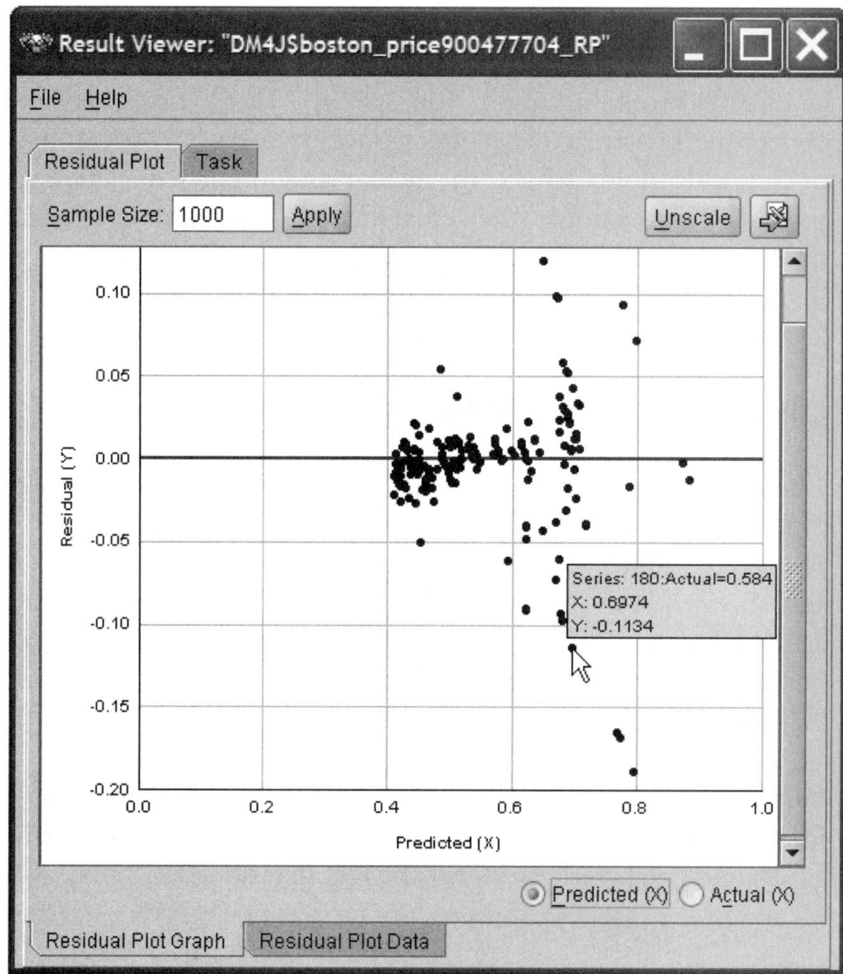

Figure 3.18: *Predicted Residual Plot Graph for NOX.*

The statistical measures of goodness of fit are found under the Test Metric Result (Figure 3.19). Here the Root Mean Square Error (RMSE) is shown which is also known as the standard error of the regression. An RMSE closer to zero means that the model is a better predictor.

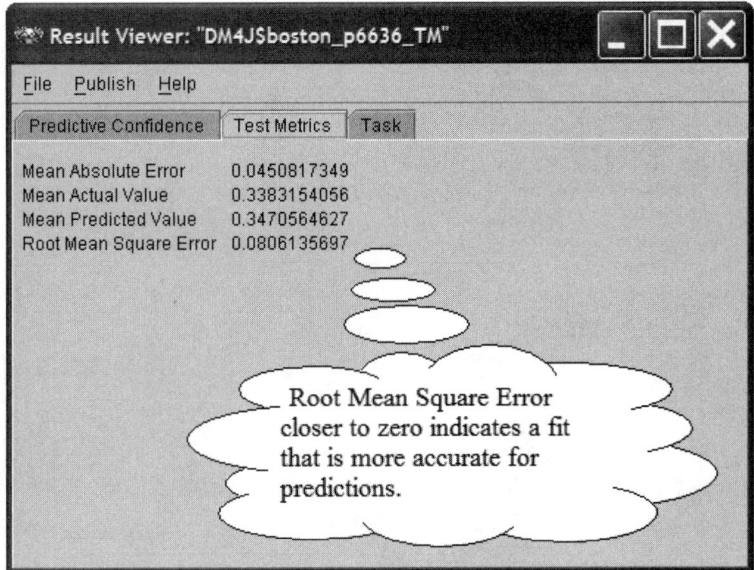

Figure 3.19: *Test Metrics for NOX.*

Compare this result to that of using TAX as the target for a regression model. Here we see that the majority of points are tightly clustered around the horizontal zero line, the RMSE is 0.0418, and the predictive confidence is very good at 87%.

A model built on the same dataset with TAX as the target is a very highly accurate model for predicting tax rates for properties in the Boston housing dataset.

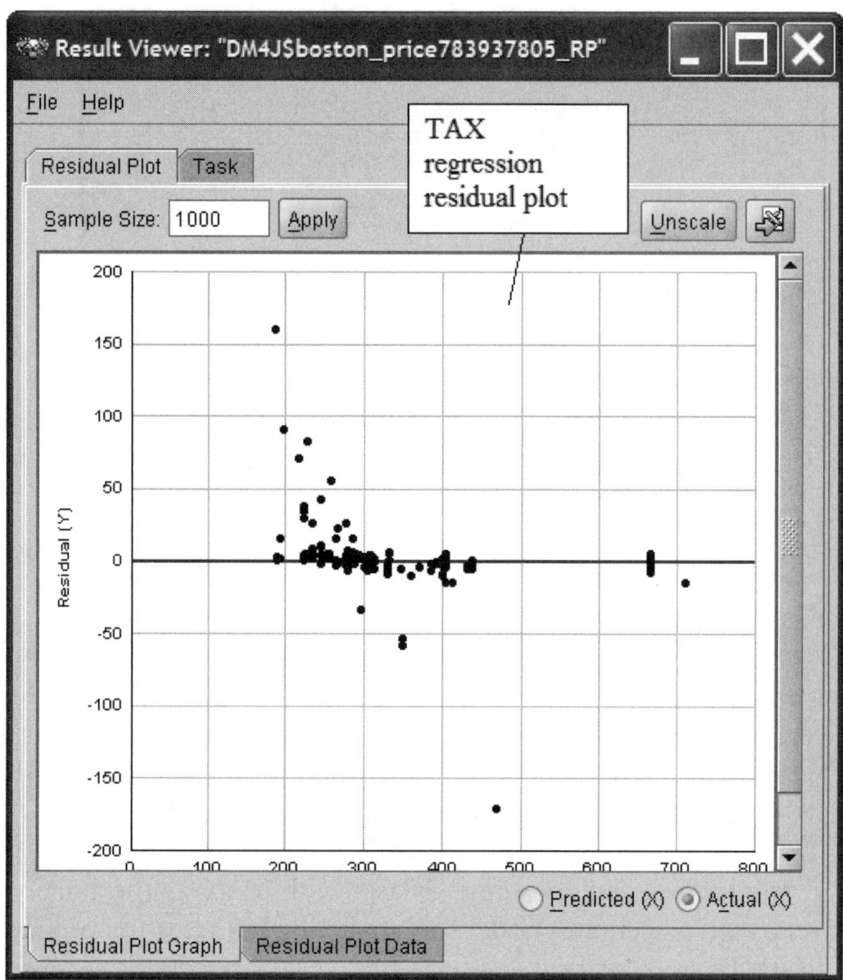

Figure 3.20: *Residual Plot Graph for TAX.*

Drilling into the SVM Data

Taking the high variability of the NOX data into account, we are still not sure whether settling near the Charles River would be associated with higher air pollution or not. Running the following SQL statement for the towns with highest and lowest coefficients in our linear SVM model reveals that towns more likely near the river have on average lower nitric oxide concentrations than those that are not.

```
select AVG(NOX) from "BOSTON_PRICE" where TOWN IN ('Somerville',
'Arlington', 'Belmont', 'Brookline') = 5.822.

select AVG(NOX) from " BOSTON_PRICE " where TOWN IN ('Dedham',
'Waltham', 'Dover', 'Watertown') = 4.905.
```

Given these results, we can conclude that lower levels of pollution appear to be associated with properties that border the Charles River, and that higher levels of pollution are highly variable and perhaps not well modeled with the 20 attributes in our case dataset.

Using Text Data in SVM Predictive Models

The usefulness of the SVM algorithm for modeling categorical and continuous data has been shown, and how to utilize text data in predictive models will now be examined. The dataset is found at http://kdd.ics.uci.edu/summary.task.type.html and is the Syskill Webert Web Data, which contains HTML source web pages along with the ratings of a single user on these web pages.

Type the following string into the Google search engine to find more information: : **uci kdd archive summary**

The web pages are on four separate subjects which are bands of recording artists, goats, sheep, and biomedical information. Users looked at each web page and rated the content on a three point scale (hot, medium, cold). However, there were very few ratings for medium, indicating that the rater's opinions were highly polarized.

The Web rating data is organized into 4 folders which are bands, biomedical, goats, and sheep. The folders have a number of files containing web page content and a single file named index which relates viewer ratings to each of the web pages. We will create a table with the web content stored as CLOB type data, and then match this with the index file so that we have a case dataset with an ID field, viewer rating, category of web page, and the web page content.

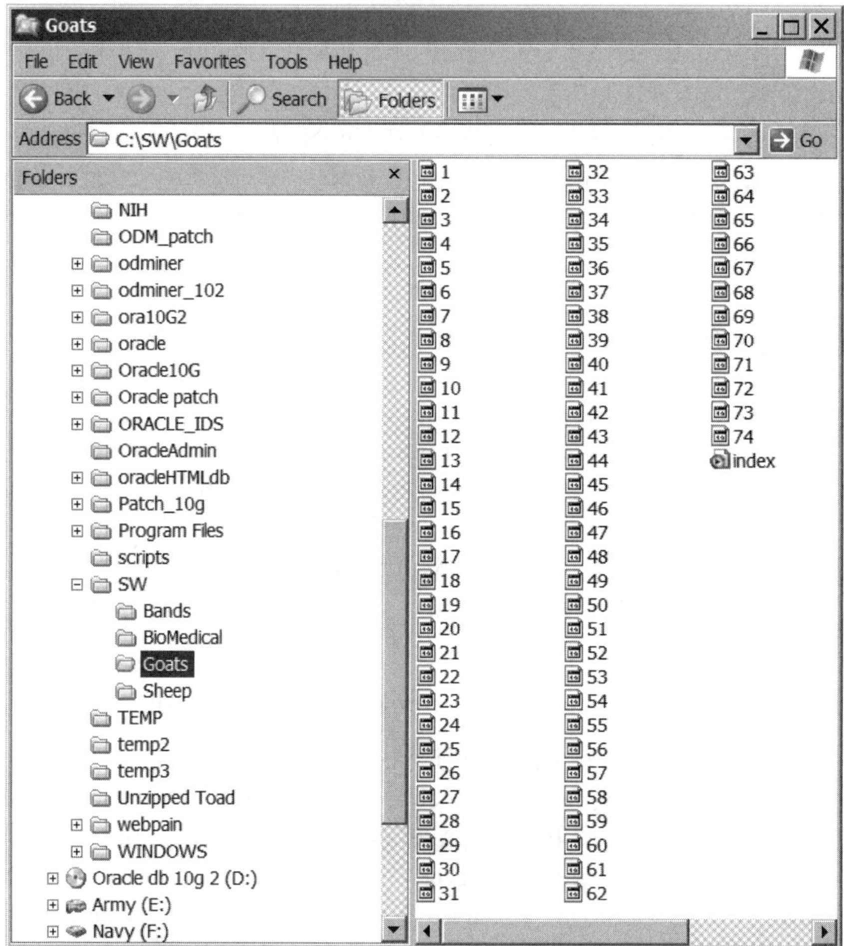

Figure 3.21: *Directory of Goats.*

The steps in arriving at the case dataset are as follow:

1. Import the index table for each subject using the import wizard in Data Miner.

2. Create a table for importing the CLOB data.
3. Use *sqlldr* to import the web content as CLOB fields.
4. Create views for each category of web page by joining the index and CLOB tables for each subject.
5. Union all four views together into a final table.
6. Create a unique identifier for the cases in this table.

Using the Import Wizard in Data Miner is straightforward. Rename the index file with a .dat extension before attempting the import and specify Vertical Bar (|) as the delimiter. The field names are file_name, rating, url, date_rated, and title. Import each file into a separate table such as web_rating_goats, web_rating_sheep, web_rating_bands, and web_rating_biomed.

Importing CLOB Data

Next, create 4 tables for importing the CLOB data in each subject area, using the code example below. Using sqlplus, log on as the Data Miner user and run these scripts:

```
create table web_desc_sheep (seqnum int primary key, type
varchar2(10), location varchar2(20), filename varchar2(20),text
CLOB);
create table web_desc_goats (seqnum int primary key, type
varchar2(10), location varchar2(20), filename varchar2(20),text
CLOB);
create table web_desc_bands (seqnum int primary key, type
varchar2(10), location varchar2(20), filename varchar2(20),text
CLOB);
create table web_desc_biomed (seqnum int primary key, type
varchar2(10), location varchar2(20), filename varchar2(40),text
CLOB);
```

Now that the tables are created, use *sqlldr* to import CLOB data from each directory using the code below. First, create control files using the programs as shown.

We are creating two new fields, seqnum for matching the CLOB files with the index, and type, designating a constant for each subject area. Go to the directory where the CLOB files are located, substitute the directory listing for each folder as appropriate, and change the filename position to read the filename for your system.

Loading CLOB Data into the Oracle Database

For example, if your files are located at c:/sw/bands/1 ensure that the numbers following filename position are the columns in the control file where this is listed. Once you have created and saved your control files, type the following SQL*Loader (sqlldr) syntax from the command line, substituting your ODM username and password, and the location of the control files that you created:

```
Sqlldr dmuser/pswd control = c:/loader_bands.ctl
log=c:/loader_bands.log

LOAD DATA
   INFILE *
   replace
   into table web_desc_bands
   (seqnum recnum,
    type constant bands,
    filename position(63:79),
    text LOBFILE (filename)
    terminated by EOF)
BEGINDATA
10/13/1995  06:21 PM  6,897 DSCWEBDEV\Decision Suppc:\sw\bands\1
10/17/1995  12:01 PM  4,382 DSCWEBDEV\Decision Suppc:\sw\bands\2
10/17/1995  12:05 PM  4,654 DSCWEBDEV\Decision Suppc:\sw\bands\3
10/17/1995  12:11 PM  5,051 DSCWEBDEV\Decision Suppc:\sw\bands\4
10/17/1995  12:12 PM  9,086 DSCWEBDEV\Decision Suppc:\sw\bands\5
10/17/1995  12:15 PM  2,585 DSCWEBDEV\Decision Suppc:\sw\bands\6
```

For Step 4, create views using the following scripts:

```
create or replace view bands_v as
select a."file_name", a."rating", b.type, b.text
from "web_rating_bands" a join web_desc_bands b
on a."file_name" = b.location;

create or replace view goats_v as
```

```
select a."file_name", a."rating", b.type, b.text
from "web_rating_goats" a join web_desc_goats b
on a."file_name" = b.location;

create or replace view sheep_v as
select a."file_name", a."rating", b.type, b.text
from "web_rating_sheep" a join web_desc_sheep b
on a."file_name" = b.location;

create or replace view biomed_v as
select a."file_name", a."rating", b.type, b.text
from "web_rating_biomed" a join web_desc_biomed b
on a."file_name" = b.location;
```

The Oracle Application Express (APEX, formerly HTMLDB) program in Figure 3.22 shows a listing of records with the filename, seqnum, and type (biomed). The numbers in the seqnum column are links to the clob data stored in the case dataset.

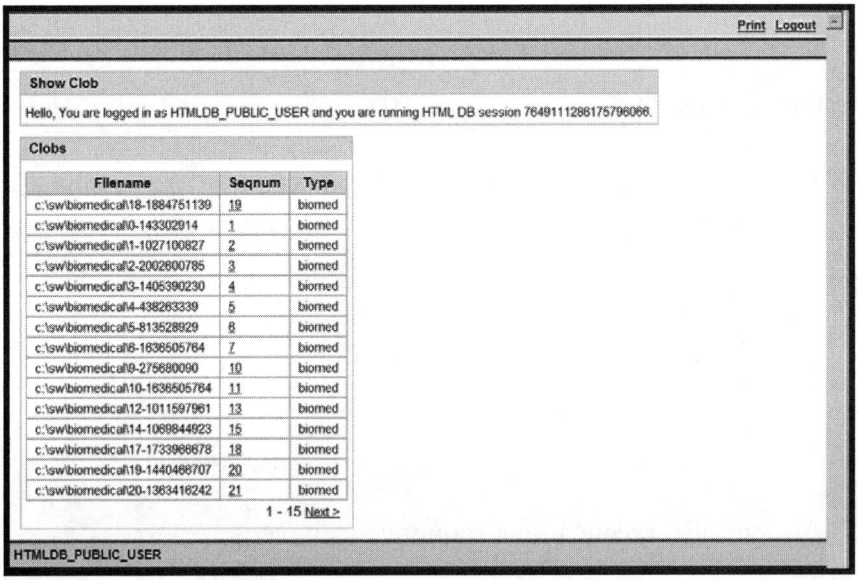

Print Logout

Show Clob

Hello, You are logged in as HTMLDB_PUBLIC_USER and you are running HTML DB session 7649111286175796066.

Clobs

Filename	Seqnum	Type
c:\sw\biomedical\18-1884751139	19	biomed
c:\sw\biomedical\0-143302914	1	biomed
c:\sw\biomedical\1-1027100827	2	biomed
c:\sw\biomedical\2-2002600785	3	biomed
c:\sw\biomedical\3-1405390230	4	biomed
c:\sw\biomedical\4-438263339	5	biomed
c:\sw\biomedical\5-813528929	6	biomed
c:\sw\biomedical\8-1636505764	7	biomed
c:\sw\biomedical\9-275680090	10	biomed
c:\sw\biomedical\10-1636505764	11	biomed
c:\sw\biomedical\12-1011597961	13	biomed
c:\sw\biomedical\14-1069844923	15	biomed
c:\sw\biomedical\17-1733966678	18	biomed
c:\sw\biomedical\19-1440466707	20	biomed
c:\sw\biomedical\20-1363416242	21	biomed

1 - 15 Next >

HTMLDB_PUBLIC_USER

Figure 3.22: *Application Express Application showing CLOB fields.*

Clicking on seqnum #2 brings up a new Web page with the clob content for biomedical record #2.

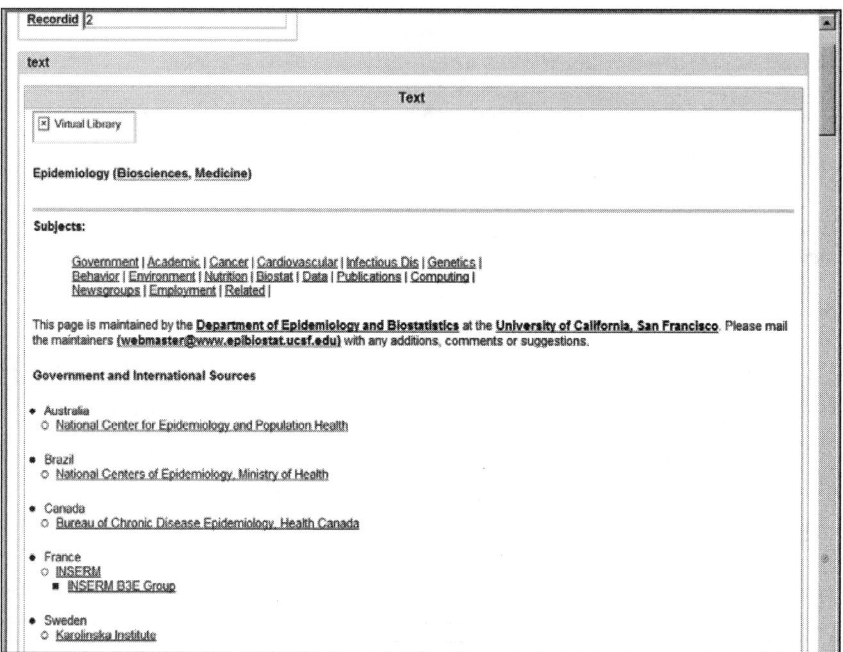

Figure 3.23: *Application Express Application view of CLOB fields.*

Next, we create a new table by executing the union SQL statements below:

```
Create table web_union as
Select "file_name", "rating", type, text from bands_v
UNION ALL
Select "file_name", "rating", type, text from sheep_v
UNION ALL
Select "file_name", "rating", type, text from goats_v
UNION ALL
Select "file_name", "rating", type, text from biomed_v;
```

And we also create a new sequence web_seq:

```
create sequence
  web_seq
  start with 1
  increment by 1;
```

Finally, we create the case table for web ratings.

```
create table
   WEB_RATE
as
select
   web_seq.nextval file_id,
   a.*
from
   WEB_UNION a;
```

Building a SVM Text Model

Now that we have a table with a sequence (file_id), file_name, rating, type, textual data (CLOB), and 327 rows of data, we can proceed with the new data mining activity.

- As before, choose the classification function type and use the SVM algorithm. The unique identifier is file_id. In the select columns box, de-select file_name from the column list.
- On the Review Data Usage Settings page (Step 3 of 5) ensure that the CLOB (text) field, type, and rating are checked as input attributes for the model.
- Using type as the target, run the SVM data mining activity, keeping the build parameters at the default settings.

Interpreting the SVM text Data

The SVM classification mining activity shows two new steps labeled Text and Text (Test). The algorithm detected the CLOB field and correctly identified it as a text attribute. In this step the algorithm applies context indexing or feature extraction to the text attribute, and uses the same settings for the test text fields.

Clicking the Result of the Build step you can see that the algorithm used a linear kernel and the words that were used to classify the type target are listed along with their coefficients.

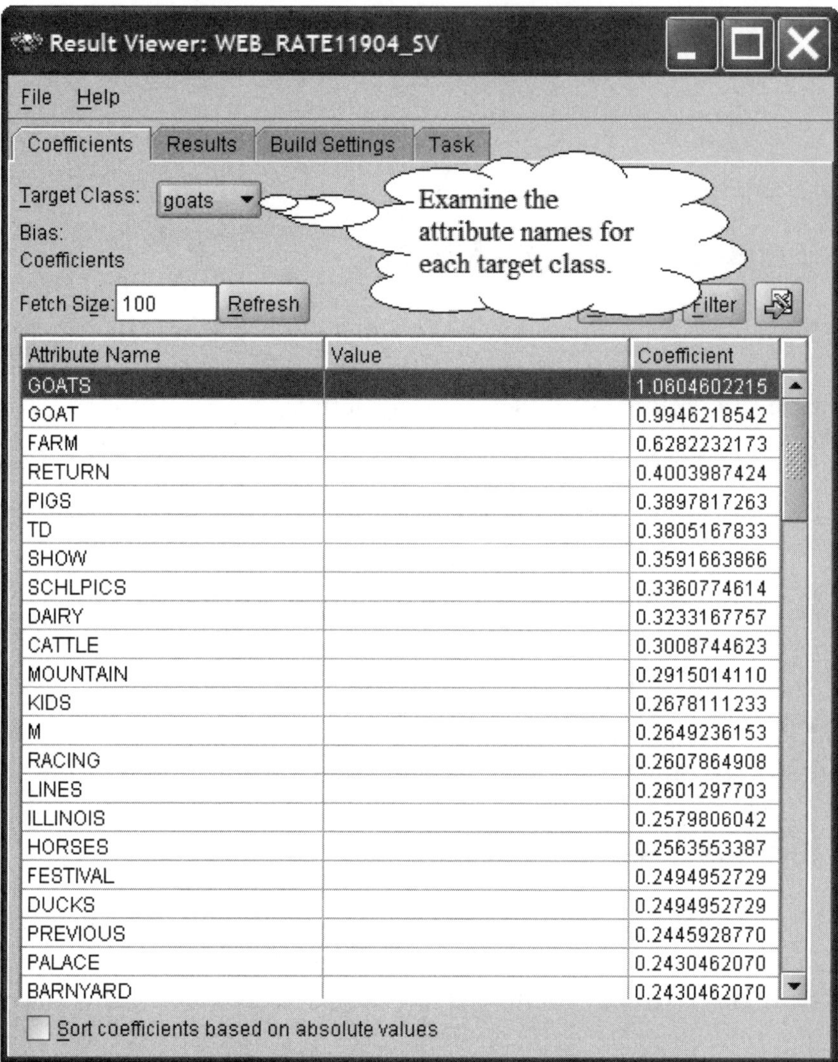

Attribute Name	Value	Coefficient
GOATS		1.0604602215
GOAT		0.9946218542
FARM		0.6282232173
RETURN		0.4003987424
PIGS		0.3897817263
TD		0.3805167833
SHOW		0.3591663866
SCHLPICS		0.3360774614
DAIRY		0.3233167757
CATTLE		0.3008744623
MOUNTAIN		0.2915014110
KIDS		0.2678111233
M		0.2649236153
RACING		0.2607864908
LINES		0.2601297703
ILLINOIS		0.2579806042
HORSES		0.2563553387
FESTIVAL		0.2494952729
DUCKS		0.2494952729
PREVIOUS		0.2445928770
PALACE		0.2430462070
BARNYARD		0.2430462070

Figure 3.24: *SVM Text Coefficients.*

Not surprisingly, "GOATS" and "GOAT" were the top attributes for the goat target class, "SHEEP" was the highest for sheep target class, "INFORMATION" and "MEDICAL" were the best for biomed, and "IUMA" was the top for bands.

Checking the Result of the Test Metrics step shows that the model was in the "best" range at 82% predictive confidence.

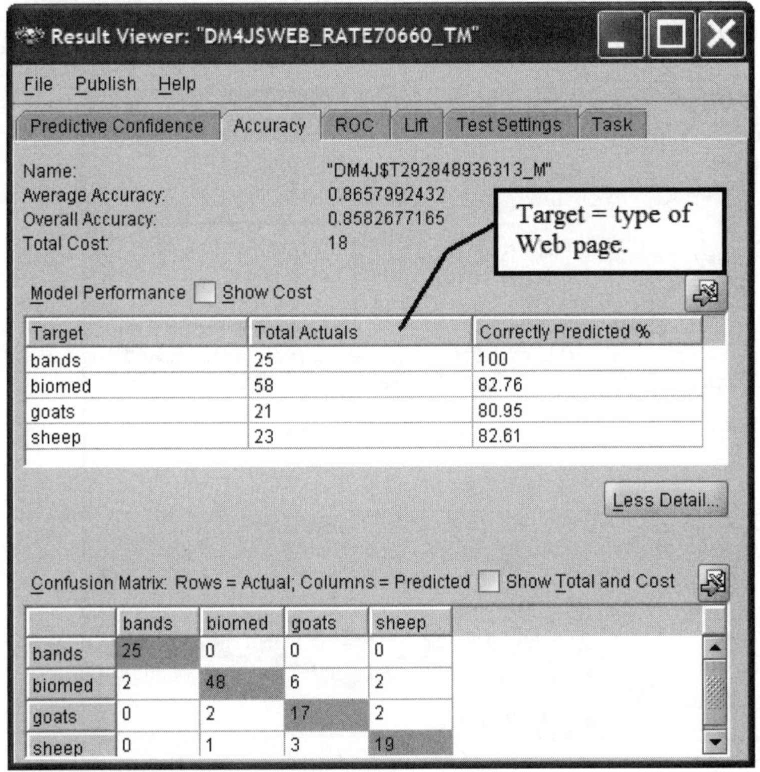

Figure 3.25: *SVM Text Confusion Matrix.*

The confusion matrix shows that the model predicted bands with 100% accuracy, and the other web pages ranged from 81% to 83% correctly predicted.

Now the SVM classification will be repeated choosing "rating" as the target. Since there are only 11 web ratings equal to "medium" we have recoded these to "cold" using the Recode Transformation. Repeat the steps as above and keep the default settings, picking text and rating as the input attributes. The preferred target value will be hot.

The result of the test metrics show that predicting the users rating of Web pages is in the good range at 35%, and 41% of the hot ratings were correctly predicted.

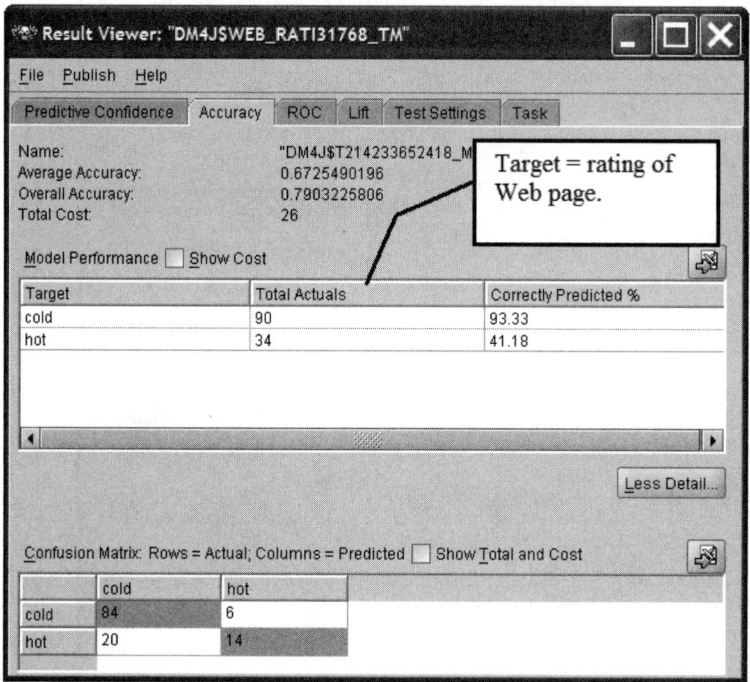

Figure 3.26: *SVM Text Model Accuracy.*

The Build results show the words that were used in the model to classify the test cases. There were 84 cold ratings classified as cold; 14 hot were classified as hot. There were a total of 26 ratings misclassified; most of these were 20 hot ratings that were misclassified as cold.

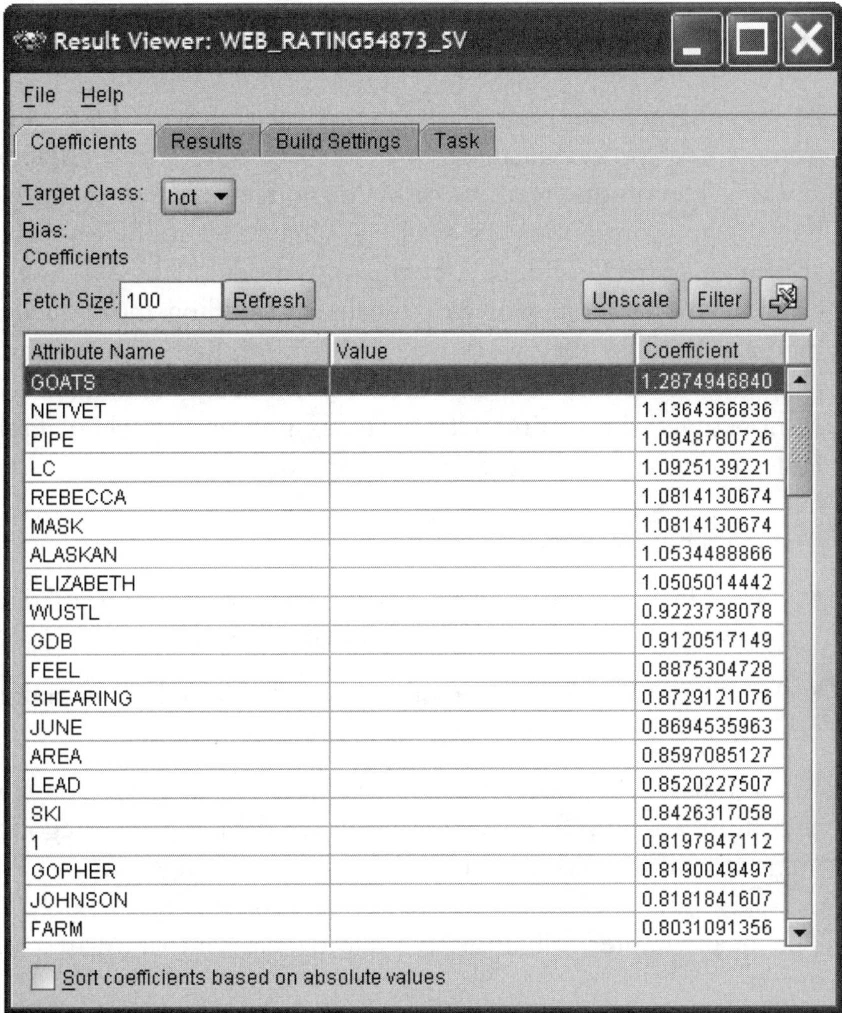

Attribute Name	Value	Coefficient
GOATS		1.2874946840
NETVET		1.1364366836
PIPE		1.0948780726
LC		1.0925139221
REBECCA		1.0814130674
MASK		1.0814130674
ALASKAN		1.0534488866
ELIZABETH		1.0505014442
WUSTL		0.9223738078
GDB		0.9120517149
FEEL		0.8875304728
SHEARING		0.8729121076
JUNE		0.8694535963
AREA		0.8597085127
LEAD		0.8520227507
SKI		0.8426317058
1		0.8197847112
GOPHER		0.8190049497
JOHNSON		0.8181841607
FARM		0.8031091356

Figure 3.27: *SVM Text Model Coefficients.*

If we repeat the SVM Activity Build and include type along with rating and text in the model, we find that the predictive confidence of the model actually decreases to 28%.

Conclusion

In this chapter we built classification models with Data Miner using a very powerful algorithm: the Support Vector Machine (SVM). The unique features of SVM models are that they can be built from continuous as well as binary or multiclass target attributes. After building a regression model, we saw how to examine the residual plot as a means of building more accurate models. Because they work well with sparse, high dimensionality data, this algorithm is well-suited for modeling text data. We demonstrated importing CLOB data into an Oracle database table, and using a text attribute for data mining.

The main points of this chapter are:

- The two kernels, linear and Gaussian are automatically chosen to maximize the accuracy of the model.
- SVM is a highly accurate algorithm that avoids over-training and can work on data with thousands of attributes.

In summary, Support Vector Machine is a very adaptable algorithm able to fit a wide variety of data types: categorical, numeric or continuous, and text.

The next chapter will look at creating clusters of related data items.

Creating Clusters and Cohorts

CHAPTER

Clustering data is a very common technique in data mining as well as many other fields, including statistics, bioinformatics, pattern recognition, and machine learning. Clustering is the unsupervised classification of data into subsets, where the subsets of data share common traits. In previous chapters we have discussed supervised classification, meaning that a target was identified and the accuracy of the prediction followed from how many cases were correctly classified according to the target values. With clustering algorithms no target is specified, you simply see what patterns are discovered by the technique.

Clustering and Cohorts

Clusters may be found in a large group of hospital patients, which are comprised of those with similar characteristics, such as coronary patients, pediatric patients and so on. Furthermore, certain cancer patients may exhibit a type of tumor characterized by a certain gene that is sensitive to a specific type of drug treatment. Clustering can reveal interesting correlations among drugs, genes and the disease, and how these may respond best to a specific therapy.

Oracle Data Mining has two algorithms for performing cluster analysis, the k-Means algorithm and Orthogonal Partitioning Clustering (O-Cluster). In this chapter each clustering algorithm will be described, and an example will be provided using k-Means.

The k-Means Cluster

The enhanced k-means algorithm randomly defines initial centroids, which approximate a center of gravity and uses distance measures to calculate the distance between centroids and data objects. ODM uses either the Euclidean, Cosine, or Fast Cosine distance metrics. From the Oracle Data Mining Forum in response to "How does ODM cluster algorithm work?" posted May 2, 2006:

> "ODM k-means builds a hierarchical tree. When a new cluster is added, the parent node is replaced with two new nodes. Both children have the same centroid as the parent except for a small perturbation in the dimension with most variablility. Then a few k-means iterations are run on the two children and the points belonging to the parent are distributed among the two new nodes.
>
> There are a couple of different strategies how to choose which node to split (e.g., size, dispersion). Once the desired number of leaf nodes is reached, we run k-means across all leaf nodes.
>
> The advantage is that all clusters have reasonable initial centroids and we are unlikely to get dead/empty clusters. We explode categorical attributes into multiple binary dimensions and compute distances using these new dimensions."

Using O-Cluster

O-Cluster is a density-based algorithm that does not use distance formulas. O-Cluster is an Oracle proprietary algorithm. Technical details about the O-Cluster algorithm can be found in Milenova and Campos' paper "Clustering Large Databases with Numeric and Nominal Values Using Orthogonal Projections" at http://www.oracle.com/technology/products/bi/odm/pdf/ocluster_wnominal_data.pdf.

Type the following string into the Google search engine to find more information: **nominal values using orthogonal**

According to the Oracle Data Miner Tutorial, O-Cluster finds natural clusters by identifying areas of density within the data, up to the maximum number entered as a parameter. That is, the algorithm is not forced into defining a user-specified number of clusters, so the cluster membership is more clearly defined.

O-Cluster Sensitivity Settings

The sensitivity setting determines how sensitive the algorithm is to differences in the characteristics of the population. O-Cluster determines areas of density by looking for a valley separating two hills of density in the distribution curve of an attribute. A lower sensitivity requires a deeper valley; a higher sensitivity allows a shallow valley to define differences in density.

Thus, a higher sensitivity value usually leads to a higher number of clusters. If the build operation is very slow, you can increase the Maximum Buffer Size in an attempt to improve performance.

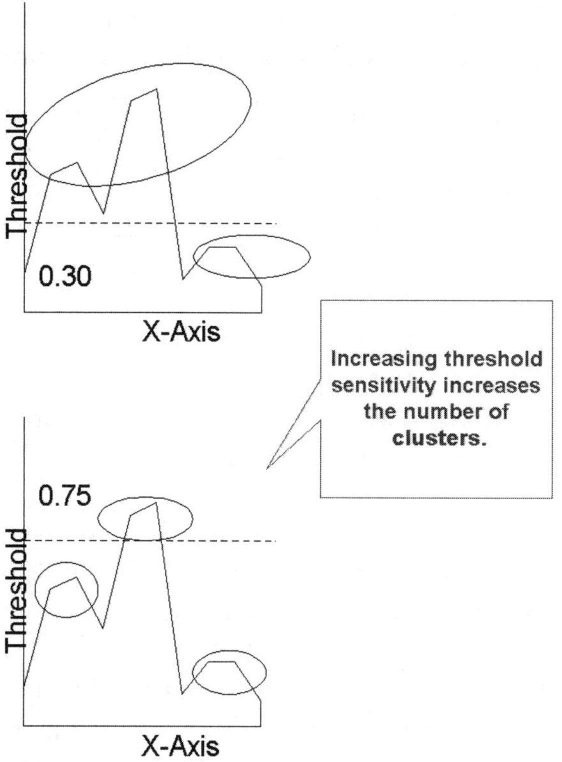

Figure 4.1: *Cluster Density.*

Using K-Means for Clustering

The k-means algorithm is the most well-known and commonly used partitioning method, and has been widely studied in biology, marketing, machine learning, and spatial databases, to name a few. K-Means is important because it does not depend on pre-defined notions of classifications existing in the dataset. The data mining analyst determines only the number of clusters that will be derived, removing any potential bias about how the resulting clusters may be grouped together.

When data contains clusters of greatly different sizes or unusual shapes (non-spherical groupings), has many outlier data points or random observations (noise), then k-means will have trouble discovering clusters. In the following sections we will show an example of applying k-means to a dataset with a large number of attributes. We will demonstrate the use of stratified sampling to help the algorithm find clusters for an attribute we want to examine.

Examining the CoIL Data

The k-Means algorithm will be used to find clusters in the CoIL dataset, found at http://kdd.ics.uci.edu/databases/tic/tic.html. The build dataset used in the CoIL 2000 Challenge has 86 attributes and 5822 descriptions of customers from a Dutch insurance company. The target attribute is #86, "CARAVAN" which is the number of mobile home policies.

Type the following string into the Google search engine to find more information: **CoIL 2000**

At the start, be sure to name the file with the .dat extension and save as comma delimited if you use the Data Miner Import Wizard.

After importing the dataset, we will examine the histogram of the target attribute by right-clicking the case table and choosing Show Summary Single Record.

You will see that there are 348 cases where CARAVAN = 1, approximately 6% of the total. In order to more clearly distinguish clusters around the target value of interest, we will stratify the case table so that we have a more even distribution of 1's and 0's for the CARAVAN attribute.

Stratified Sampling Transformation Wizard

Use the transform wizard Stratified Sample to create a new table with 1/3 of the target attribute = 1 (having insurance) and 2/3 of the cases for customers who don't have mobile home insurance.

The new case table will have a total sample count of 1044 cases, 348 with insurance and a random sample of uninsured customers equaling 696 cases.

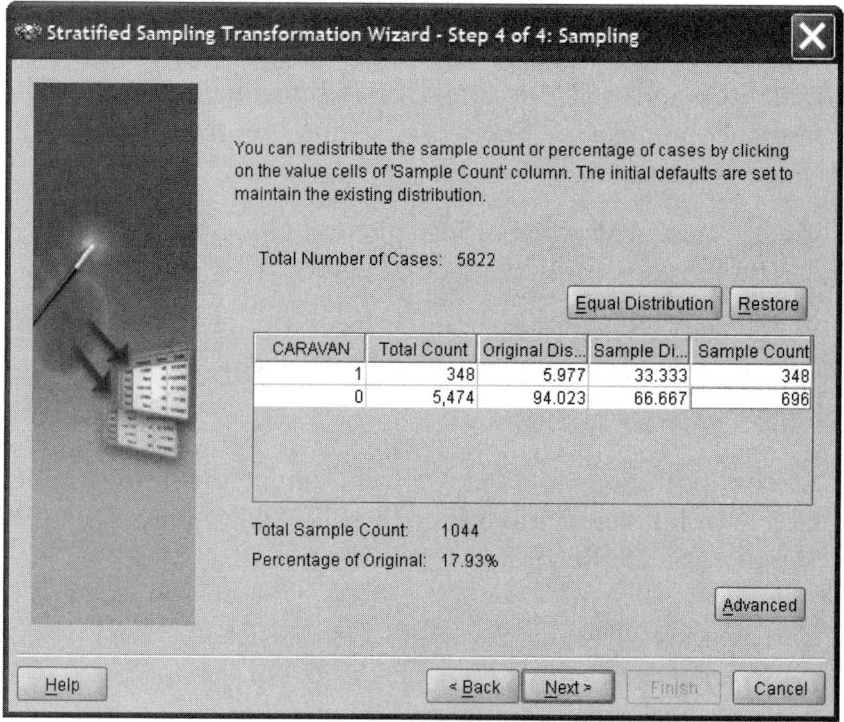

Figure 4.2: *Stratified Sampling.*

Now a new cluster model will be built using the stratified sample, choosing K-means for the algorithm. There is no unique key for the case data, so we choose Compound or None for the Unique

Identifier. Note that in-contrast to the classification models, you do not choose a target variable in the Activity Wizard.

Building a K-Means Cluster

The Wizard will automatically trim outliers and impute missing data by substituting the mean for numerical attributes and the mode for categorical attributes. Normalization of numerical values is also performed using the Min/Max technique. You can change these default settings by clicking on Advanced Settings when you finish the New Activity Wizard. In the Build Tab, the default number of clusters is set at 10. K-means must have a number of clusters to start with, in contrast to O-Cluster, which finds the number of clusters best suited to the dataset. Keep the default build settings and build the model with 10 clusters.

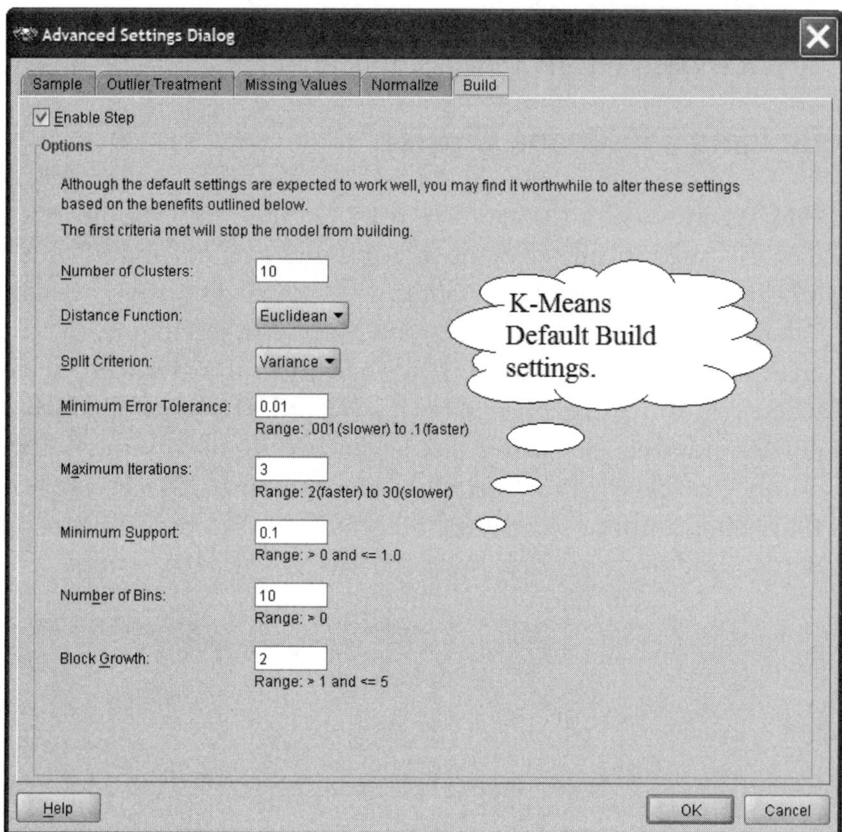

Figure 4.3 *K-Means Default Build Settings.*

After the Mining Activity completes, click on Build results to view the clusters. In this view, all clusters are shown. Cluster #1 has all 1044 cases. Cluster #2 is an intermediate cluster created from Cluster #1, with 615 cases, and Cluster #4 was created from Cluster #3. The check box Show Leaves Only will display the final clustering.

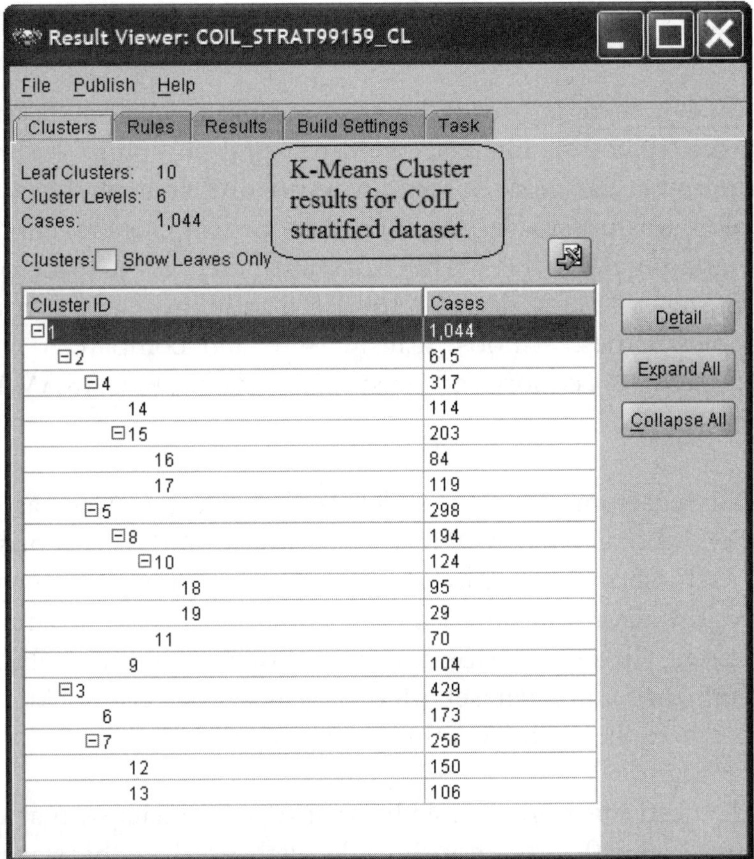

Figure 4.4: *K-Means Cluster Results.*

Next, highlight a cluster and click the Detail button to view a histogram of the cluster centroid attributes and corresponding values. Keeping in mind that clustering is an unsupervised data mining technique, meaning that there was no target attributes to predict. We can learn more about the similarities of customers who purchased insurance if by chance the clustering algorithm split on the target attribute.

Finding majority cohort values

Even though there is usually no pure sample of customers with the target value of interest, we may find a cohort of the population that has more or less a majority of that attribute value. To explore this possibility, select each of the leaf clusters, choose Detail, and highlight the CARAVAN attribute. As it turns out, three clusters (#11, #14 and #16) are mostly insurance carriers for mobile homes. Choose Cluster #16 and compare it with Cluster #18, a cohort of customers without CARAVAN insurance.

You can see from the cluster details that Cluster #16 has 84 customers who all have insurance while Cluster #18 is comprised of 95 customers without insurance. These divisions were not planned, the algorithm found these naturally occurring clusters in the dataset. In fact, performing the cluster algorithm without stratifying the entire dataset of 5822 cases does not yield any clusters where the CARAVAN target equals all 1.

We influenced this pure sample by stratifying the data so that the values of 1 and 0 were more evenly distributed in the starting cluster, Cluster #1. You might use this technique to discover subsets of the case dataset, defining very homogeneous populations or cohorts of customers, hospital patients, sales executives or whatever business you may be investigating.

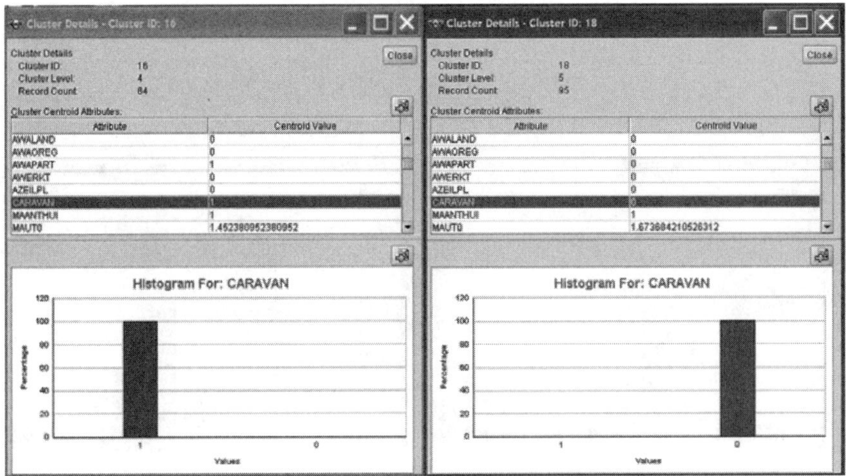

Figure 4.5: *Cluster Details for CARAVAN Insurance.*

Next, we proceed by clicking through each attribute to find those whose values are most different between the cohorts, as shown in figures 4.6 through 4.8. To quickly review the values, you can place each Cluster Detail window side by side.

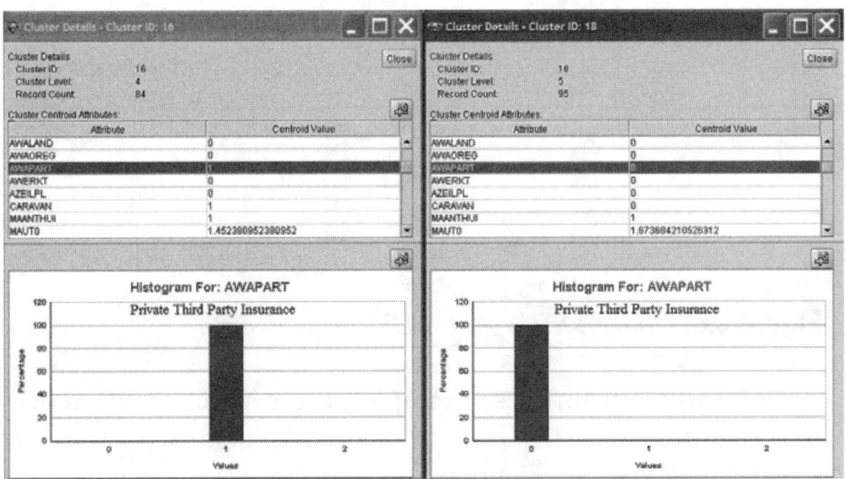

Figure 4.6: *Cluster Details for Private Third Party Insurance.*

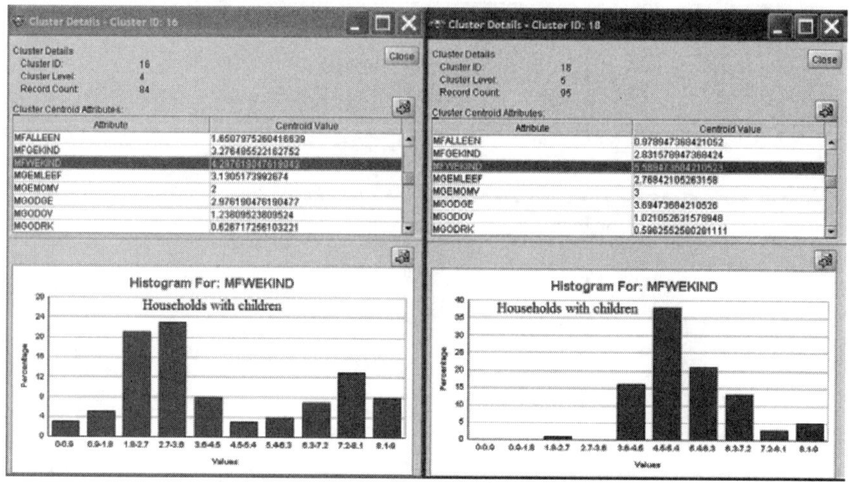

Figure 4.7: *Cluster Details for Households with Children.*

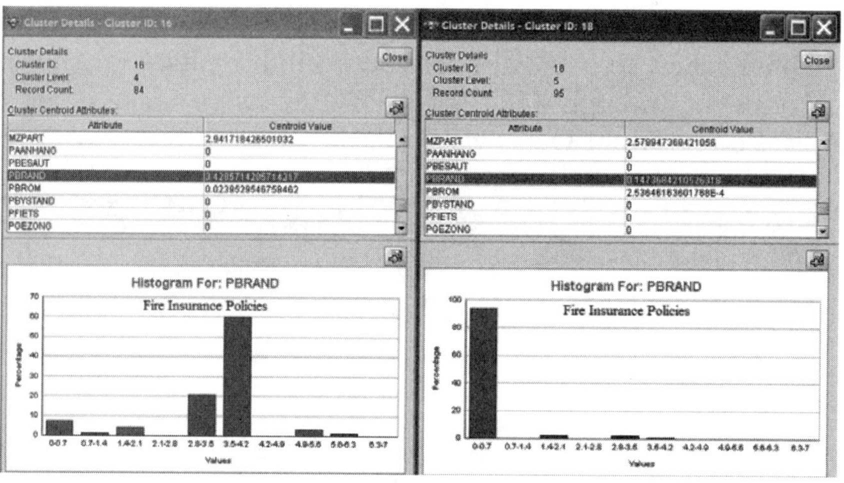

Figure 4.8: *Cluster Details for Fire Insurance Policies.*

As you can see from these examples, there are clear differences in various attributes between those customers who purchased CARAVAN insurance and those who did not. This includes any other insurance purchased, size of household, number of children in the household, and amount of money spent on third party insurance.

Comparing data sub-sets with K-Means

Although the numbers of customers in these clusters are a small percentage of the whole sample, insights as to how subsets of cases behave in relation to others may help target areas where taking some action may substantially impact the overall business practice.

K-Means gives you the rules for deriving each cluster, so that you may apply the rules to another dataset. For example, the rule for Cluster #16 is shown below. For clarity, the top 10 attributes as determined from the Attribute Importance algorithms are displayed. The algorithm provides probabilistic scoring and gives you the confidence and percent support. Note that the rule is written in such a manner that IF A implies (THEN) B (Cluster = 16).

The confidence of the rule is the conditional probability of B given A (A implies B) = probability (B given A). Support for a rule is an estimate of the number of cases in the training dataset for which the rule is true. For Cluster #16 the confidence is 82% and the support estimate is 69 cases.

```
IF
APERSAUT in (1.0) and PBRAND >= 2.8 and AWAPART in (1.0) and
MKOOPKLA >= 1.70 and PWAPART in (2.0) and APLEZIER in (0.0) and
MOPLHOOG <= 4.2 and MOSTYPE <= 41.0 and MOSHOOFD >= 1.0 and MHHUUR
>= 0.0

THEN
Cluster equal 16

Confidence (%)=82.1428571428571
Support =69
```

Choosing the Appropriate Data Mining Algorithm

One of the strategies of the data analyst is to try many approaches when searching for patterns and clusters in the data.

The beauty of Oracle Data Mining is that these tools are easily applied to datasets, without requiring the user to have any data mining training since ODM uses the appropriate filters and settings for you. Still, the question of using one algorithm versus another will arise and the answer as to which is most appropriate is not always straightforward. Sometimes the type of data limits the analysis, as in the case of text data, which is very sparse and highly dimensional. For unsupervised data mining the number of cases and number of attributes (dimensionality) are two features that should be taken into consideration when choosing between k-Means and O-cluster. Keep in mind that there are no hard and fast rules for determining high and low numbers of attributes or large and small data sets. The following guidelines for when to use k-Means and O-cluster are taken from Oracle Data Mining Concepts (10g Release 2 (10.2)) as well as other sources.

When to use K-Means Analysis

K-Means is recommended for datasets with low numbers of attributes (less than 500). The number of clusters is specified by the user (the default is 10), and normalization of the dataset is recommended to prepare the data for analysis. The advantages of using enhanced k-Means clustering (the algorithm included in ODM) is that it provides results based on the algorithm that are superior to the results obtained with traditional k-Means techniques utilized in other data mining programs.

When to use O-Cluster Analysis

O-Cluster, a proprietary Oracle algorithm, has the advantage of handling large numbers of attributes (high dimensionality), and is more appropriate for large numbers of cases, say for instance more than 500. Although this does not seem like very many cases, this is the figure given by Oracle Data Mining Concepts documentation. The number of leaf clusters is determined automatically. The points where splits occur can provide insight to the way data is structured and is helpful in selecting features that help discriminate among cohorts of cases.

Be aware that O-Cluster does not necessarily use all the input data when it builds a model. The algorithm reads 50,000 rows in a batch and will only read in another batch if there is reason to suspect that more clusters exist. Therefore, O-Cluster may stop building the model before all the data is read in, and it is highly recommended that the data be randomized, and discretized using equi-width binning after clipping to handle outliers. Of course, the Build Activity Wizard in Oracle Data Miner takes care of all data preparation for you.

Applying the Cluster

Now that we have defined the population, we are interested in applying the cluster definition to a new dataset. Use this link, http://kdd.ics.uci.edu/databases/tic/ticeval2000.txt, to download the CoIL dataset. Using the Copy Table Wizard in Data Miner, create an exact copy of the CoIL build dataset, naming the dataset coil_test. Then delete all rows in the table using the following SQL statements in the SQL Worksheet:

```
delete from coil_test;
commit;
```

Next, create a control file for SQLLDR with the following. Note that the target attribute CARAVAN is not included:

```
load data
infile '\\folder\shareddocs\coil_test.dat.csv'
replace
into table dmuser_book.coil_test
fields terminated by ','
(
MOSTYPE, MAANTHUI, MGEMOMV, MGEMLEEF, MOSHOOFD, MGODRK, MGODRP,
MGODOV, MGODGE, MRELGE, MRELSA, MRELOV, MFALLEEN,
MFGEKIND, MFWEKIND, MOPLHOOG, MOPLMIDD, MOPLLAAG, MBERHOOG,
 MBERZELF, MBERBOER, MBERMIDD, MBERARBG, MBERARBO, MSKA,
```

```
 MSKB1, MSKB2, MSKC, MSKD, MHHUUR, MHKOOP, MAUT1, MAUT2,
MAUT0,  MZFONDS,  MZPART,  MINKM30, MINK3045, MINK4575, MINK7512,
 MINK123M, MINKGEM, MKOOPKLA, PWAPART, PWABEDR, PWALAND,
 PPERSAIT, PBESAUT, PMOTSCO, PVRAAUT, PAANHANG, PTRACTOR,
 PWERKT, PBROM, PLEVEN, PPERSONG, PGEZONG, PWAOREG, PBRAND,
 PZEILPL, PPLEZIER, PFIETS, PINBOED, PBYSTAND, AWAPART, AWABEDR,
 AWALAND, APERSAUT, ABESAUT, AMOTSCO, AVRAAUT, AAANHANG,
 ATRACTOR, AWERKT, ABROM, ALEVEN, APERSONG, AGEZONG,      AWAOREG,
ABRAND, AZEILPL, APLEZIER, AFIETS, AINBOED, ABYSTAND
)
```

Now, execute this line of code at the command prompt in the directory where the SQLLDR control file is located, substituting your password and database sid as appropriate.

```
C:\scripts>sqlldr dmuser /pswd@database control=coil.ctl
log=coil.log
```

You can also use the File Import Wizard in Oracle Data Miner to import the test dataset into your case data table, and let ODM write the SQLLDR scripts for you.

The apply or test dataset contains 4000 records and 86 attributes. From the Activity menu, choose Apply and select the Cluster Build Model that was built previously.

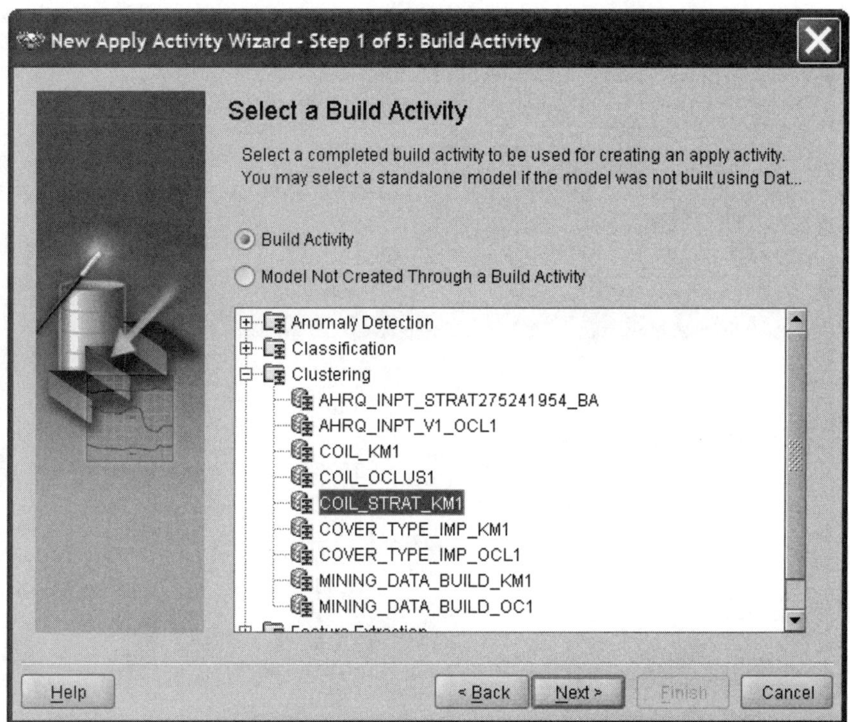

Figure 4.9: *Selecting the Build Activity.*

Select the table just created for the Apply Data Source (coil_test), and pick any attributes that you want included in the result set. The CoIL test data table does not have a unique identifier, so Data Miner will create one for you. In step 4 of 5 in the Apply Activity Wizard, you have the choice of Most Probable Cluster, Specific Cluster ID, and Number of Best Cluster ID's as output options.

The Most Probable Cluster ID will assign the cluster with highest probability to each record, the default choice. These results are shown in Figure 4.10. Each case in the result table is assigned to a cluster with a certain probability attached.

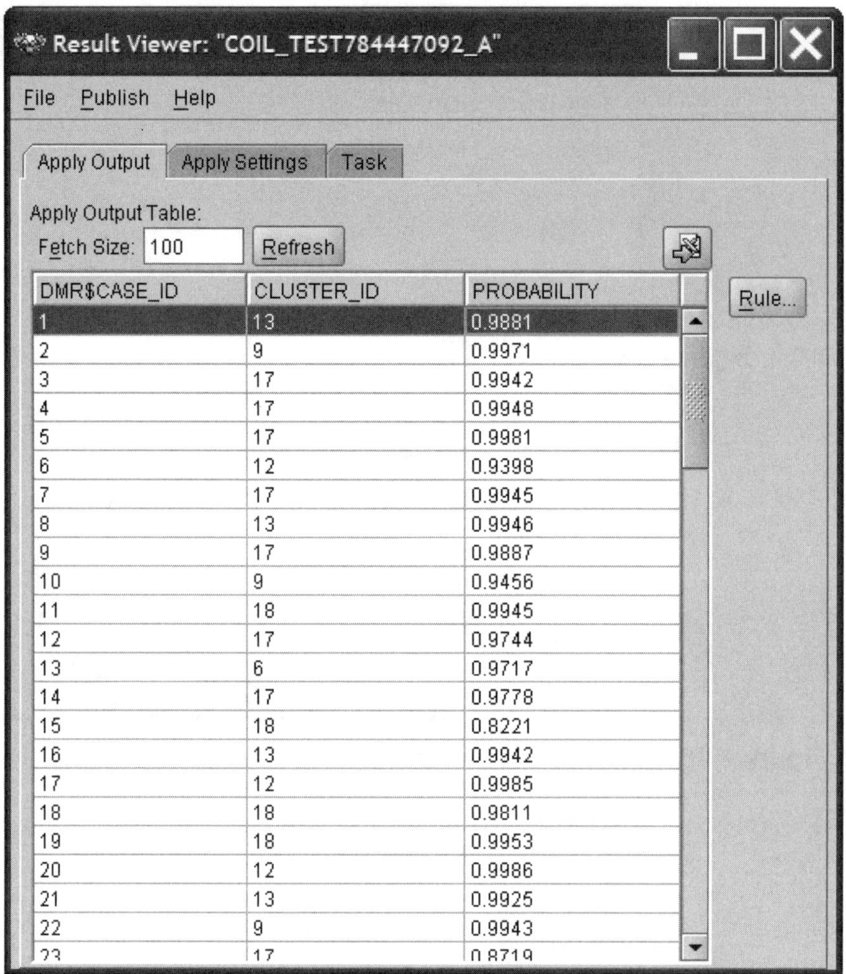

Result Viewer: "COIL_TEST784447092_A"

File Publish Help

Apply Output | Apply Settings | Task

Apply Output Table:

Fetch Size: 100 Refresh

Rule...

DMR$CASE_ID	CLUSTER_ID	PROBABILITY
1	13	0.9881
2	9	0.9971
3	17	0.9942
4	17	0.9948
5	17	0.9981
6	12	0.9398
7	17	0.9945
8	13	0.9946
9	17	0.9887
10	9	0.9456
11	18	0.9945
12	17	0.9744
13	6	0.9717
14	17	0.9778
15	18	0.8221
16	13	0.9942
17	12	0.9985
18	18	0.9811
19	18	0.9953
20	12	0.9986
21	13	0.9925
22	9	0.9943
23	17	0.8719

Figure 4.10: *Apply using Most Probable Cluster ID*

When specific clusters are chosen, the output is shown in Figure 4.11. For each cluster chosen, Data Miner displays a column with the probability of that case fitting into the cluster. Selecting the records with probability greater than .85, for instance, will result in a cohort of customers who fit a particular profile.

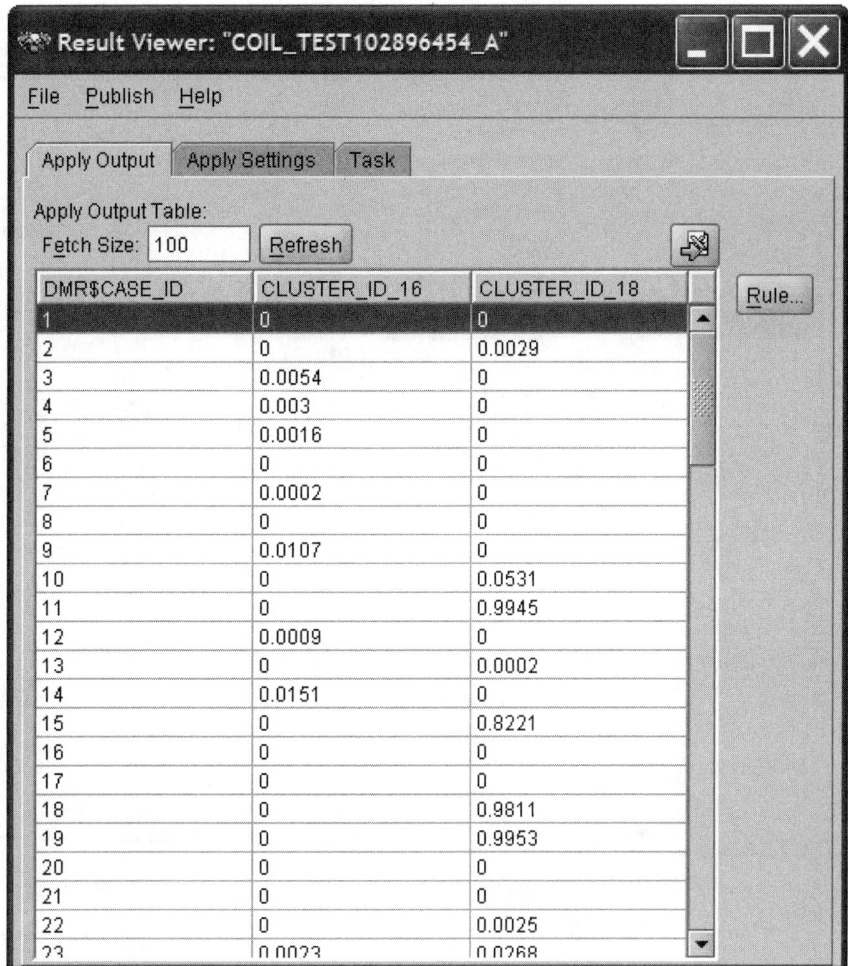

DMR$CASE_ID	CLUSTER_ID_16	CLUSTER_ID_18
1	0	0
2	0	0.0029
3	0.0054	0
4	0.003	0
5	0.0016	0
6	0	0
7	0.0002	0
8	0	0
9	0.0107	0
10	0	0.0531
11	0	0.9945
12	0.0009	0
13	0	0.0002
14	0.0151	0
15	0	0.8221
16	0	0
17	0	0
18	0	0.9811
19	0	0.9953
20	0	0
21	0	0
22	0	0.0025
23	0.0023	0.0268

Figure 4.11: *Apply using Specific Cluster ID*

If you choose the Number of Best Cluster ID's, you will get a listing of the number of best clusters with corresponding probabilities as shown in Figure 4.12. Each case will have multiple cluster cohorts and their respective probabilities.

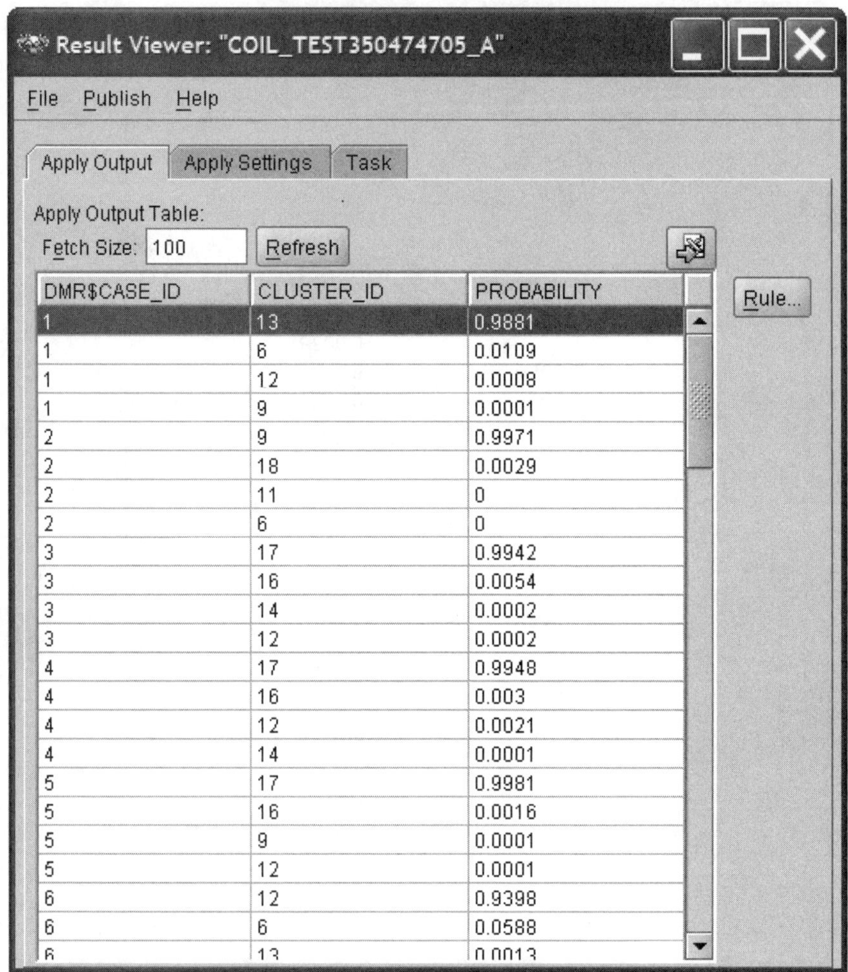

Figure 4.12: *Apply using Number of Best Cluster ID's*

Publishing the Cluster Results

Data Miner gives you three ways to deploy the results of the applied models. You can save the result as a text file or spreadsheet, publish the result to Oracle Discoverer, or export the model to another Oracle database for scoring.

In the clustering apply examples shown above, the result viewer features this button:

Figure 4.13: *Result Viewer Icon.*

Publishing to a File

Selecting this button launches a wizard that lets you choose either Excel format (tab delimited) or Text format (comma, vertical bar, hyphen, period or space delimited), allowing you to store the data on your local hard drive or network.

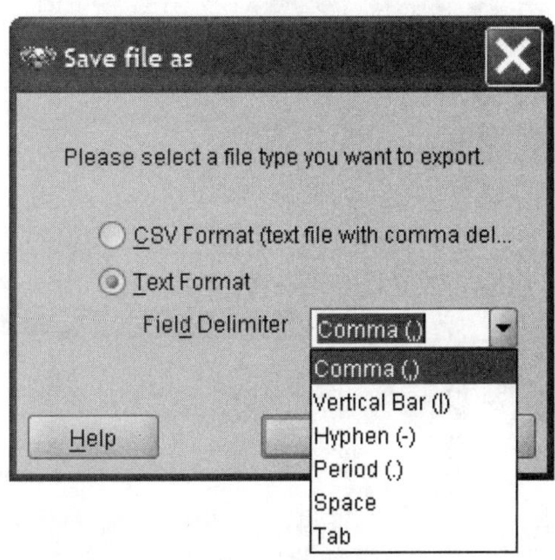

Figure 4.14: *Save File Window.*

Using the Discoverer Gateway for Publication

The second way to deploy your results is via Publish to Discoverer Gateway.

This is a good way to publish because the table is made available for ad hoc queries to any application. Although the documentation currently refers to a Discoverer Gateway, Siebel Answers can make use of this data table as well.

In the result viewer you will see a Publish tab, which starts the Publish to Discoverer wizard. You can choose to create either a table or view, and after creating the output you can see the object in the Data Miner navigator tree under Discoverer Objects.

Having the table or view in a location separate from the other tables in the schema makes it easier for Oracle Discoverer Gateway to pick the table and add it to an End User Layer.

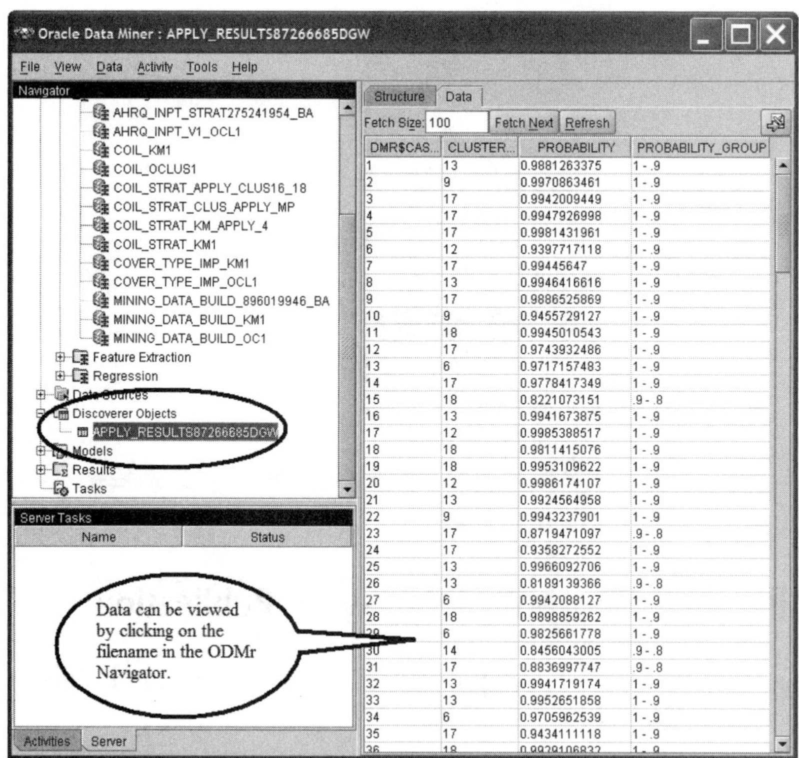

Figure 4.15: *Apply Results.*

Publishing to an Oracle Database

The third method for deployment involves exporting a model to another Oracle database for scoring. Using Data Pump technology, Data Miner supports export and import of all models. If you export and import an entire database or schema using Oracle Data Pump, all data mining models created in that database will be transferred.

When you want to export your models to another database, you must use the Oracle Data Mining API at the command line level, since there is no wizard in Oracle Data Miner to assist with the export. The two functions are aptly named EXPORT_MODEL and IMPORT_MODEL.

To view a listing of all models, type the following sql statement after connecting to sqlplus as dmuser:

```
Select name from dm_user_models;
```

Export a single model specifying the dump file, directory object, and model using the following syntax:

```
EXECUTE DBMS_DATA_MINING.EXPORT_MODEL('MODEL.DMP',
'mining_dump','name = ''COIL59865_CL''');
```

> Note: The model name is surrounded by two single quotes, not double quotes.

You can export an individual model, several, or all models using the Oracle Data Mining API at the command line level. To export all models, use 'NULL' or 'ALL' in place of the metadata_filter parameter 'name = ''model name'''. Export all models starting with 'COIL' using the following syntax:

```
EXECUTE DBMS_DATA_MINING.EXPORT_MODEL('MODEL.DMP',
'mining_dump','name LIKE ''COIL%''');
```

The dump file is located in the directory mapped to the directory object 'mining_dump'. A directory object is a logical name in the database that is mapped to a file location, for example c:\ODMr_files.

The next section will show how to import and use the data mining model.

Importing the model to a different Oracle database

The model can be imported and used by executing the following command.

```
SQL> exec dbms_data_mining.import_model('MODEL.DMP', 'NEW_DIR');
```

Since no model name is entered as an argument, all models in the dumpfile are imported.

The model is now available for use in the new environment. For a step by step explanation of exporting and importing ODM models refer to the Oracle 10G Rel 2 Tutorial available at: http://www.oracle.com/technology/products/bi/odm/odminer.html.

Type the following string into the Google search engine to find more information: otn oracle data miner 10.2.0.2

Conclusion

In summary, this chapter explored the two types of cluster analysis available in Data Miner, the k-Means and O-Cluster algorithms.

Advantages of using each was discussed in relation to the data being mined, and we showed an example of using k-Means clustering on data downloaded from the internet and imported into our Oracle database. The cluster model was applied to new data, and three deployment methods were shown.

The main points of this chapter include:

- Understanding the differences between a partitioning type of clustering algorithm (k-Means) and a density clustering technique such as O-cluster.
- Comparing clusters using Data Miner's cluster detail histogram.
- Utilizing stratified sampling techniques to understand differences between clusters.

We are now ready to dive into more details and take a closer look at the internals of the Oracle Data Mining tool. This will show how to customize the data mining tool to suit the constraints of the data model or the case dataset.

Inside Oracle Data Miner

CHAPTER 5

Exploring Data Miner

We have explored the Data Miner tool utilizing the Activity wizard to construct data mining activities. This approach, new to the 10g release 2 of Data Miner, takes care of prepping the data (normalizing, eliminating outlier data, discretizing), creating build and test datasets, building the model, and finally testing the results. Transformation wizards are available in 10gR2 that allow analysts to customize the data mining tasks to their liking.

The following sections will demonstrate how to:

- Examine in detail the steps in the Oracle Data Miner Build Activity.
- Learn about different binning strategies using the discretize wizard.
- Learn how to use functions such as sum, count and average to generate summary reports
- Re-code data values
- Review stratified sampling techniques
- Use wizards to perform advanced techniques for filtering, sampling and preparing datasets.

Data Miner Activity Builder Tasks

Clicking the Data Mining Activity in the Navigator pane shows a listing of activities that were created under each of the algorithms. Selecting an activity shows the details of all the steps and the output, build, and test data created for each step. In previous releases, these tasks were not automated, leaving the data mining analyst to prep the data and create the interim data tables or views before building and testing each model. The analyst kept notes of all the tables and views generated by this process in order to document the process and replicate the resultant datasets and analyses.

Next, we will examine the Support Vector Machine Activity created for the Boston housing market. The model produced output data for the outlier treatment, missing values, normalization, split, build and test steps.

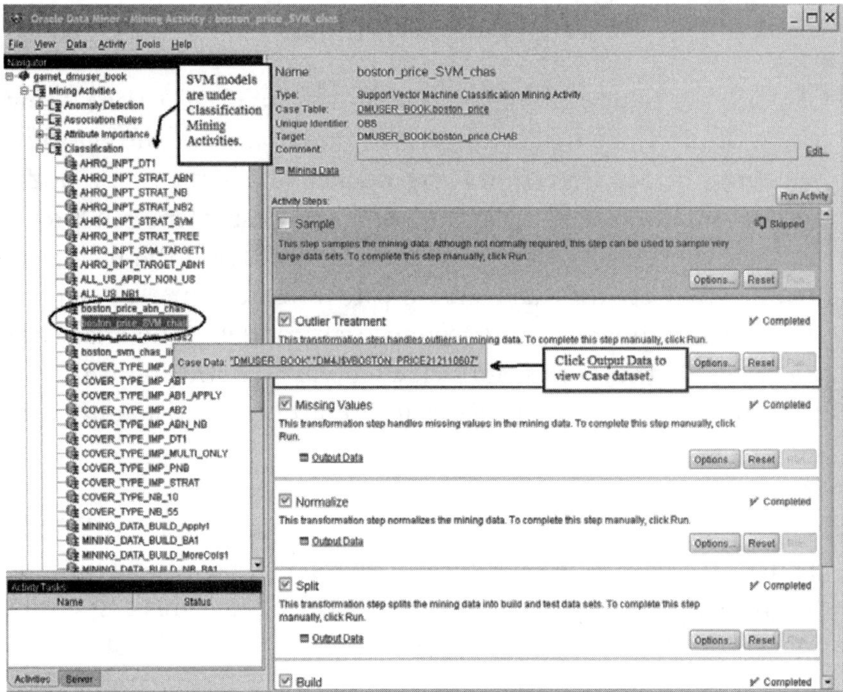

Figure 5.1: *Oracle Data Mining Activity.*

As shown in Figure 5.1, the outlier treatment created an output dataset named:

```
"DMUSER_BOOK"."DM4J$VBOSTON_PRICE212110607"
```

The data in this view can be examined using the Data Viewer by clicking on the output data name. You can view the structure of this dataset, scroll through the data, and see the lineage. This dataset is then used as input for the next step in the Activity list, Missing Values, which is used as input to the splitting algorithm and results in a new output dataset named:

```
"DMUSER_BOOK"."DM4J$VBOSTON_PRICE569386744"
```

Each step in the Activity generates an output table that is used in the following step. This feature is a huge help to the analyst for keeping track of the many steps of building the final result set.

For many business applications, the default settings used by the Activity Builder will be sufficient to guide data mining activities. For normalizing and treating outlier data, you probably do not want to change the settings given by the product defaults. However, you may want to change the binning to something else that might have more meaning for the business rules you are interested in.

In that case, you will want to use the Discretize wizard to prepare the data more to your liking. There may also be situations where you choose to use a different normalization scheme. These transformation wizards will be examined in this chapter. First, the Naïve Bayes Mining Activity that was created in Chapter One will be reviewed. Recall that we created an Activity named ALL_US_NB1. Selecting this Activity brings up the Data Mining Activity steps. The Mining Activity pane shows the case table named DMUSER_BOOK.MINING_DATA_BUILD_V_US, with the Unique Identifier CUST_ID, target attribute of AFFINITY_CARD, and comment "Naïve Bayes classification for all US customers".

Note that Case Table is a link that opens a Data Viewer window where you can see the Structure, Data, and View Lineage. Data Miner uses a naming convention to ensure a unique table name. Table names will appear similar to the following:

```
"DMUSER_BOOK"."DM4J$VMINING_DATA_28226663"
```

You can also link directly to this case table by clicking on MINING DATA underneath the comment.

In the View Lineage tab, the SQL statement defining the case table for the Mining Activity can be seen:

```
SELECT
"MINING_DATA_BUILD_V_US"."CUST_ID" as "DMR$CASE_ID",  TO_CHAR(
"MINING_DATA_BUILD_V_US"."AFFINITY_CARD") AS "AFFINITY_CARD",
"MINING_DATA_BUILD_V_US"."AGE" AS "AGE",  TO_CHAR(
"MINING_DATA_BUILD_V_US"."BOOKKEEPING_APPLICATION") AS
"BOOKKEEPING_APPLICATION",  TO_CHAR(
"MINING_DATA_BUILD_V_US"."BULK_PACK_DISKETTES") AS
"BULK_PACK_DISKETTES",  "MINING_DATA_BUILD_V_US"."CUST_GENDER" AS
"CUST_GENDER",  "MINING_DATA_BUILD_V_US"."CUST_INCOME_LEVEL" AS
"CUST_INCOME_LEVEL",  "MINING_DATA_BUILD_V_US"."CUST_MARITAL_STATUS"
AS "CUST_MARITAL_STATUS",  "MINING_DATA_BUILD_V_US"."EDUCATION" AS
"EDUCATION",  TO_CHAR(
"MINING_DATA_BUILD_V_US"."FLAT_PANEL_MONITOR") AS
"FLAT_PANEL_MONITOR",  TO_CHAR(
"MINING_DATA_BUILD_V_US"."HOME_THEATER_PACKAGE") AS
"HOME_THEATER_PACKAGE",  "MINING_DATA_BUILD_V_US"."HOUSEHOLD_SIZE"
AS "HOUSEHOLD_SIZE",  "MINING_DATA_BUILD_V_US"."OCCUPATION" AS
"OCCUPATION",  TO_CHAR( "MINING_DATA_BUILD_V_US"."OS_DOC_SET_KANJI")
AS "OS_DOC_SET_KANJI",  "MINING_DATA_BUILD_V_US"."YRS_RESIDENCE" AS
"YRS_RESIDENCE",  TO_CHAR( "MINING_DATA_BUILD_V_US"."Y_BOX_GAMES")
AS "Y_BOX_GAMES"
FROM "DMUSER_BOOK"."MINING_DATA_BUILD_V_US"
```

The Sample Step was skipped in this example, so we go on to Discretize and click on the Output Data link to view the data. Note that the AGE attribute has been binned so that ages have been coded as 1, 2 and 3. We can see what was done to bin the data by reviewing the SQL statement in the View Lineage tab:

```
SELECT
"AFFINITY_CARD",( CASE WHEN "AGE" < 32 THEN 1
WHEN "AGE" <= 44 THEN 2
WHEN "AGE" > 44 THEN 3
 end)  "AGE", "BOOKKEEPING_APPLICATION", "BULK_PACK_DISKETTES",
"CUST_GENDER", "CUST_INCOME_LEVEL", "CUST_MARITAL_STATUS",
"DMR$CASE_ID", "EDUCATION", "FLAT_PANEL_MONITOR",
"HOME_THEATER_PACKAGE", "HOUSEHOLD_SIZE", "OCCUPATION",
"OS_DOC_SET_KANJI",( CASE WHEN "YRS_RESIDENCE" < 3 THEN 1
WHEN "YRS_RESIDENCE" <= 5 THEN 2
WHEN "YRS_RESIDENCE" > 5 THEN 3
 end)  "YRS_RESIDENCE", "Y_BOX_GAMES"
FROM "DMUSER_BOOK"."DM4J$VMINING_DATA_28226663"
```

Quantile Binning

Data Miner recognized that the two numerical data attributes AGE and YRS_RESIDENCE should be binned, and discretized the data so that these fields were categorized into 3 different bins: 1, 2, and 3.

Clicking on the Options button in the Discretize section will show these options: Quantile Binning, Equal Width Binning, and None.

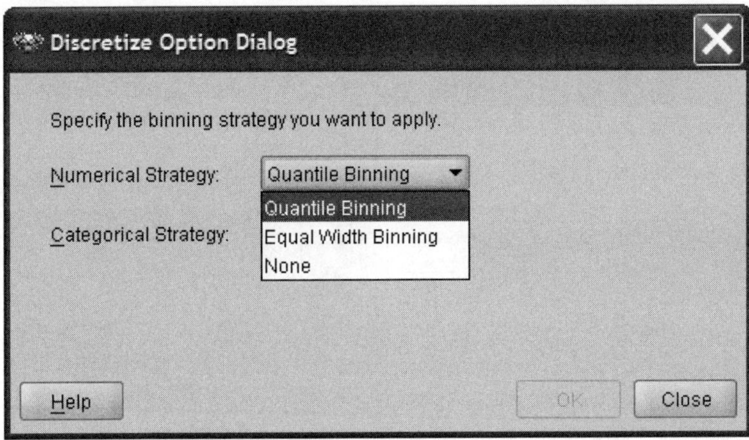

Figure 5.2: *Quantile Binning.*

We can illustrate the difference between the quantile and equal width binning by using the discretize wizard. The histogram for the attribute AGE in the MINING_DATA_BUILD_V_US case dataset using the equal width binning strategy is shown in Figure 5.2.

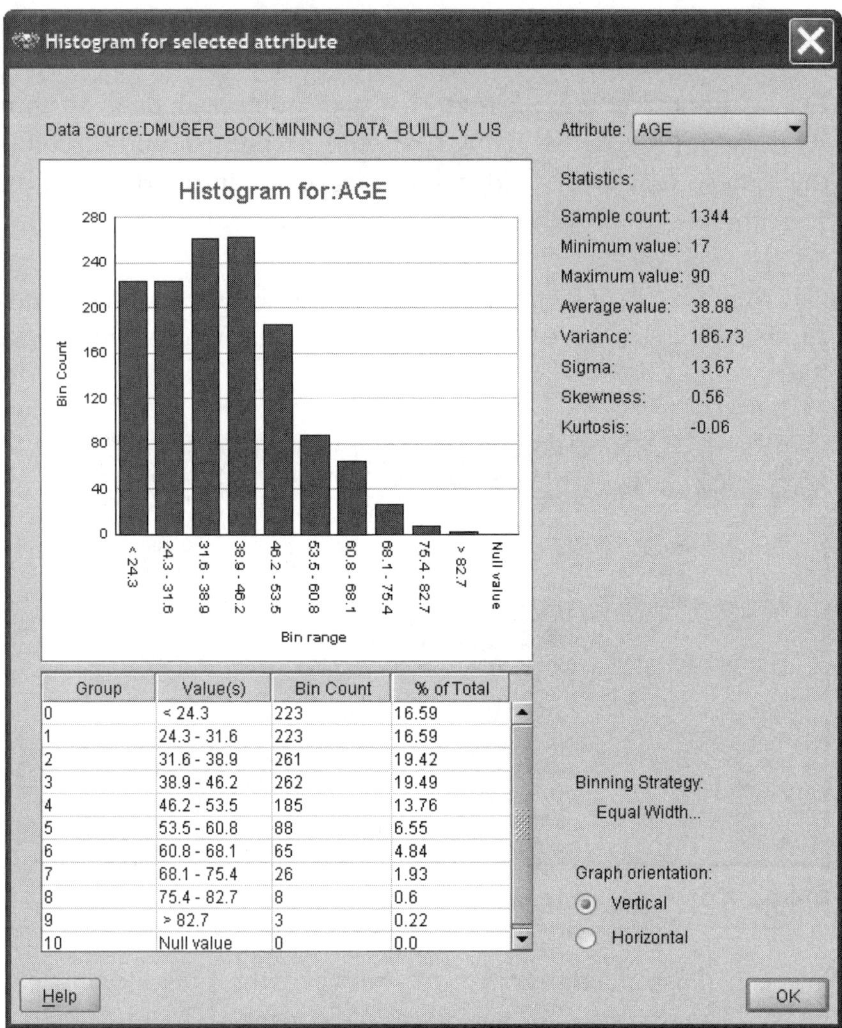

Group	Value(s)	Bin Count	% of Total
0	< 24.3	223	16.59
1	24.3 - 31.6	223	16.59
2	31.6 - 38.9	261	19.42
3	38.9 - 46.2	262	19.49
4	46.2 - 53.5	185	13.76
5	53.5 - 60.8	88	6.55
6	60.8 - 68.1	65	4.84
7	68.1 - 75.4	26	1.93
8	75.4 - 82.7	8	0.6
9	> 82.7	3	0.22
10	Null value	0	0.0

Figure 5.3: *Histogram for Age – Equal Width Binning.*

Each group in the histogram view is composed of age values in increasing increments of 7.3 years. As age increases, the number of customers in the bins decreases from a maximum of 19.49% in group 3 to 0.22% in group 9. An uneven type of distribution that tails off is not usually a good choice for data mining analysis, as it becomes difficult to interpret results due to bins with very large or small numbers. A more desirable histogram has uniform distribution of ages across all groups, as in the quantile binning method shown in Figure 5.3.

Decision Tree classification is extremely sensitive to data skewing, and when distribution of the target values are severely skewed, the tree classification is not reliable. On the other hand, you may be very interested in the outliers, as in finding credit card fraud or Web intrusions. Where anomaly detection is your goal, keeping the uneven distribution is the key to successfully locating suspect cases.

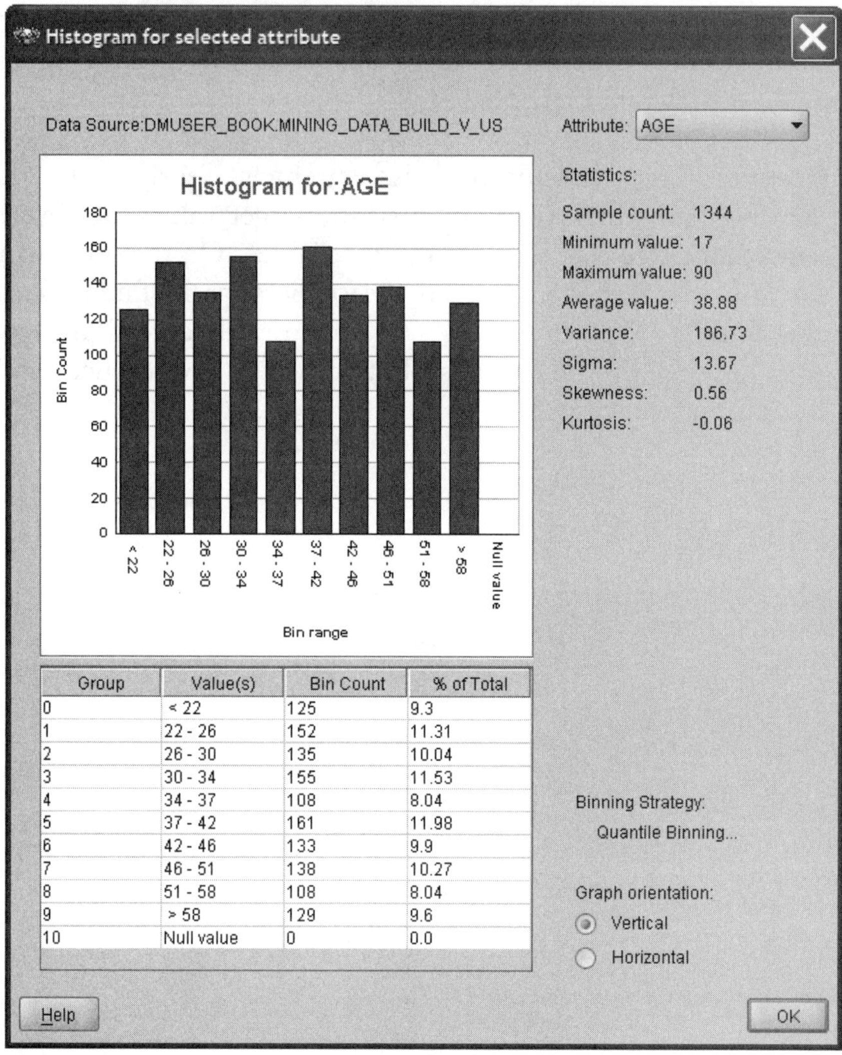

Group	Value(s)	Bin Count	% of Total
0	< 22	125	9.3
1	22 - 26	152	11.31
2	26 - 30	135	10.04
3	30 - 34	155	11.53
4	34 - 37	108	8.04
5	37 - 42	161	11.98
6	42 - 46	133	9.9
7	46 - 51	138	10.27
8	51 - 58	108	8.04
9	> 58	129	9.6
10	Null value	0	0.0

Figure 5.4: *Histogram for Age – Quantile Binning*

Using the Discretize Transform Wizard

You can view the histograms of data using different binning methods in the discretize wizard. We will illustrate the use of the discretize wizard by customizing the age ranges in a new binning strategy.

In Step 3 of the Wizard, note that there are 3 attributes identified as numerical mining types: AGE, CUST_ID, and YRS_RESIDENCE. In this step you can change the mining type if necessary by clicking numerical or categorical and choosing the appropriate type. Numerical data can be binned. Click Next to continue the wizard.

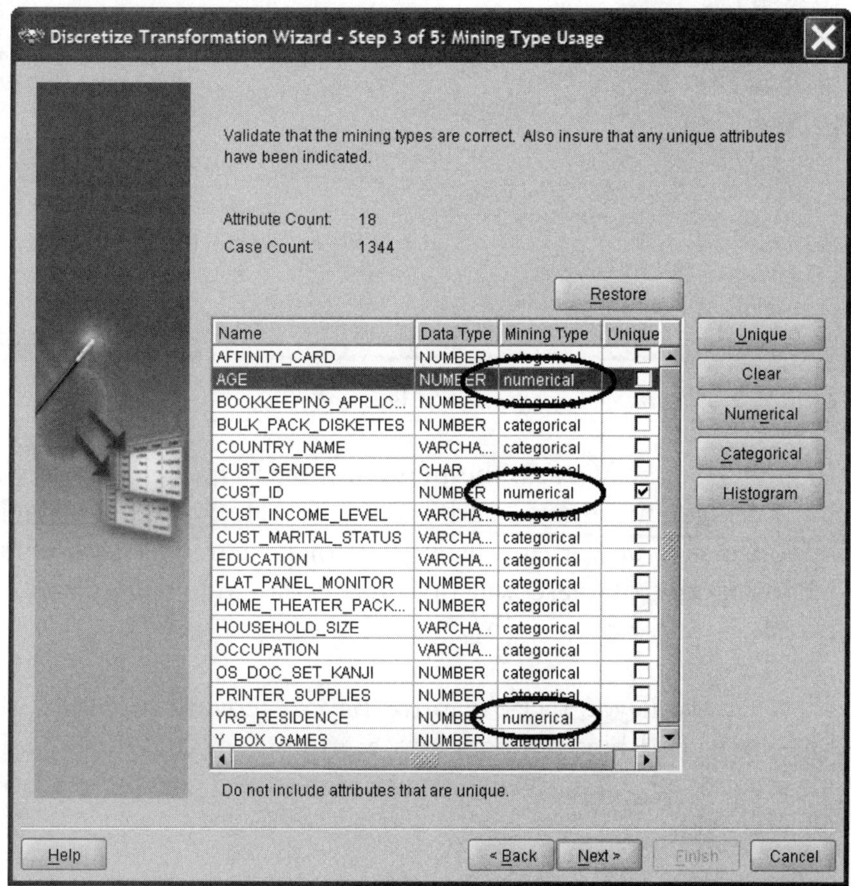

Figure 5.5: *Data Mining Types.*

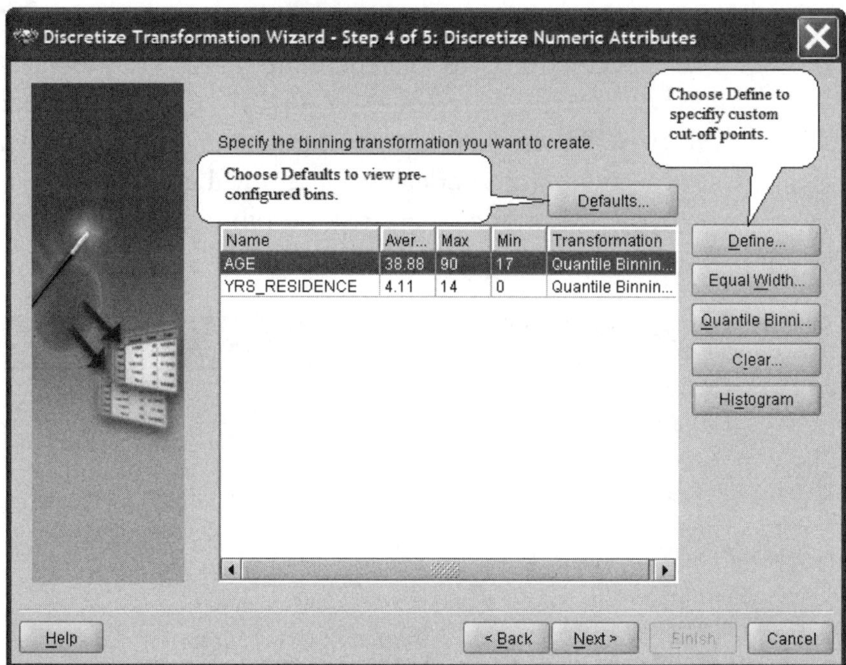

Figure 5.6: *Binning Transformation Wizard.*

In step 4 of the Wizard, the numerical data types are listed with the average, maximum, and minimum values. The Defaults option brings up a menu listing a choice of mining algorithms. Choosing any of these will optimize a binning strategy specific for the algorithm.

For example if you pick Adaptive Bayes Network for AGE, the binning wizard bins the data into 5 groups: < 26, 26-34, 34-42, 42-51, and >51. The Naïve Bayes defaults to 3 groups: <32, 32-44, and >44.

Customizing Discretize Transformations

To customize AGE cut-offs, choose the Define button. Finding it easier to edit one of the default settings, choose Generate Default Bins, and enter 4 as the number of bins. You may have an Application Warning appear that tells you 3 is a better binning choice; click OK to proceed.

The lower bounds for each of the 4 bins listed can be edited, so to adjust the bins to these ranges, <25, 25-40, 40-50, and >50, type 25, 40, and 50. The resulting histogram shows that there are a disproportionate number of cases in the 25-40 range (41%).

Although not optimal for building a model, you may need to use this binning strategy for your business application. By changing the lower boundary to 30 the histogram is more uniformly distributed with each of the bins having 29, 28, 23, and 21% of the total number of cases, respectively.

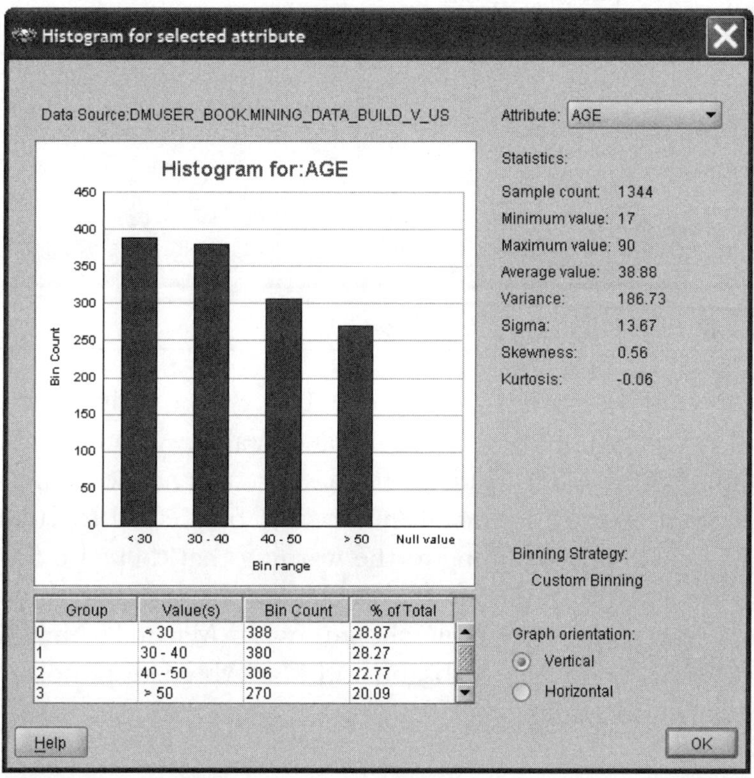

Group	Value(s)	Bin Count	% of Total
0	< 30	388	28.87
1	30 - 40	380	28.27
2	40 - 50	306	22.77
3	> 50	270	20.09

Figure 5.7: *Histogram for AGE.*

In Step 5 of 5 of the Discretize Transformation Wizard, you can change the bins of the categorical attributes. For instance, to change the CUST_MARITAL_STATUS attribute, highlight the name and click Define.

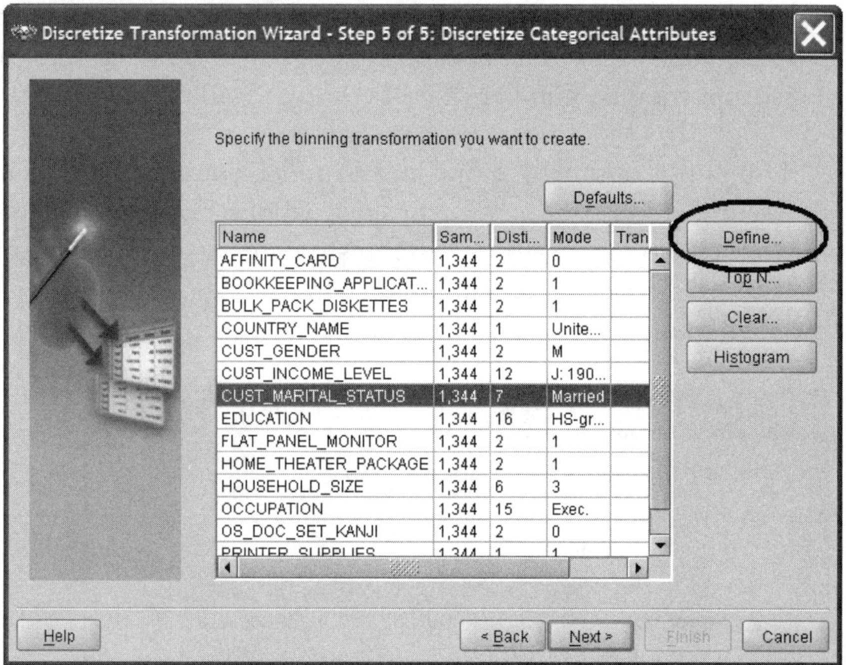

Name	Sam...	Disti...	Mode	Tran
AFFINITY_CARD	1,344	2	0	
BOOKKEEPING_APPLICAT...	1,344	2	1	
BULK_PACK_DISKETTES	1,344	2	1	
COUNTRY_NAME	1,344	1	Unite...	
CUST_GENDER	1,344	2	M	
CUST_INCOME_LEVEL	1,344	12	J: 190...	
CUST_MARITAL_STATUS	1,344	7	Married	
EDUCATION	1,344	16	HS-gr...	
FLAT_PANEL_MONITOR	1,344	2	1	
HOME_THEATER_PACKAGE	1,344	2	1	
HOUSEHOLD_SIZE	1,344	6	3	
OCCUPATION	1,344	15	Exec.	
OS_DOC_SET_KANJI	1,344	2	0	

Figure 5.8: *Define Binning Transformation.*

A window with existing strategies (if any) for that attribute appears showing the Bin Category and Value. You can add definitions by choosing Add, or for a shortcut choose Generate Default Bins. Keep the default number of bins equal to 10 and choose OK when responding to the warning that there are fewer than 10 bins in the case data if you choose the generate option. The bin categories are now shown, with Married, NeverM, Divorc, Separ, Widowed, Mabsent, and Mar-AF corresponding to the category and values.

To re-bin the attribute to Married and Not_Married, highlight Married and click the Edit button. The Married bin category corresponds to Married, so choose Divorc, Mabsent, Mar_AF, Separ to add to the Married category. Click OK to complete the Married category. Now there are 3 categories: NeverM, Widowed, and Married. Highlight NeverM and click Edit. Re-name NeverM in the Bin Category to Not_Married, and add Widowed to the selected Bin Values.

After clicking OK, the bin categories are now Married with values Divorc, Mabsent, Mar-AF, Married, and Separ; Not_Married with the values NeverM and Widowed. Click OK and Next to finish.

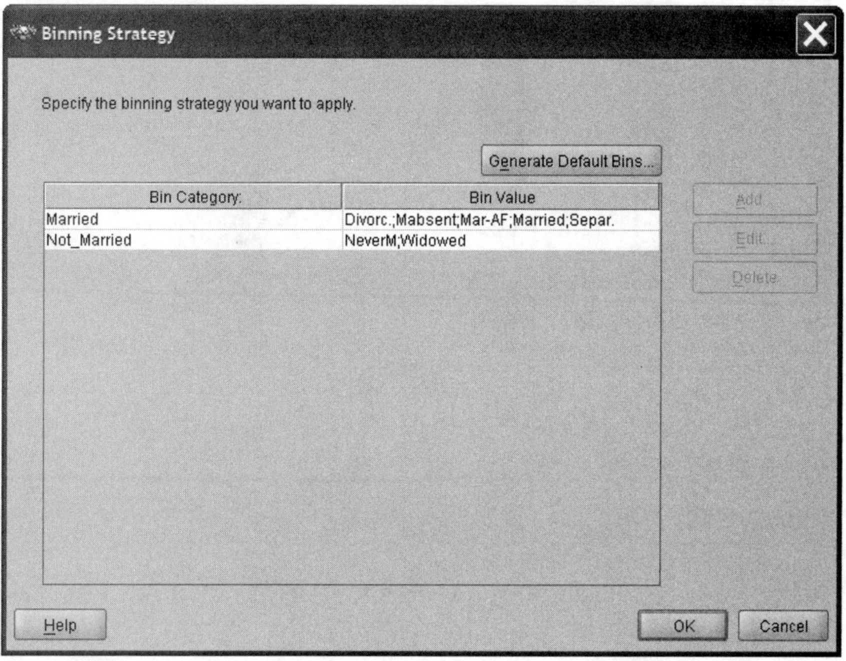

Figure 5.9: *Specify Binning Strategy.*

Right click on the new view created, choose Show Summary Single-Record, and view the histograms for AGE and CUST_MARITAL_STATUS.

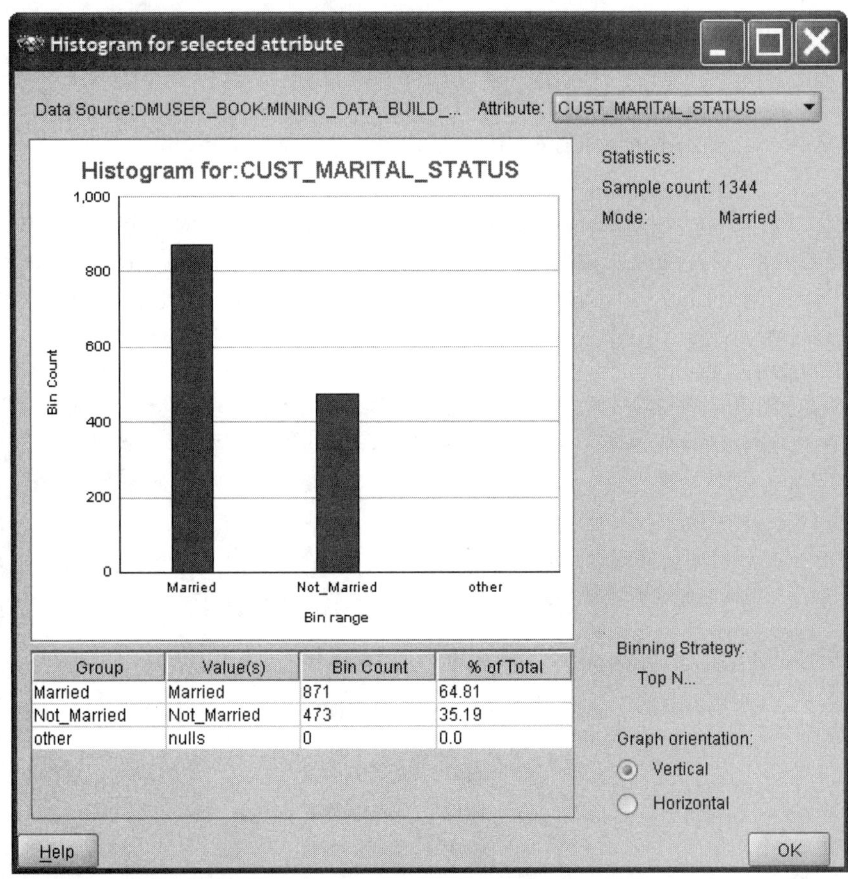

Group	Value(s)	Bin Count	% of Total
Married	Married	871	64.81
Not_Married	Not_Married	473	35.19
other	nulls	0	0.0

Figure 5.10: *Histogram for Marital Status.*

Now, we right click the new view and choose Show Lineage to see details of the disretize transformation. We do this because Data Miner generates the SQL code for us. We may want to use this code in a query. The wizard used a CASE and DECODE statement to create the bins.

```
SELECT
```

```
"AFFINITY_CARD",( CASE WHEN "AGE" < 30 THEN ' < 30'
WHEN "AGE" <= 40 THEN '30 - 40'
WHEN "AGE" <= 50 THEN '40 - 50'
WHEN "AGE" > 50 THEN ' > 50'
else null end)  "AGE", "BOOKKEEPING_APPLICATION",
"BULK_PACK_DISKETTES", "COUNTRY_NAME", "CUST_GENDER", "CUST_ID",
"CUST_INCOME_LEVEL", DECODE ("CUST_MARITAL_STATUS"
,'Divorc.','Married'
,'Mabsent','Married'
,'Mar-AF','Married'
,'Married','Married'
,'Separ.','Married'
,'NeverM','Not_Married'
,'Widowed','Not_Married'
,NULL,NULL,'other') "CUST_MARITAL_STATUS", "EDUCATION",
"FLAT_PANEL_MONITOR", "HOME_THEATER_PACKAGE", "HOUSEHOLD_SIZE",
"OCCUPATION", "OS_DOC_SET_KANJI",
"PRINTER_SUPPLIES",( CASE WHEN "YRS_RESIDENCE" < 3 THEN ' < 3'
WHEN "YRS_RESIDENCE" <= 5 THEN '3 - 5'
WHEN "YRS_RESIDENCE" > 5 THEN ' > 5'
else null end)  "YRS_RESIDENCE", "Y_BOX_GAMES"
FROM "DMUSER_BOOK"."MINING_DATA_BUILD_V_US"
```

Using the Discretize wizard gives you the ability to easily create new attributes and bin the data to your liking. The view created is used as the case table for data mining activities. How many bins you choose when doing the data prep depends on the nature of the data you are processing. It is sometimes easy to categorize variables into High, Medium and Low to simplify interpretation of the data mining results.

Using the Aggregate Transformation Wizard

For times when you want to group your data, a useful way to transform in Data Miner is the Aggregate Transformation Wizard. For example, in the Mining_Data_Build_V_US dataset you can count how many of each item was sold to customers with an affinity card.

You may want to view trends in sales by aggregating daily sales to the week, month, or year level. You can calculate, store, and export aggregated values such as sum, average, max, min, standard deviation, and variance. This information may be saved in a view or table, or exported in csv or text format.

In this example, the Aggregate Transform Wizard is used to visualize customer buying habits grouped by occupation in the Mining_Data_Build_V_US dataset. For every level of OCCUPATION, data was aggregated using the average, count and max functions. The wizard provides an easy interface for adding and editing functions for any attribute in the case dataset, and gives you a preview of the result. After viewing the preview you can go back and delete, edit, or add more functions before finishing the transform. The SQL statement shown is provided by the transform wizard for creating the resulting view.

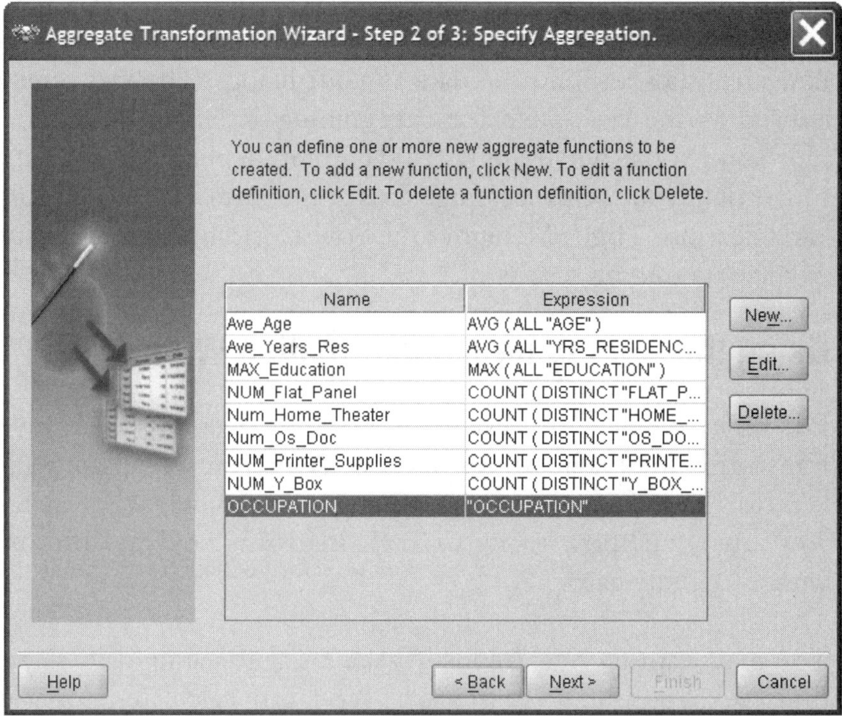

Figure 5.11: *Aggregate Functions.*

```
CREATE VIEW "DMUSER_BOOK"."MINING_DATA_BUILD_980685885"
AS
SELECT AVG ( ALL "AGE" ) AS "Ave_Age", AVG ( ALL "YRS_RESIDENCE" )
AS "Ave_Years_Res", MAX ( ALL "EDUCATION" ) AS "MAX_Education",
COUNT ( DISTINCT "FLAT_PANEL_MONITOR" ) AS "NUM_Flat_Panel", COUNT (
DISTINCT "HOME_THEATER_PACKAGE" ) AS "Num_Home_Theater", COUNT (
DISTINCT "OS_DOC_SET_KANJI" ) AS "Num_Os_Doc", COUNT ( DISTINCT
"PRINTER_SUPPLIES" ) AS "NUM_Printer_Supplies", COUNT ( DISTINCT
"Y_BOX_GAMES" ) AS "NUM_Y_Box", "OCCUPATION" AS "OCCUPATION"
 FROM "DMUSER_BOOK"."MINING_DATA_BUILD_V_US" GROUP BY "OCCUPATION"
```

The resulting aggregated data is shown in Table 5.1:

OCCUPATION	AVE_ AGE	AVE_ YEARS_ RES	MAX_ EDUCATION	NUM_ FLAT_ PANEL	NUM_ OS_ DOC
?	42	3.25	PhD	2	1
Armed-F	35	3.50	Masters	2	1
Cleric.	35	3.66	PhD	2	1
Crafts	40	4.27	Presch.	2	1
Exec.	43	5.19	Profsc	2	1
Farming	40	4.54	Profsc	2	1
Handler	31	2.88	HS-grad	2	1
House-s	49	3.25	HS-grad	2	1
Machine	38	3.89	HS-grad	2	2
Other	34	2.91	HS-grad	2	1
Prof.	41	4.73	Profsc	2	1
Protec.	41	4.41	Masters	2	1
Sales	39	4.21	Profsc	2	1
TechSup	38	3.83	Masters	2	2
Transp.	42	4.63	HS-grad	2	1

Table 5.1: *Aggregated Data*

The next section will examine how to recode values in a dataset using the Recode Transformation Wizard.

Recode Transformation Wizard

A similar transformation to the Discretize transformation is the Recode transformation. Recoding refers to the process of replacing data elements with other, more meaningful values or characters.

The Recode Wizard supports the relational operators =, <=, and >=. This makes it difficult to partition values at a particular numerical value (example: Latitude <= 4.2 vs. Latitude > 4.2). Recode is really meant for use with strings and integers so Discretization can be used to accomplish the same purpose for real numbers.

Single values, NULL values, ranges of values, and Other values can be recoded. For single values and ranges of values, you can pick the values from the dropdown that has been populated with all possible attribute values, or you can enter new values that have a compatible data type.

The new or recode value can have a different data type from the old value. Ffor example, you could recode the number 0 as the character n. Recode definitions are sorted in the following order in the listbox: NULL values (first), single values, ranges of values, and Other values last. If the wizard detects problems when you are defining a recode scheme, it generates a message explaining the problem.

The next section will show a wizard that you will probably never use in Oracle 10G Data Mining. The inclusion of the split transformation wizard in the Activity Build is a great time saver for the Data Mining analyst. However, there may be times when you will need to split your data into build and test data sets explicitly. For example, you may use this tool to create a build data table that can be used across multiple model builds to ensure the exact same records are being used for test, and to possibly avoid the overhead of splitting the data each time.

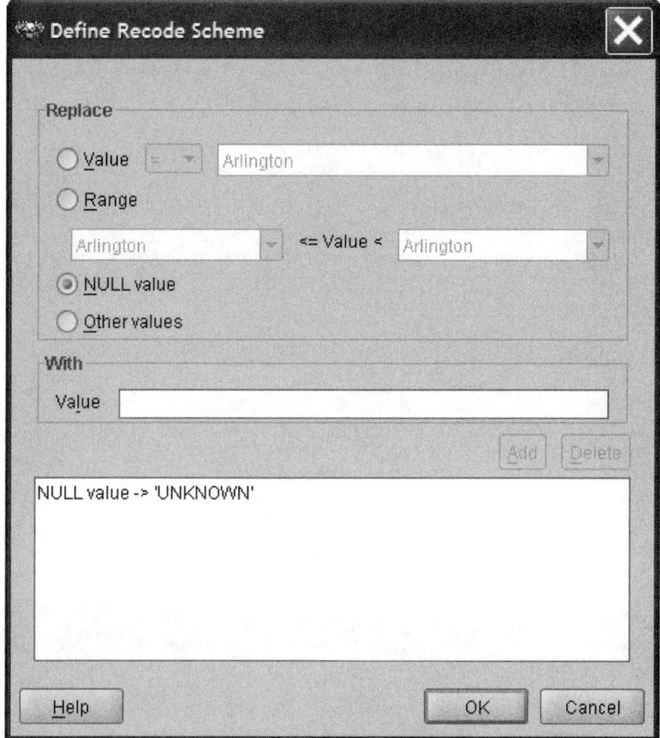

Figure 5.12: *Define Recode Scheme.*

Using the Split Transformation Wizard

If you are using a version of Data Miner prior to 10gR2, you will also need to create the build and test datasets. This is done by using the split transformation to generate build and test tables or views of randomized data from a single case table.

The use of the split transformations is straightforward. Select the case table or view that you are analyzing, and select Split in the transformation menu. Re-name each table from the default if desired to a more meaningful name. For example, "boston_priceT103959454" could be more meaningfully renamed as BOSTON_PRICE_TEST1. In the final step of the wizard, select the percent of cases desired in each table. The wizard defaults to 60% for the build table and 40% for the test table. The SQL code used to create the build and test tables is shown below:

```
CREATE TABLE "DMUSER_BOOK"."BOSTON_PRICE_BUILD1" AS
SELECT "OBS", "TOWN", "TOWN#", "TRACT", "LON", "LAT", "MEDV",
"CMEDV", "CRIM", "ZN", "INDUS", "CHAS", "NOX", "RM", "AGE", "DIS",
"RAD", "TAX", "PTRATIO", "B", "LSTAT" FROM (SELECT /*+ no_merge */
t.*, ROWNUM RNUM
FROM "DMUSER_BOOK"."boston_price" t)
WHERE ORA_HASH(RNUM,99,0) < 60

CREATE TABLE "DMUSER_BOOK"." BOSTON_PRICE_TEST1" AS
SELECT "OBS", "TOWN", "TOWN#", "TRACT", "LON", "LAT", "MEDV",
"CMEDV", "CRIM", "ZN", "INDUS", "CHAS", "NOX", "RM", "AGE", "DIS",
"RAD", "TAX", "PTRATIO", "B", "LSTAT" FROM (SELECT /*+ no_merge */
t.*, ROWNUM RNUM
FROM "DMUSER_BOOK"."boston_price" t)
WHERE ORA_HASH(RNUM,99,0) >= 60
```

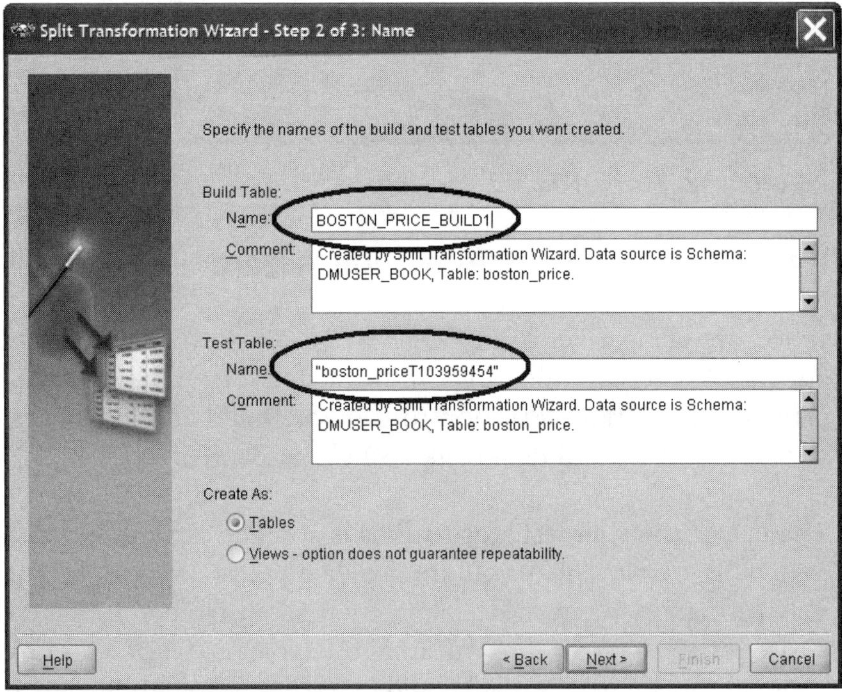

Figure 5.13: *Specify Build and Test Tables.*

The next section reviews using the stratified sampling technique to change the proportion of attribute values in a dataset.

Using the Stratified Sample Transformation Wizard

In 2000, the Department of Health and Human Services reported to the House Budget Committee a report detailing the methodology for detecting improper payments and fraud in the Medicare program. According to the report, Medicare and Medicaid costs consumed 33.7 cents of every dollar spent on healthcare in the United States. A methodology was developed to determine the national rate of erroneous Medicare payments. The analysts utilized a stratified sample design including 600 beneficiaries with 5,223 claims valued at $5.4 million. By projecting the results of this study sample, the Department found that payment errors totaled an estimated $13.5 billion, or 7.97 percent of total Medicare fee-for-service benefit payments. You can review the briefing at the following address: http://oig.hhs.gov/reading/testimony/2000/00712fin.htm. This section will show how to use the stratified sample technique in your dataset.

Type the following string into the Google search engine to find more information: **stratified sample fraud**

The stratified sample transformation is useful when your target attribute constitutes a small percentage of cases. This transformation was utilized in Chapter 4 to create a dataset for clustering. In that example, we used the CoIL dataset and increased the percentage of the target CARAVAN from 6% to 33% of the sampled data.

We kept all attributes where CARAVAN = 1 (348 cases) and randomly selected cases where CARAVAN = 0 which made up 2/3 of the total sample. An alternate method is using percentage of cases in Step 3 of the stratified sample wizard. Click Percent of Cases, leaving 100% as the default. In step 4 of 4, click the Equal Distribution button to create a case dataset with a 50% distribution of the target attribute. The total sample count is 696 cases, which is 12% of the original CoIL dataset.

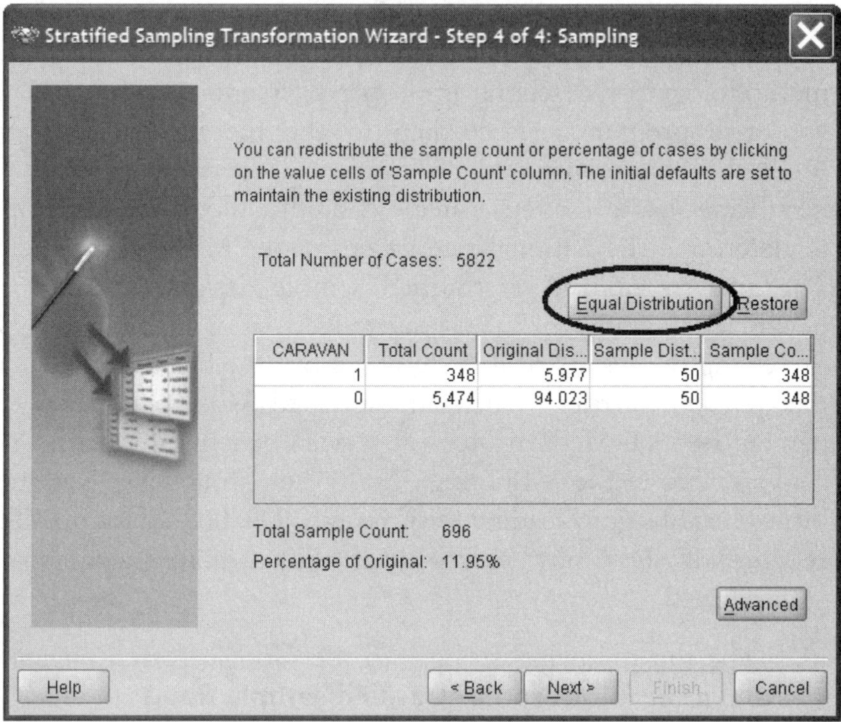

Figure 5.14: *Equal Distribution Sampling.*

The SQL used to create this transformation is shown below:

```
CREATE TABLE "DMUSER_BOOK"."COIL128895151"
AS
SELECT "MOSTYPE", "MAANTHUI", "MGEMOMV", "MGEMLEEF", "MOSHOOFD",
"MGODRK", "MGODRP", "MGODOV", "MGODGE", "MRELGE", "MRELSA",
"MRELOV", "MFALLEEN", "MFGEKIND", "MFWEKIND", "MOPLHOOG",
"MOPLMIDD", "MOPLLAAG", "MBERHOOG", "MBERZELF", "MBERBOER",
"MBERMIDD", "MBERARBG", "MBERARBO", "MSKA", "MSKB1", "MSKB2",
"MSKC", "MSKD", "MHHUUR", "MHKOOP", "MAUT1", "MAUT2", "MAUT0",
"MZFONDS", "MZPART", "MINKM30", "MINK3045", "MINK4575", "MINK7512",
"MINK123M", "MINKGEM", "MKOOPKLA", "PWAPART", "PWABEDR", "PWALAND",
"PPERSAIT", "PBESAUT", "PMOTSCO", "PVRAAUT", "PAANHANG", "PTRACTOR",
"PWERKT", "PBROM", "PLEVEN", "PPERSONG", "PGEZONG", "PWAOREG",
```

```
"PBRAND", "PZEILPL", "PPLEZIER", "PFIETS", "PINBOED", "PBYSTAND",
"AWAPART", "AWABEDR", "AWALAND", "APERSAUT", "ABESAUT", "AMOTSCO",
"AVRAAUT", "AAANHANG", "ATRACTOR", "AWERKT", "ABROM", "ALEVEN",
"APERSONG", "AGEZONG", "AWAOREG", "ABRAND", "AZEILPL", "APLEZIER",
"AFIETS", "AINBOED", "ABYSTAND", "CARAVAN"
FROM (SELECT /*+ no_merge */ t.*, ROWNUM RNUM FROM
"DMUSER_BOOK"."COIL" t)
WHERE
( "CARAVAN"='1' and ORA_HASH(RNUM,(348-1),12345) < 348 )
 OR ( "CARAVAN"='0' and ORA_HASH(RNUM,(5474-1),12345) < 348 )
```

Using the Filter Single-Record Transformation Wizard

Where the stratified sampling technique enabled you to change the percentage of cases, filtering allows you to examine a subset of the case dataset. You may see some interesting results in a cohort of diabetic patients, or want to explore more about customers in a specific region of the country. The Filter Single Record transformation creates a view for the filtered dataset. Filter conditions are specified using a Where clause, which is easy to construct using the expression builder.

In Figure 5.14, using the case dataset for the Boston housing data, which can be found at http://lib.stat.cmu.edu/datasets/, CRM is set for less than 8.0 and NOX greater than 5.5.

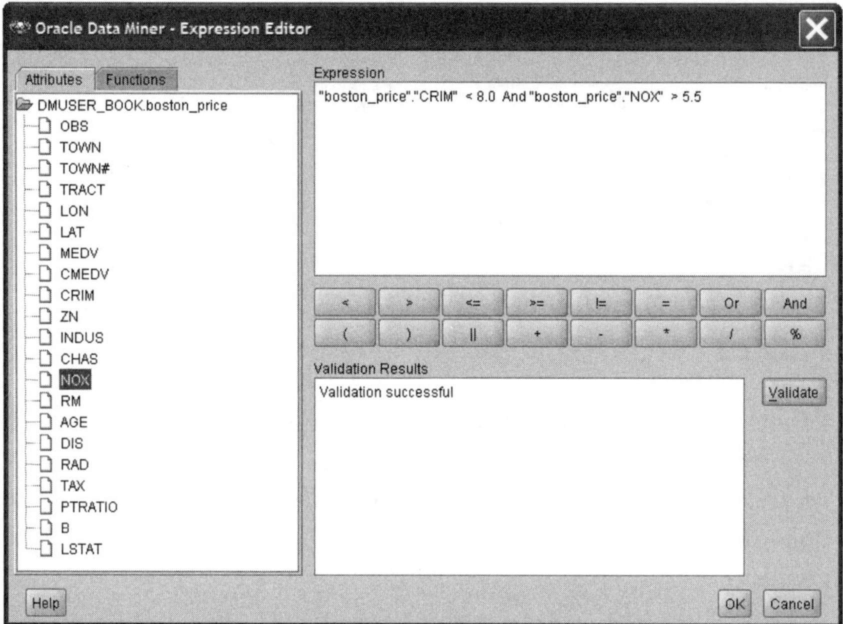

Figure 5.15: *Expression Builder.*

The resulting SQL to create the view is shown below:

```
CREATE VIEW "DMUSER_BOOK"."boston_price261754772" AS
SELECT * FROM "DMUSER_BOOK"."boston_price"
WHERE "boston_price"."CRIM"  < 8.0  And "boston_price"."NOX"  > 5.5
```

The next section will illustrate creating a randomized sample of data. This technique is useful for creating subsets of data for testing hypotheses, or validating a statistical analysis.

Inside the Sample Transformation Wizard

The Sample Transformation wizard creates a random sample of a table or view. The generated random sample can be either a table or a view. You can specify the sample size either as a number of records or as a percentage of records. You can also specify a random seed. A random sample is created by choosing a sample of cases picked at random.

The random sample is smaller than the set that it is based on. Using the smaller sample can result in improved performance in building a model. If the sample is representative of the whole set, results generated using the sample will be compatible with the results generated using the whole set.

The next sections shows advanced features available for preparing data prior to applying data mining algorithms. These techniques are fully automated in the Build Activity, and the wizards are also available as separate menu items.

Preparing datasets for Data Mining Activities

The Missing Values, Normalize, Numeric, and Outlier Treatment wizards are useful for prepping the data prior to applying data mining algorithms. Most algorithms have a preferred method for handling missing values, normalizing, and outliers, so in most data mining tasks you can relax and let the Activity wizard take care of this. In certain situations you may wish to take advantage of these wizards to help prepare your data for analysis.

Using the Missing Values Transformation Wizard

In the Missing Values Numerical Strategy, you have many choices for replacing the missing values, including None, Mean, Max, Min, and Custom Value. The Mean treatment replaces a missing value with the average of the values for that attribute; max substitutes missing values with the maximum of the values, and min replaces missing values with the minimum of the values. The default custom value is zero; you can replace this with any appropriate value.

If the value is NULL, you can drop the case entirely by specifying Drop attribute.

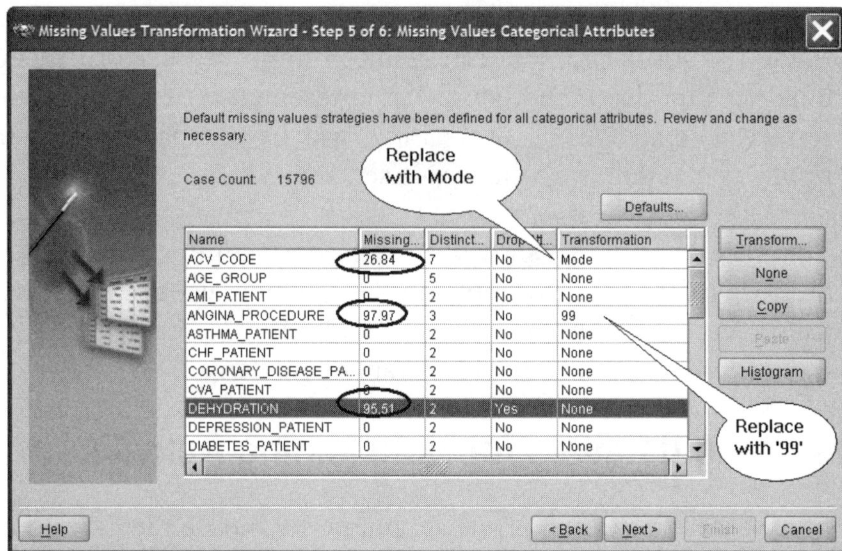

Figure 5.16: *Missing Values Transformation Wizard.*

The SQL statement shown below was automatically generated by the Missing Values Transformation Wizard for clinical patient data. Missing values for attribute ACV_CODE is replaced with the mode ('E'), ANGINA_PROCEDURE is replaced by '99', and rows are dropped when ADULT_ASTHMA, BACTERIAL_PNEUMONIA, CHF, and COPD are NULL.

We do this because we may need to improve data quality, or simplify and consolidate data prior to analysis.

```
CREATE VIEW "DMUSER_BOOK"."AHRQ_INPT_STRAT406981843"
AS
SELECT
  "ADMISSION_COUNT",
  "ADMISSION_TYPE_HIGHEST",
  "ADULT_ASTHMA",
  "BACTERIAL_PNEUMONIA",
  "CHF",
  "COPD",
  "DIABETES_LONG_TERM_CX",
  "ER_VISIT_COUNT",
  "PATIENT_KEY",
```

```
   DECODE ( "ACV_CODE" , NULL, 'E' , "ACV_CODE" ) "ACV_CODE" ,
   DECODE ( "ANGINA_PROCEDURE" , NULL, 99 , "ANGINA_PROCEDURE" )
  "ANGINA_PROCEDURE" ,
  "ASTHMA_PATIENT",
  "CHF_PATIENT",
  "SLEEP_APNEA_PATIENT",
  FROM "DMUSER_BOOK"."AHRQ_INPT_STRAT"
   WHERE
"ADMISSION_COUNT" NOT IN (
SELECT
"ADMISSION_COUNT"
FROM "DMUSER_BOOK"."AHRQ_INPT_STRAT"
WHERE   "ADULT_ASTHMA" IS NULL  AND
   "BACTERIAL_PNEUMONIA" IS NULL  AND
   "CHF" IS NULL  AND
   "COPD" IS NULL  )
```

Next, we will use the normalize transformation to scale data to a uniform distribution of values. Normalization was described for Support Vector Machines in Chapter 3.

Using the Normalize Transformation Wizard

The Normalize transform is used to normalize data using a predefined scheme, or you can select a transformation for any numeric attribute. The available transformations include:

- (x-MIN(x)) / (MAX(x) - MIN(x)) * (new max – new min) + new min
- (x – AVG(x)) / SQRT(VARIANCE(x))
- (x / MAX(ABS(MIN(x)), ABS(MAX(x))))

For example, if the {(x-MIN(x)) / (MAX(x) - MIN(x)) * (new max – new min) + new min} normalization scheme is chosen, for an average value 253.5, standard deviation 146.21, with minimum value = 1 and maximum value = 506, the transformed average value is 0.5, standard deviation 0.29, minimum value = 0 and maximum value = 1.

For the {(x – AVG(x)) / SQRT(VARIANCE(x))} scheme, the transformed values average 0.0 with standard deviation 1, minimum value = -1.73 and maximum = 1.73.

The {(x / MAX(ABS(MIN(x)), ABS(MAX(x))))} transformation results in an average of 0.5 with standard deviation 0.29, minimum value = 0 and maximum = 1.

The next sction will explore the numeric transformation, which is similar to the normalize transformation, with exponential (EXP), log (LOG), log natural (LN) and square root (SQRT) functions for normalizing data.

Using the Numeric Transformation Wizard

The Numeric Transformation wizard allows you to create a view by applying one of a list of predefined functions to one or more numeric attributes. These functions modify the data distribution characteristics and normalize the data values. You can select one of the following predefined schemes:

- EXP(x), where x <= 70 (Oracle database limit)
- 1 / EXP(AVG(x) - x), where AVG(x) - x <= 70 (Oracle database limit)
- LN(x + a), where a is a user-supplied numeric constant and x + a > 0; LN is natural logarithm. Use this scheme when you are dealing with large numbers; this transformation makes the distribution more like a normal distribution.
- LN((x - a) / (b - x)), where a and b are user-supplied numeric constants and (x - a) / (b - x) > 0; LN is the natural logarithm.
- LOG(10, x + a), where a is a user-supplied numeric constant and x + a > 0; LOG(10, z) is the logarithm to the base 10 of z. Use this scheme when you are dealing with large numbers;

this transformation makes the distribution more like a normal distribution.

- SQRT(x), where x >= 0. Use this function to linearize a distribution.

The next section will examine options for handling extreme or outlying data points.

Using the Outlier Treatment Transformation Wizard

The Outlier Treatment Transformation is used to generate recommended outlier treatments based on the mining algorithm that you plan to use. If you invoke this wizard from a Mining Activity, the appropriate default treatments are specified automatically.

The default algorithm settings are shown in Figure 5.16. An outlier is a data point that is located far from the rest of the data. An outlier is typically several standard deviations from the mean. Some data mining algorithms are sensitive to outliers in data. The Outlier Treatment wizard identifies outliers and lets you specify how to treat them.

You specify a treatment by defining what constitutes an outlier, for example, all values in the top and bottom 5% of values, and how to replace outliers, either with NULL or edge values. The wizard can generate default treatments based on the algorithm that you are planning to use.

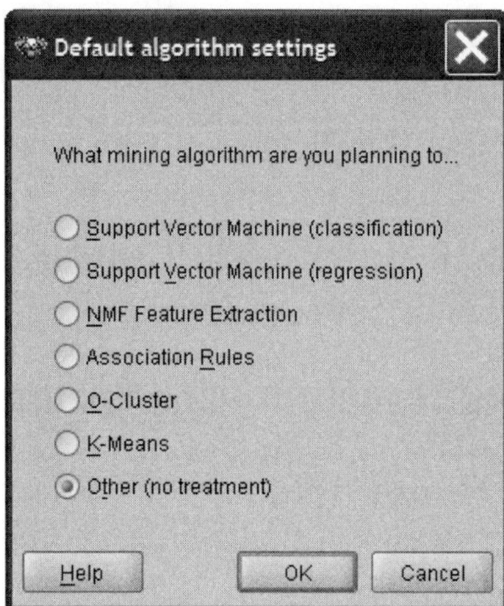

Figure 5.17: *Default Algorithm Settings.*

You can also specify how to identify outliers using the wizard, as shown in Figure 5.17.

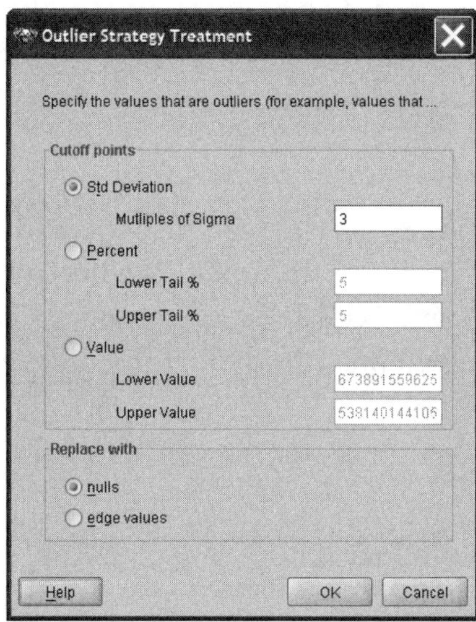

Figure 5.18: *Outlier Strategy Treatment.*

The SQL statement shows the wizard-generated code when the attribute CMEDV in the Boston price dataset is set to Standard Deviation, Multiples of Sigma = 3.

```
CREATE VIEW "DMUSER_BOOK"."boston_price58837524"
 AS SELECT
"AGE","B","CHAS",( CASE WHEN "CMEDV" < -5.02 THEN NULL
WHEN "CMEDV" >= -5.02 AND "CMEDV" <= 50.08 THEN "CMEDV"
WHEN "CMEDV" > 50.08 THEN NULL
end)  "CMEDV"
,"CRIM","DIS","INDUS","LAT","LON","LSTAT","MEDV","NOX","OBS","PTRATI
O","RAD","RM","TAX","TOWN","TOWN#","TRACT","ZN" FROM
"DMUSER_BOOK"."boston_price"
```

Conclusion

Oracle Data Miner provides a powerful and useful toolbox for analyzing, aggregating, prepping, and transforming data. You can customize the discretization of data to fit your business rules, create new data, and leverage powerful analytic functions available in SQL. While the new Data Miner tool automates the important functions necessary for each data mining algorithm, the transformation wizards give you the flexibility to modify datasets, use advanced statistical techniques to improve data quality, and enhance the predictive accuracy of classification models.

We are now ready to take a look at Oracle's predictive analytics, which provides a simple way of predicting and explaining data using data mining techniques.

Predictive Analytics

CHAPTER 6

Predictive Analytics in Data Mining

Predictive analytics concerns the prediction of future probabilities. With predictive analytics, the data mining analyst takes the case dataset, identifies two key components, and voila a model is built and applied to the data. Previous chapters have shown how to use Oracle Data Miner to perform these tasks. Now Oracle has taken data mining to a new level by introducing data-centric automated data mining.

At a recent BioIT World meeting, Mr. Charles Berger stated:

> Predictive analytics -- or "one-click data mining" through the simplification and automation of the data-mining process -- enables advanced analytics to be applied across the entire life sciences spectrum -- from drug discovery through marketing. Researchers, for example, can use predictive analytics to find factors associated with a disease or predict which patient might respond best to an experimental treatment.

Type the following string into the Google search engine to find more information: **Predictive Analysis is Data Mining's Future Berger**

In contrast to the methods previously described in this text, using predictive analytics requires no decisions on the part of the data analyst in terms of preprocessing the data, picking an algorithm, building and testing a model, and applying the model to identify important attributes or predict which cases fall into the target values. In essence, predictive analytics simplifies the process and fully automates data mining.

Oracle Predictive analytics is based on Oracle 10G Release 2's PL/SQL package DMBS_PREDICTIVE_ANALYTICS. Oracle provides an interface to this package with both Data Miner and the predictive analytic spreadsheet add-in for MS Excel.

Predictive Analytics accomplishes two tasks important to the data mining analyst: explaining the importance of attributes and classifying cases.

Explain Procedure

The Explain procedure identifies attributes important for explaining the target attribute. The analyst may be interested in answering these questions:

- Which demographic characteristics are important in their customer database for individuals who are likely to churn?
- What symptoms do patients exhibit who eventually succumb to disease?
- What environmental changes suggest global warming?

The EXPLAIN procedure has the following specification:

```
DBMS_PREDICTIVE_ANALYTICS.EXPLAIN (
data_table_name                   IN VARCHAR2,
explain_column_name               IN VARCHAR2,
result_table_name                 IN VARCHAR2,
data_schema_name                  IN VARCHAR2
DEFAULT NULL);
```

This procedure simplifies the data mining process to these steps:

1. Specify the case dataset.
2. Identify the target attribute to explain.
3. Generate results.

The procedure automates the complex data mining methodologies and generates results with minimal user input. The procedure discretizes numeric data (if needed), uses quantile binning, and writes the results (explanatory power and rank) to a table.

Predict Procedure

The predict procedure provides predictions of a specific attribute for all records in the input data. The analyst may be interested in answering these types of questions:

- Which customers might buy a certain product?
- What is the probability a customer will respond to an ad campaign?
- What is the probability a patient may acquire a certain disease?

The predict procedure input consists of a data table and target attribute (values to predict). The PREDICT procedure has the following specification:

```
DBMS_PREDICTIVE_ANALYTICS.PREDICT (
accuracy                    OUT NUMBER,
data_table_name             IN VARCHAR2,
case_id_column_name         IN VARCHAR2,
target_column_name          IN VARCHAR2,
result_table_name           IN VARCHAR2,
data_schema_name            IN VARCHAR2
DEFAULT NULL);
```

The procedure samples and performs statistical computations on the dataset, determines the attribute data type (categorical or numeric), selects an algorithm and model, determines skewness of the dataset and adjusts parameters to prevent trivial results, calculates a performance measure (accuracy), and applies the model to the entire input dataset.

Next, we will take a closer look at Oracle Data Miner's interface for Predictive Analytics. You can find the Predict and Explain wizards under the Data toolbar. We will use the Mining_Data_Build_V dataset that was introduced in Chapter One.

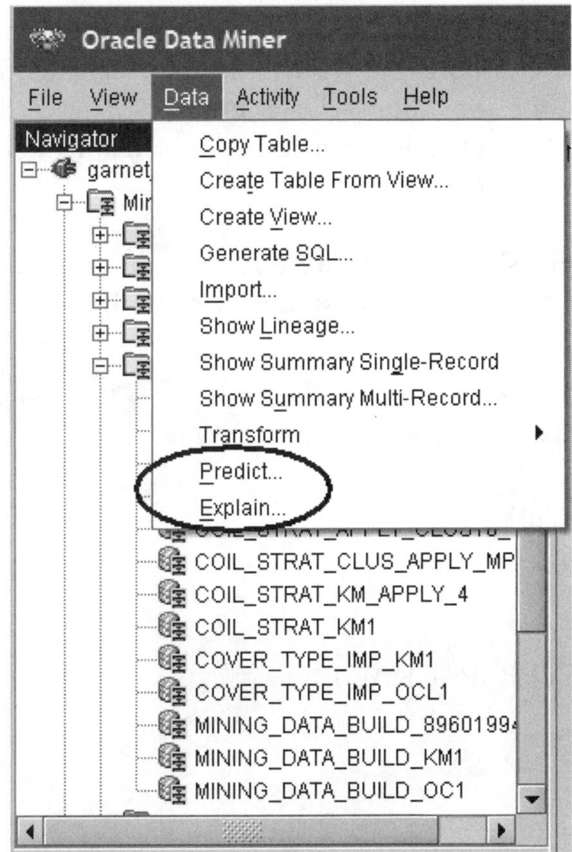

Figure 6.1: *Predict and Explain in Oracle Data Miner*

Explain Wizard

The steps taken by the explain wizard include analyzing the input table, prepping the data, building the model, analyzing the model to identify important attributes, and creating a table with the attributes rank ordered in importance. The output table lists the attributes sorted in decreasing order of importance for explaining the target values. Importance is a number between 0 and 1, with 1 being most important.

After identifying the case dataset, Step 2 of the Explain Wizard asks you to select the attribute you wish to explain. This is the target attribute, and for the Mining_Data_Build_V dataset the target is AFFINITY_CARD. All that is left is to pick a name for the output table, and click Finish.

In the Explain Output shown in Figure 6.2, the top 10 ranking attributes for predicting whether a customer has an affinity card are:

- HOUSEHOLD_SIZE
- CUST_MARITAL_STATUS
- YRS_RESIDENCE
- Y_BOX_GAMES
- EDUCATION
- HOME_THEATER_PACKAGE
- OCCUPATION
- CUST_GENDER
- AGE
- BOOKKEEPING_APPLICATION

The model sets the importance of the remaining columns to zero.

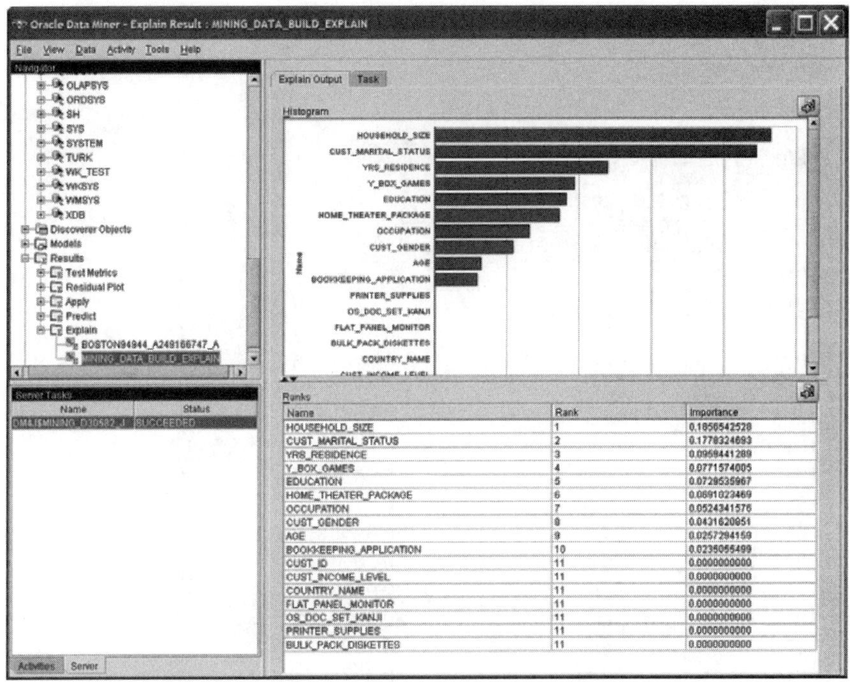

Figure 6.2: *Explain Output.*

Predict Wizard

The Predict Wizard assigns probabilities and predictions of the target value for every case in the dataset. Predict uses the existing data in the dataset to train the model, with the requirement that there must be some existing values for the target attribute (not all values can be NULL). The Predict Wizard analyzes the input table, preps the data, builds the model, analyzes the model, and creates a table with three columns: Case ID, Prediction of the target value, and the Probability of the prediction.

Shown in Figure 6.3 is a portion of the Predict table showing the CUST_ID, PREDICTION, and PROBABILITY of the OCCUPATION attribute for the Mining_Data_Build_V dataset.

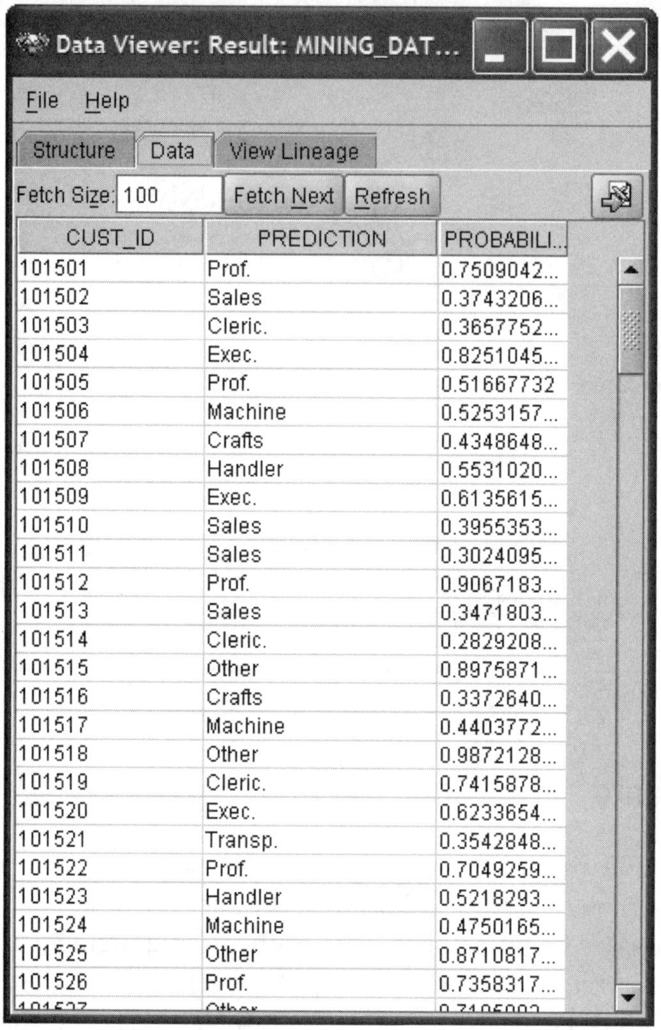
Data Viewer: Result: MINING_DAT...
File Help
Structure
Data
View Lineage
Fetch Size: 100
Fetch Next
Refresh

CUST_ID	PREDICTION	PROBABILI...
101501	Prof.	0.7509042...
101502	Sales	0.3743206...
101503	Cleric.	0.3657752...
101504	Exec.	0.8251045...
101505	Prof.	0.51667732
101506	Machine	0.5253157...
101507	Crafts	0.4348648...
101508	Handler	0.5531020...
101509	Exec.	0.6135615...
101510	Sales	0.3955353...
101511	Sales	0.3024095...
101512	Prof.	0.9067183...
101513	Sales	0.3471803...
101514	Cleric.	0.2829208...
101515	Other	0.8975871...
101516	Crafts	0.3372640...
101517	Machine	0.4403772...
101518	Other	0.9872128...
101519	Cleric.	0.7415878...
101520	Exec.	0.6233654...
101521	Transp.	0.3542848...
101522	Prof.	0.7049259...
101523	Handler	0.5218293...
101524	Machine	0.4750165...
101525	Other	0.8710817...
101526	Prof.	0.7358317...

Figure 6.3: *Predict Table.*

The power of the Oracle Predictive Analytics approach is that the analyst needs no knowledge of a data mining algorithm to obtain useful results. The only information from the data mining analyst is the input dataset.

The following section shows some examples of predictive analytics in action.

Applying Predictive Analytics

The Explain and Predict wizards are designed to empower non-expert users to achieve reasonable results with minimum effort (Campos, Stengard, Milenova, Data-Centric Automated Data Mining:

```
http://www.oracle.com/technology/products/bi/odm/pdf/automated_data_
mining_paper_1205.pdf;
```

Type the following string into the Google search engine to find more information: **data-centric automated data mining campos**

Ritu Chinya, Data-Centric Automated Data Mining:

```
http://webpages.csus.edu/~rs248/Data_Centric_automated_Data_Mining.p
pt).
```

Oracle predictive analytics addresses the complete beginning-to-end process from input data (having known and/or unknown cases) to producing results containing predictions or explanations for specific attributes. A reasonable approach to utilizing these techniques is to utilize as many variables as possible in the dataset in order to capitalize on the strength of the model to capture the most significant attributes and provide as accurate a model as possible.

Predictive analytics has been proposed as a means for developing data mining experts in Oracle Warehouse Builder (Keith Laker, Using Predictive Analytics within Warehouse Builder, March 2006:

```
http://www.oracle.com/technology/products/warehouse/pdf/Using%20Pred
ictive%20Analytics%20within%20Warehouse%20Builder.pdf ;
```

- Type the following string into the Google search engine to find more information: **oracle using predictive analytics**

Keith Laker, ETPL – Extract, Transform, Predict and Load, March 2006:

http://www.oracle.com/technology/products/warehouse/pdf/ETPL%20-%20Extract%20Transform%20Predict%20and%20Load.pdf)

- Type the following string into the Google search engine to find more information: **oracle extract transform predict load**

Another innovative approach is using predictive analytics by intelligently building OLAP cubes with data mining (Keith Laker, The Cube Factory:

http://oraclebi.blogspot.com/2005/11/intelligently-building-olap-cubes-with.html

Laker, Obradovic, Kosuru, Adding Data Mining to Extend Your OLAP BI Solution, The Cube Factory:

http://download-east.oracle.com/oowsf2005/732wp.pdf).

- Type the following string into the Google search engine to find more information: **intelligently building olap cubes**
- Type the following string into the Google search engine to find more information: **oracle cube factory**

Conclusion

This Chapter introduced Oracle's Predictive Analytics approach to data mining. The intent is to allow one-click data mining, hiding the complexity of the underlying model building and analytics from the user. The process of data analysis, sampling, modeling, and testing is highly automated.

Oracle Data Miner has Predict and Explain wizards providing access to the Predictive Analytics package. The only selections a user needs to make are the case dataset and a target attribute.

The Predict function assigns probabilities and predictions of the target value for every case in the dataset, including those cases that already have a known target value. The Explain function lists the attributes that are important for explaining the target values.

The Predictive Analytics functionality is proposed as an exciting automation tool in a variety of applications. Perhaps you may find this tool of use in your data mining enterprise.

The next chapter is based on an intriguing presentation by Mark Hornick at Oracle, who was very kind to give us permission to include his work in this book. Oracle Data Mining is utilized in conjunction with Oracle BI Publisher to personalize and automate form letter generation.

Personalized Form Letter Generation with Oracle BI Publisher

CHAPTER

Using the Oracle Data Miner graphical interface to build models and Oracle Data Mining's SQL interface to score data, you can seamlessly integrate data mining results with Oracle BI Publisher (formerly XML Publisher).

This chapter demonstrates what is possible between BI Publisher and Oracle Data Mining.[3]

Scenarios for using ODM with BI Publisher

A few scenarios will be presented to get us stated. We began in Chapter 1 building a data model predicting which customers were to be offered an affinity card. The dataset used to build the model, MINING_DATA_BUILD_V, contains demographic and purchasing data about customers. After building a classification model, the model is applied to the actual customer population, that is, each customer is scored. Using SQL scoring functions such as PREDICTION and PREDICTION_SET, we can generate a standard form letter to customers predicted most likely to respond to our campaign. We can generate different form letters based on different customer demographics (customer segmentation). We can also personalize a form letter with customer-specific offers. Since we want to understand how predictions are made, we will use the Decision Tree (DT) algorithm to model the data.

---

[3] This Chapter is based on a presentation by Mark Hornick.

The three datasets that will be used to illustrate customer segmentation are CUST_OFFER, CUST_OFFER_APPLY, and OFFER. Unlike the datasets in previous chapters, which were downloaded and imported into Oracle tables, these datasets are simply described here.

The dataset CUST_OFFER shown in Figure 7.1 is identical to the MINING_DATA_BUILD_V case dataset as described in Chapter 1, with an additional column labeled OFFER. In the build dataset, the OFFER attribute is the item accepted by each customer in our starter campaign, and is the target attribute for the Decision Tree classification algorithm.

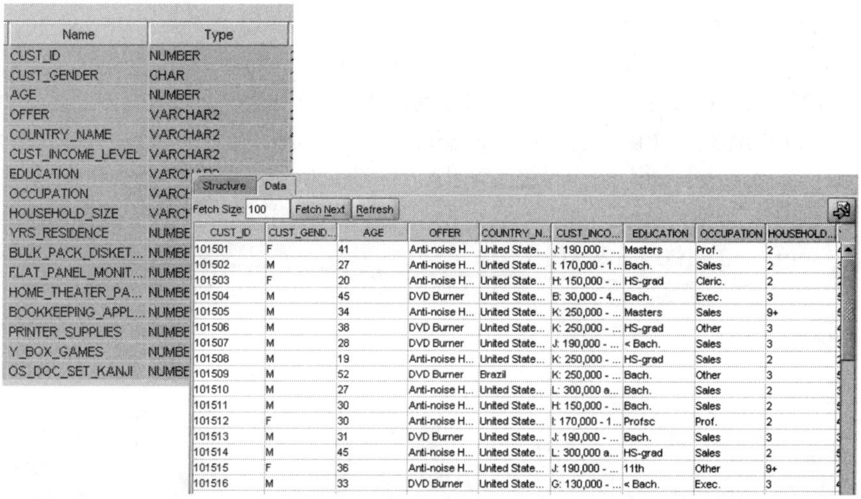

Name	Type
CUST_ID	NUMBER
CUST_GENDER	CHAR
AGE	NUMBER
OFFER	VARCHAR2
COUNTRY_NAME	VARCHAR2
CUST_INCOME_LEVEL	VARCHAR2
EDUCATION	VARCH
OCCUPATION	VARCH
HOUSEHOLD_SIZE	VARCH
YRS_RESIDENCE	NUMBE
BULK_PACK_DISKET...	NUMBE
FLAT_PANEL_MONIT...	NUMBE
HOME_THEATER_PA...	NUMBE
BOOKKEEPING_APPL...	NUMBE
PRINTER_SUPPLIES	NUMBE
Y_BOX_GAMES	NUMBE
OS_DOC_SET_KANJI	NUMBE

Structure Data

Fetch Size: 100 Fetch Next Refresh

CUST_ID	CUST_GEND...	AGE	OFFER	COUNTRY_N...	CUST_INCO...	EDUCATION	OCCUPATION	HOUSEHOLD...
101501	F	41	Anti-noise H...	United State...	J: 190,000 - ...	Masters	Prof.	2
101502	M	27	Anti-noise H...	United State...	I: 170,000 - 1...	Bach.	Sales	2
101503	F	20	Anti-noise H...	United State...	H: 150,000 - ...	HS-grad	Cleric.	2
101504	M	45	DVD Burner	United State...	B: 30,000 - 4...	Bach.	Exec.	3
101505	M	34	Anti-noise H...	United State...	K: 250,000 - ...	Masters	Sales	9+
101506	M	38	DVD Burner	United State...	K: 250,000 - ...	HS-grad	Other	3
101507	M	28	DVD Burner	United State...	J: 190,000 - ...	< Bach.	Sales	3
101508	M	19	Anti-noise H...	United State...	K: 250,000 - ...	HS-grad	Sales	2
101509	M	52	DVD Burner	Brazil	K: 250,000 - ...	Bach.	Other	3
101510	M	27	Anti-noise H...	United State...	L: 300,000 a...	Bach.	Sales	2
101511	M	30	Anti-noise H...	United State...	H: 150,000 - ...	Bach.	Sales	2
101512	F	30	Anti-noise H...	United State...	I: 170,000 - 1...	Profsc	Prof.	2
101513	M	31	DVD Burner	United State...	J: 190,000 - ...	Bach.	Sales	3
101514	M	45	Anti-noise H...	United State...	L: 300,000 a...	HS-grad	Sales	2
101515	F	36	Anti-noise H...	United State...	J: 190,000 - ...	11th	Other	9+
101516	M	33	DVD Burner	United State...	G: 130,000 - ...	< Bach.	Exec.	3

Figure 7.1: *Customer Offer Dataset.*

The OFFER dataset is comprised of seven rows, with the ID, NAME, OFFER, and DESCR (description) of the offers given to the customers. The data is shown in Figure 7.2, and is used for joining with the prediction results.

ID	NAME	OFFER	DESCR
0001	MP3 Player	Save 20% on the TOWNE MP3 Player	256MB Music MP3 Player Supports MP3 & WMA music file...
0002	DVD Player	Save 30% on the PORTPLAY DVD Player	Progressive-scan playback: When connected to a digital T...
0003	DVD	Save 50% on the purchase of 3 or more DVDs	Popular titles available and USaveDVD.com
0004	DVD Burner	Save 15% on the FIRE DVD Burner	Fast 52X writing, 24X rewriting and 52X reading speeds. ...
0005	Anti-noise H...	Save 35% on the SILENCE Anti-noise Headset	Electronically identifies and reduces unwanted noise, allo...
0006	Handheld Em...	Save 20% on the CHERRY PDA	Bluetooth Wireless Technology, full HTML browser & high...
0007	Laptop	Save 33% on the LABRADOR Laptop	Combines digital entertainment with powerful mobile comp...

Figure 7.2: *Offer Dataset.*

The CUST_OFFER_APPLY dataset corresponds to the customers that we want to predict which offer, or offers, to make. The apply dataset has all the attributes of the build dataset, except for the target attribute OFFER.

Building a Decision Tree Model

The first step is to build a decision tree (DT) model, using default DT settings. We can use any of the other classification models (Naïve Bayes, Adaptive Bayes Network, or Support Vector Machine), adjusting for needed transformations. However, the DT model will provide a rule for the leaf nodes. Note that leaf nodes are terminal nodes in the tree that describe population segment characteristics.

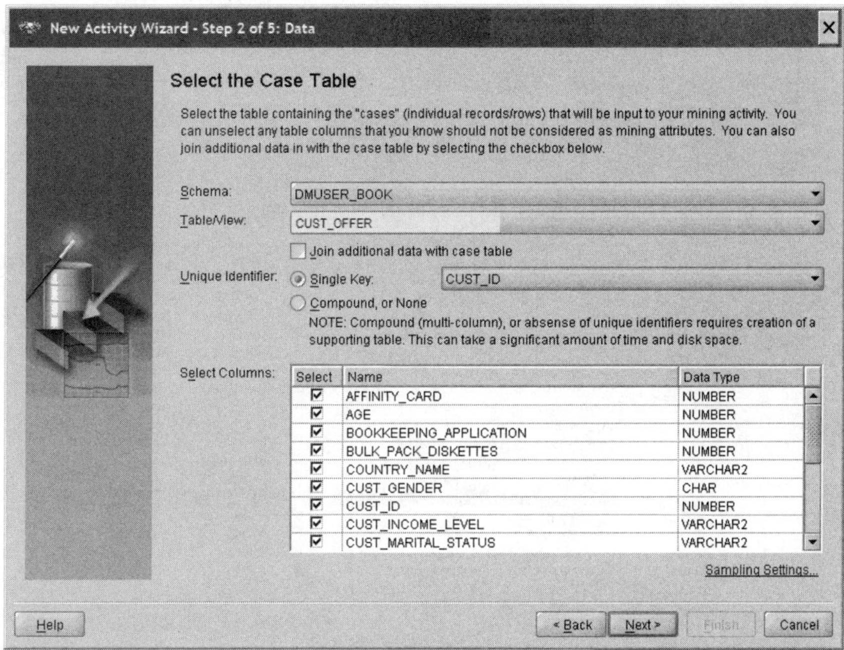

Figure 7.3: *Build Activity for Decision Tree.*

To build the DT model, start the build activity, specifying Classification for the function type using Decision Tree as the algorithm.

After selecting the CUST_OFFER case table in the Build Activity, and CUST_ID as the unique identifier, the next step is to identify OFFER as the target attribute, shown in Figure 7.4. Note that OFFER is a categorical mining type attribute.

The preferred target value can be any one of the seven shown in the OFFER dataset. For this example we pick the Laptop offer.

The last step is to choose a name for the new mining activity, and then run the model using the default settings.

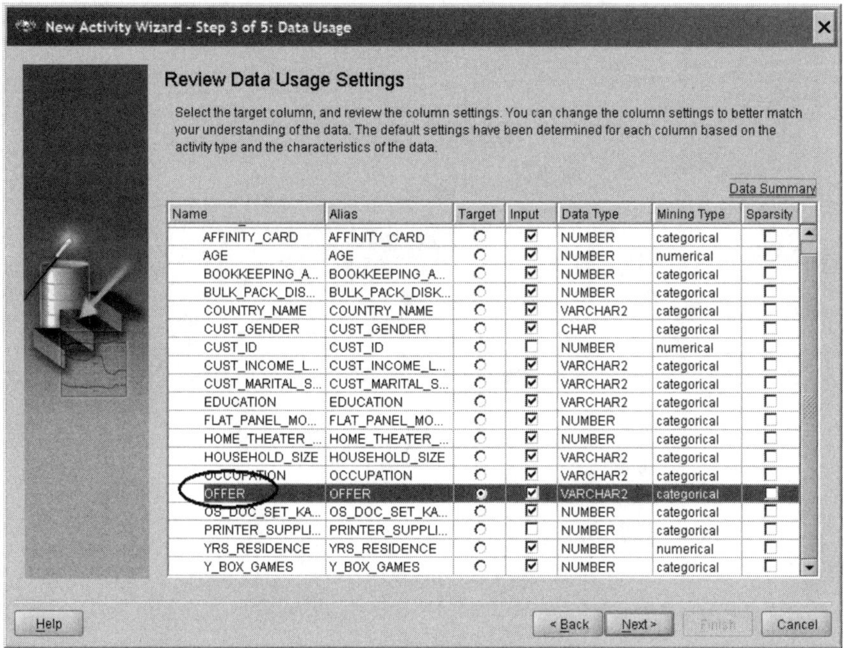

Figure 7.4: *Select OFFER as Target Attribute.*

Results of the Decision Tree Model

After building the model, the DT build results show 8 segments (leaves), with the corresponding rules that predict the various offers. Note that not all products are offered, in fact only the Headset, Laptop, and DVD Burner are offered. This results from too few customers responding to these offers in the starter campaign from where we obtained the build data.

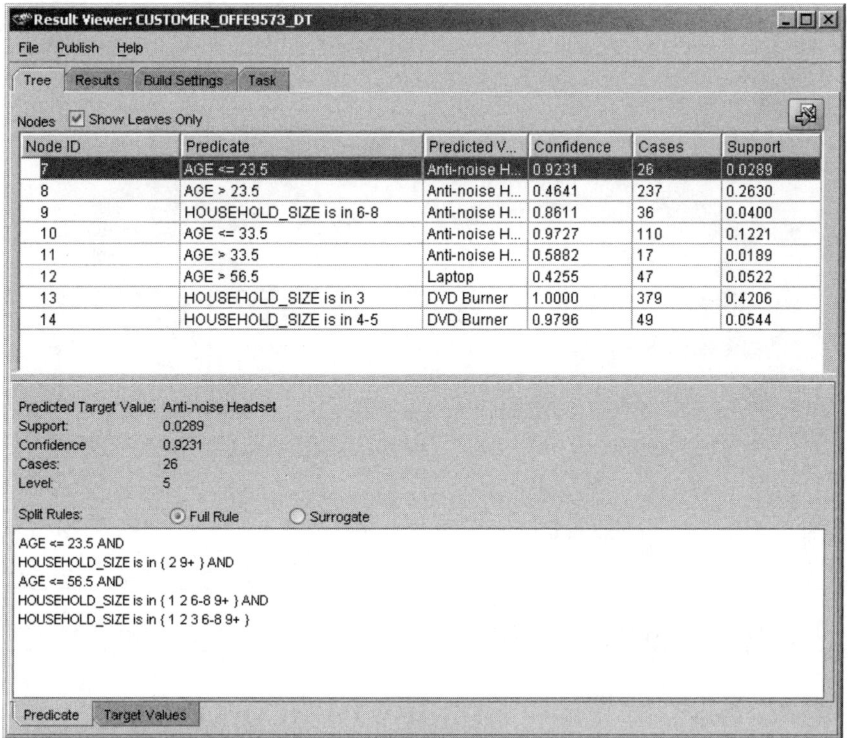

Node ID	Predicate	Predicted V...	Confidence	Cases	Support
7	AGE <= 23.5	Anti-noise H...	0.9231	26	0.0289
8	AGE > 23.5	Anti-noise H...	0.4641	237	0.2630
9	HOUSEHOLD_SIZE is in 6-8	Anti-noise H...	0.8611	36	0.0400
10	AGE <= 33.5	Anti-noise H...	0.9727	110	0.1221
11	AGE > 33.5	Anti-noise H...	0.5882	17	0.0189
12	AGE > 56.5	Laptop	0.4255	47	0.0522
13	HOUSEHOLD_SIZE is in 3	DVD Burner	1.0000	379	0.4206
14	HOUSEHOLD_SIZE is in 4-5	DVD Burner	0.9796	49	0.0544

Figure 7.5: *Decision Tree for Product Offer.*

Scoring the Apply Dataset.

The model is then applied to the dataset CUST_OFFER_APPLY, which does not have the OFFER attribute, but otherwise has the same structure as the build dataset. After scoring the dataset with the model, we can:

- Predict which top offer to make to each customer.
- Predict the top 3 offers to make to each customer.
- Include queries in BI Publisher to support response modeling and offer personalization scenarios.

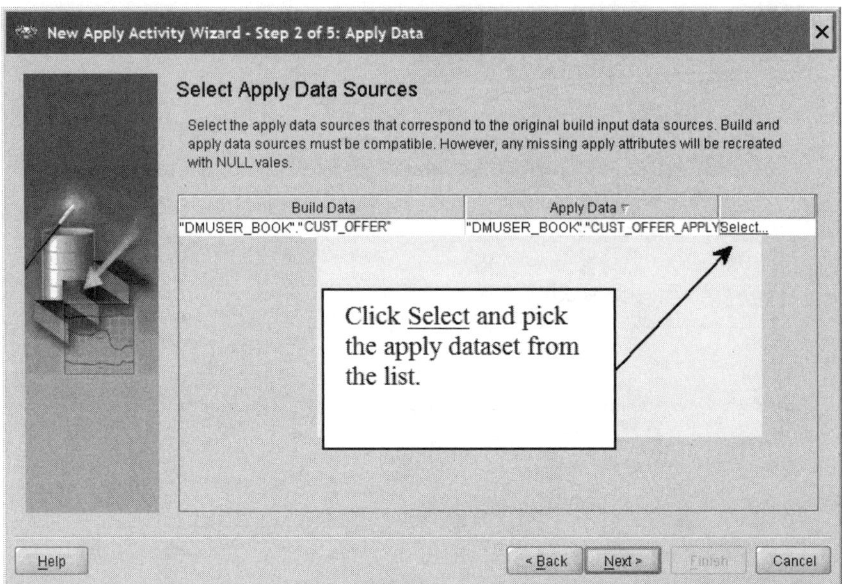

Figure 7.6: *Scoring the Apply Dataset.*

Using SQL to View Results of Scored Data

We can write an SQL query to generate offer predictions. To test the query, type SQL statements into the Oracle Data Miner SQL Worksheet, and view the results for a particular customer.

```
Select cust_id, name, offer, descr
from OFFER o, (
    select cust_id, prediction(CUST_OFFER_111787_DT using *)
prediction
    from CUST_OFFER_APPLY
    where cust_id = '100015')
where prediction = o.name
```

As depicted in Figure 7.7, the customer will be offered the Headset. Notice that we used the SQL Scoring function PREDICTION, which returns the best prediction for the target.

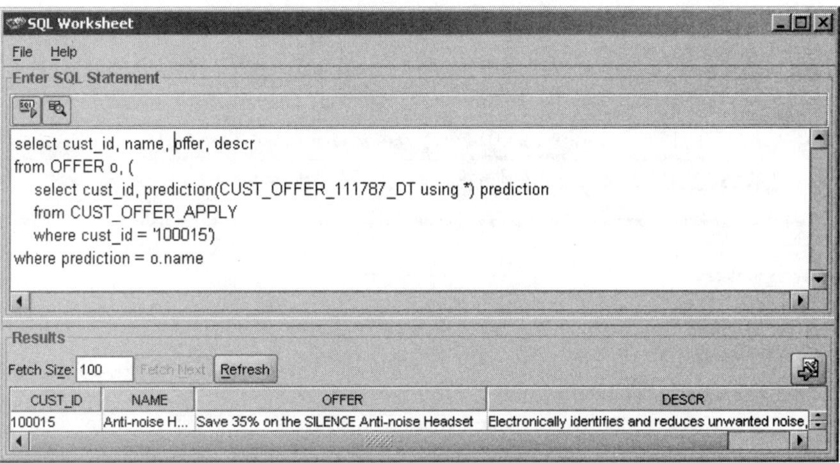

Figure 7.7: *Top Offer for Customer 100015.*

Creating a Report using BI Publisher Enterprise Server

Now, it is time to move on to Oracle BI Publisher Enterprise. You will first create a database connection, using the JDBC driver OracleDriver. The URL will have this configuration: jdbc:oracle:thin:@host:port:sid. Figure 7.8 shows an example JDBC connection in the Admin section of BI Publisher.

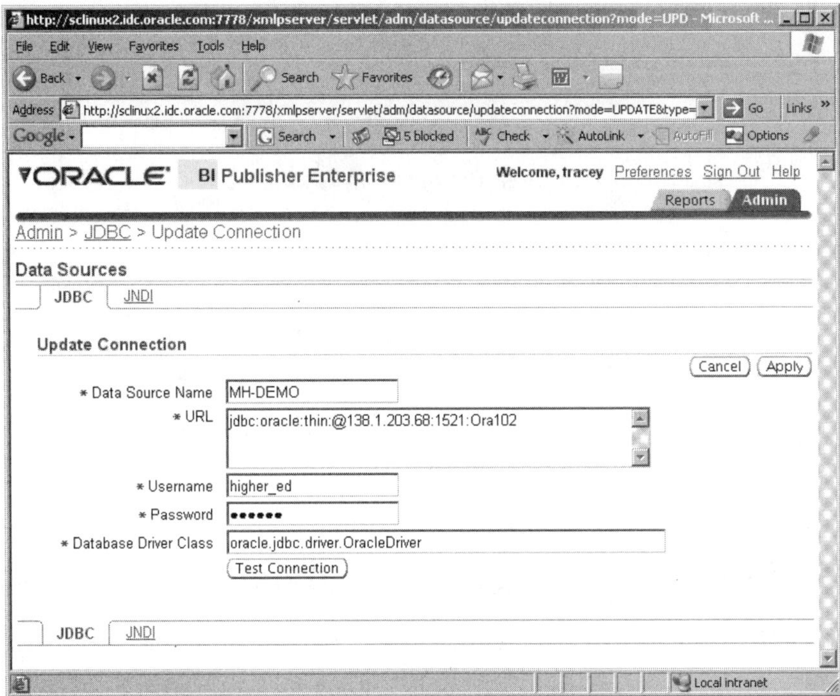

Figure 7.8: *BI Publisher Server.*

Once connected, create a new report Offers-1.

Next, specify Data Model with the data mining query. Place the ODM SQL in the box labeled SQL Query. A letter with one offer per customer will be generated for each customer in the dataset.

The next section will demonstrate creating a letter template for the Layout section of the Offers-1 report.

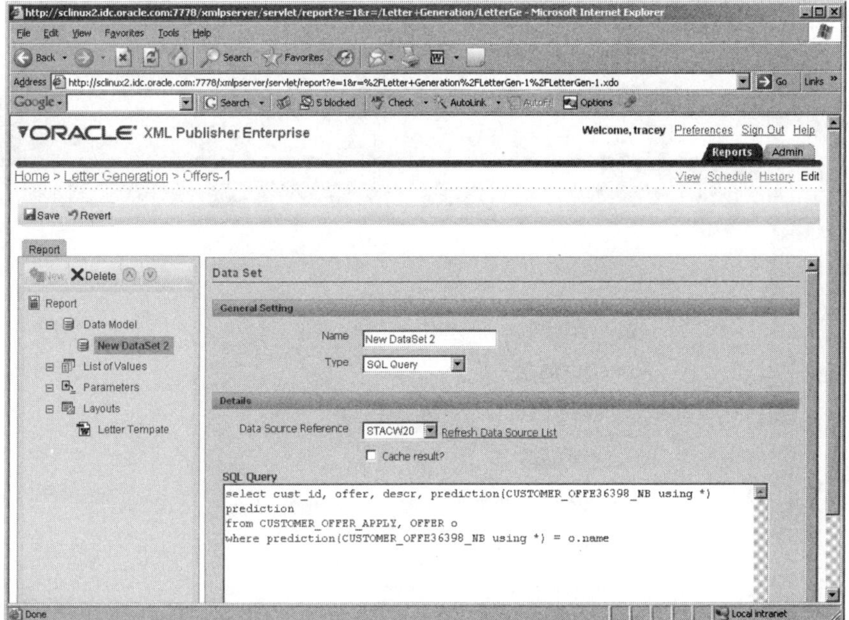

Figure 7.9: *Editing a Report in BI Publisher Enterprise.*

Using Template Builder for Oracle BI Publisher

The BI Publisher template is a client side tool for building and testing layout templates. The BI Publisher Desktop tool can be downloaded from metalink or Oracle edelivery website. Once installed, you will have a new tool bar and menu entry in MS Word. Be sure that when you install the template builder tool, you are logged in as the application user with administrative privileges.

Figure 7.10: *Template Builder Tool Bar*

Use the Word RTF file with BI Publisher Plug-in to compose a template for the letter.

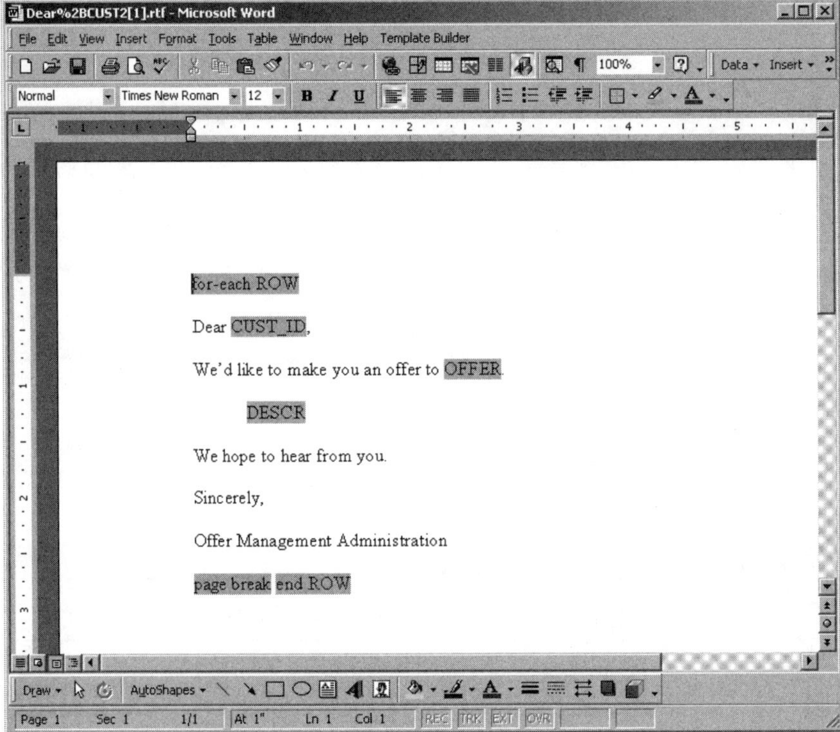

Figure 7.11: *Word RTF file with BI Publisher plug-in.*

CUST_ID, OFFER, and DESC are fields from the SQL statement. The next section illustrates the BI Publisher's drag and drop feature for inserting fields in the Template Builder.

Note that the customer ID should be replaced with the customer name. This requires joining with another customer table containing the actual names and addresses of the customers.

View the generated letters through BI Publisher Server.

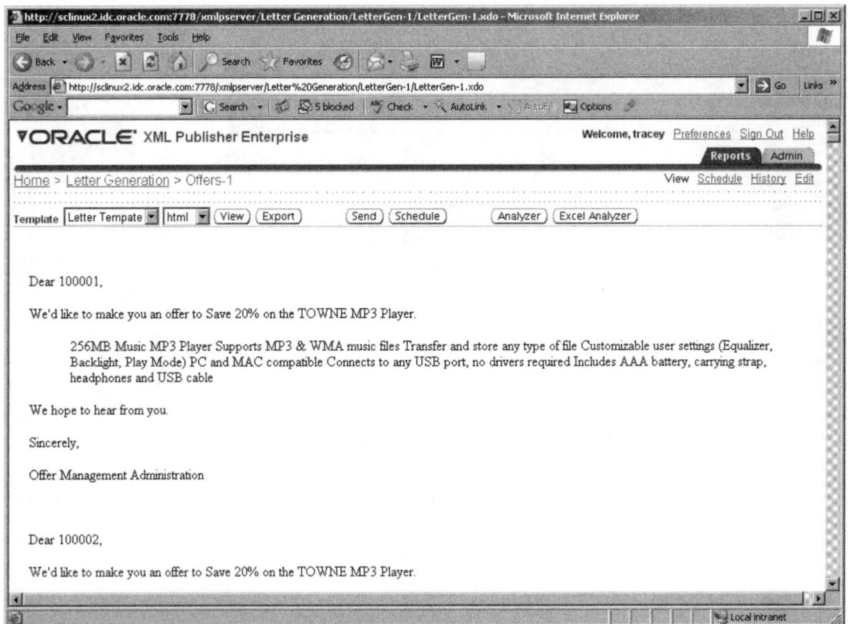

Figure 7.12: *Personalized Letter in BI Publisher Enterprise.*

This application produced 1200+ letters personalized for each customer. You can easily add logo's to your template, and make a more professional form letter, as shown in Figure 7.13.

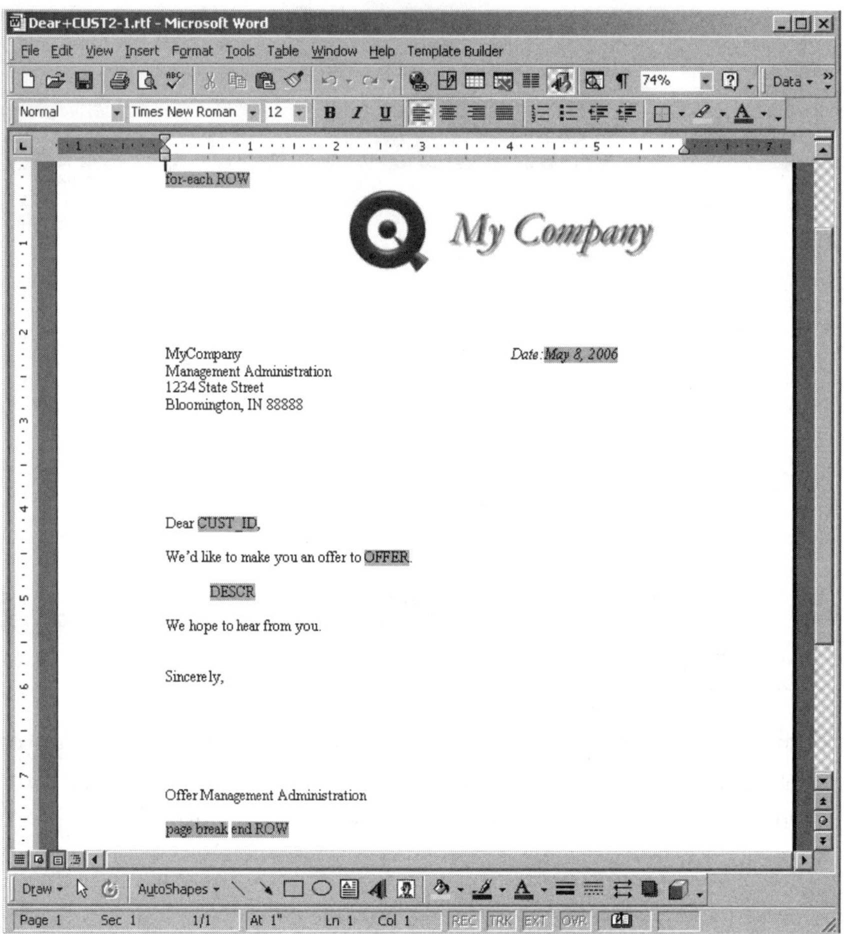

Figure 7.13: *Word RTF file with BI Publisher plug-in.*

Adding Fields to the Word Template using BI Publisher Template Builder

To create a Word template, load the XML data format into the Template Builder, then drag and drop data fields to the Word document. Add a date field, images, tables etc, and format the letter just as any other Word document.

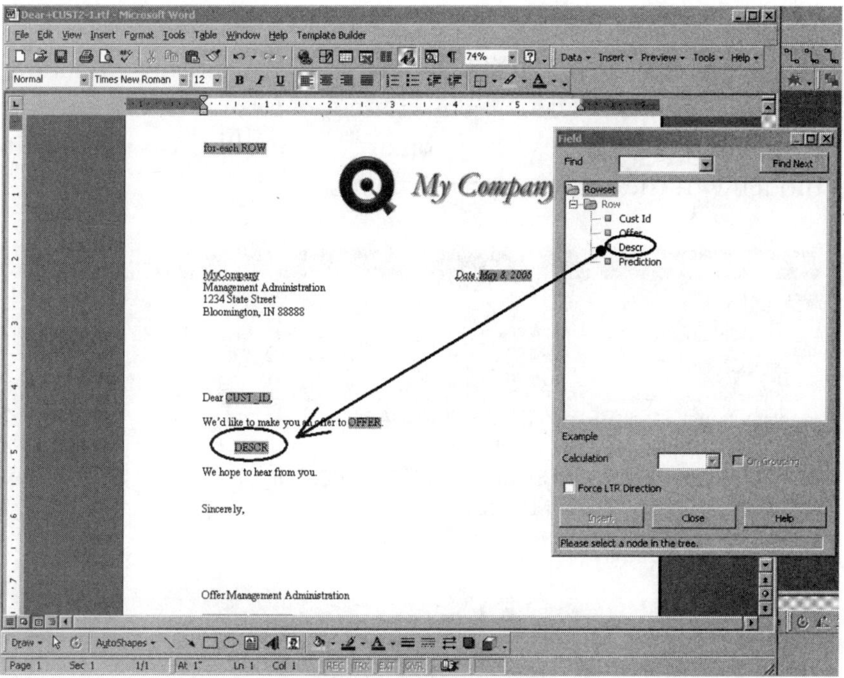

Figure 7.14: *Insert Fields from SQL Statement.*

Creating a Personalized Customer Letter with Three Offers

A form letter can contain more than one offer. The DT scored dataset can also give you the top 3 offers for each customer. Recall from Chapter 2 that one of the options when scoring data is to obtain the ranking of top three choices for each customer by clicking the radio button next to Number of Best Target Values and entering 3. Recall that this demo DT model can only predict 3 possible outcomes due to lack of support for the other offers. However, for more realistic data where more offers can be predicted the technique still applies.

Test the query in Oracle Data Miner SQL Worksheet, then cut and paste the SQL into BI Publisher.

We used the PREDICTION_SET SQL scoring function as shown in Figure 7.15. This function returns a list of objects containing all classes in a binary or multi-class classification model with the associated probability.

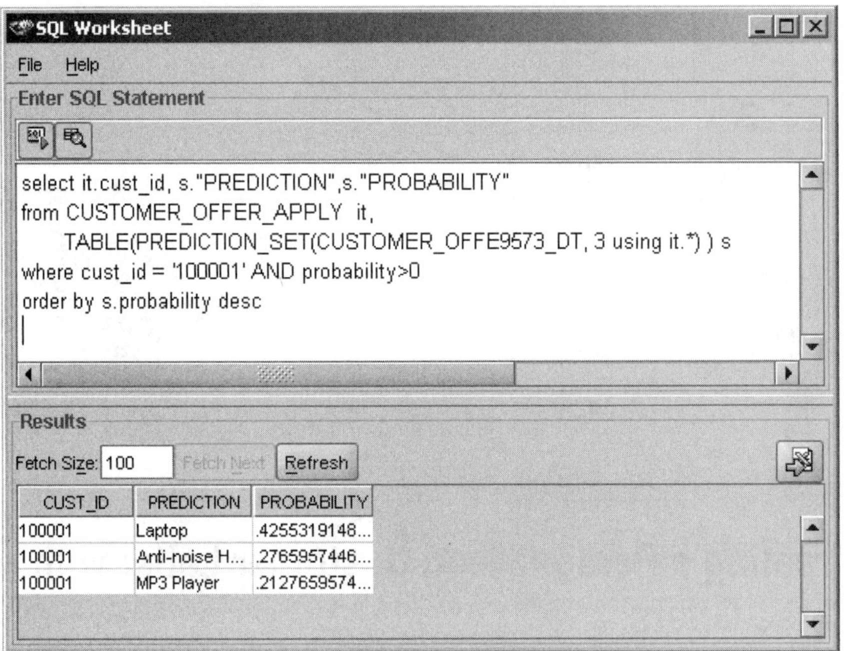

Figure 7.15: *Top 3 Offers for Customer 100001.*

Scenario for Personalizing a Form Letter

Oracle Data Mining paired with BI Publisher can also easily personalize a mail-out to customers. For this scenario, you create a DT model predicting college alumni responses to a fund raising request. You want to mail a letter only to those alumni who are most likely to respond to your fund raising campaign.

The dataset ALUMNI_RESPONSE_9 will be used to predict whether an alumnus will respond to FUND_RAISER_7, the university's latest fund raiser. The columns FUND_RAISER_1 through FUND_RAISER_6 refer to responses to previous fund raisers.

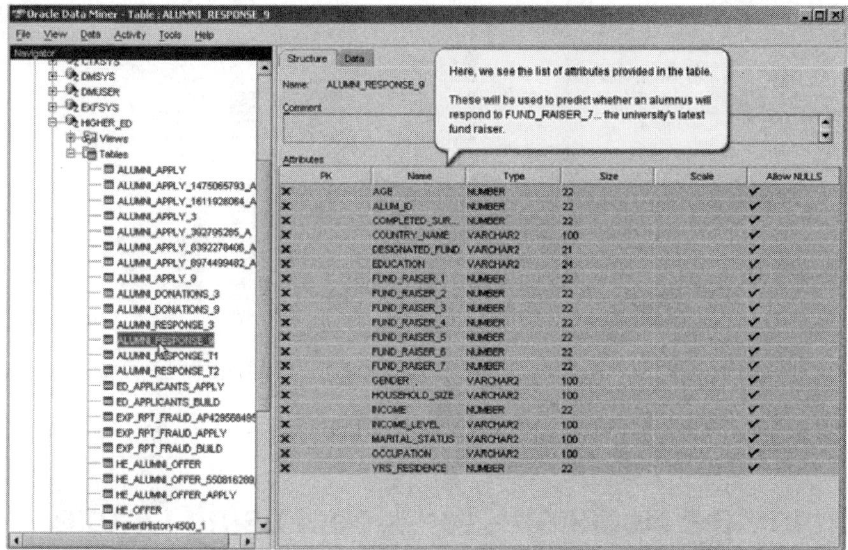

Figure 7.16: *Structure of ALUMNI_RESPONSE_9 Dataset.*

The dataset consists of one row or case per alumnus. The attributes include AGE, EDUCATION, previous responses to fund raisers, and other demographic information, as shown in Figure 7.17.

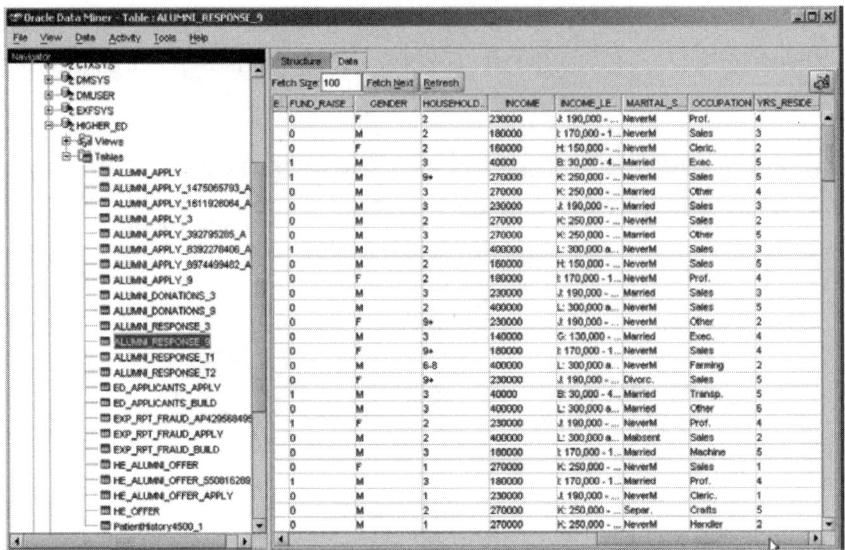

Figure 7.17: *Data in ALUMNI_RESPONSE_9 Dataset.*

Building a Decision Tree Model using Oracle Data Miner

The steps for creating personalized mail-outs are similar to those we followed previously for the customer offer dataset. First build a DT model using the table ALUMNI_RESPONSE_9, predicting a target attribute for fund raising (FUND_RAISER_7 attribute, the response to the latest fund raiser). This model will be used to predict which alumni are likely to respond to the campaign so we can focus our marketing effort on them.

Using the Activity Builder, select the case dataset, and designate the unique identifier for each alumnus, ALUM_ID.

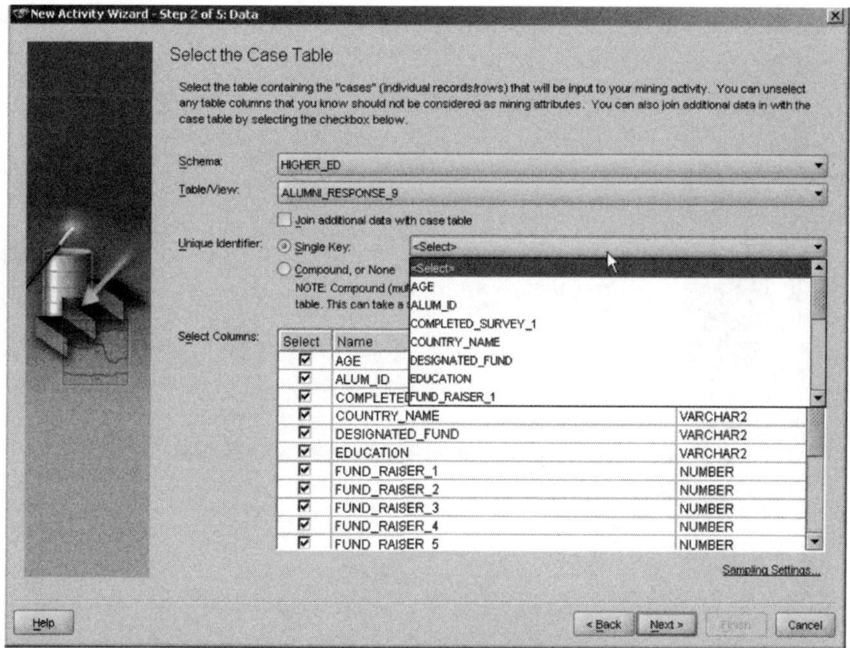

Figure 7.18: *Select Case Table for DT Classification.*

Next, select the target attribute FUND_RAISER_7. The target attribute must be designated as a categorical mining type. Note that the unique identifier ALUM_ID is automatically deselected by ODM.

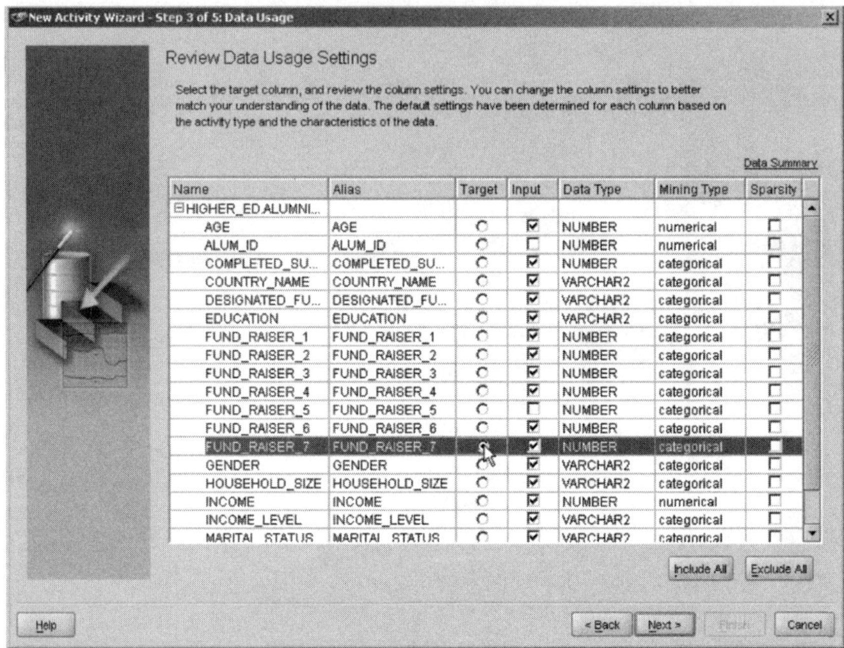

Figure 7.19: *Select Target Attribute.*

Since we are interested in those alumni who actually respond, we will select 1 for the target value, which means response.

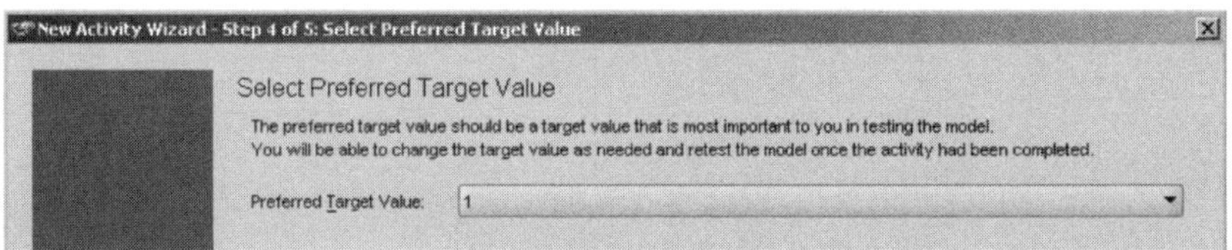

Figure 7.20: *Select Preferred Target Value.*

ODM automatically builds and tests the DT model for us.

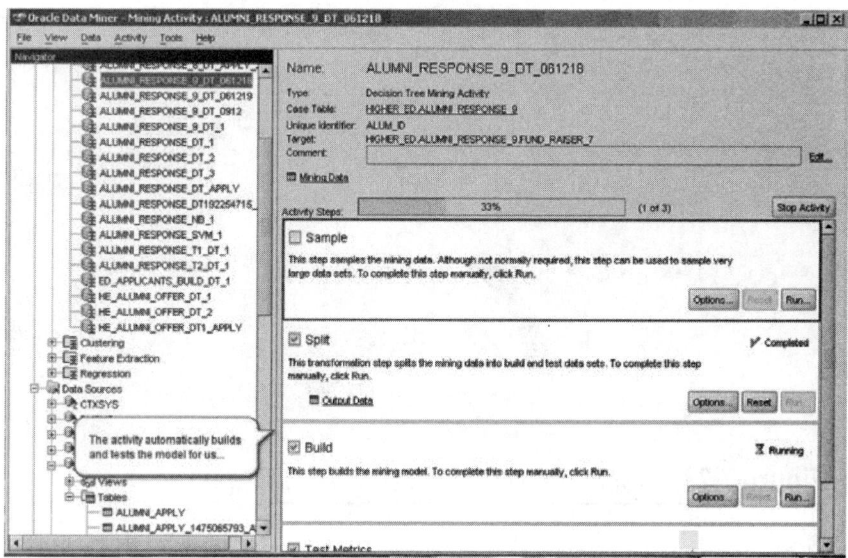

Figure 7.21: *Building the DT Classification Model*

Accuracy of the Fund Raiser DT Model

Now, we will view the test metrics which tell us how well the model can predict responses. Click Result in the Test Metrics section.

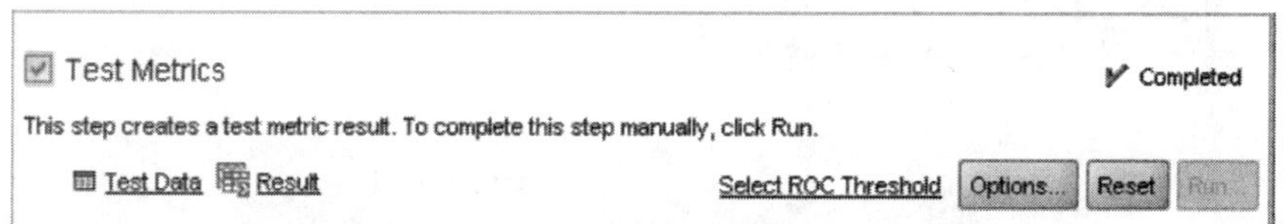

Figure 7.22: *Test Metrics Section of the DT Activity*

We see that the model is 40% better than a naïve model.

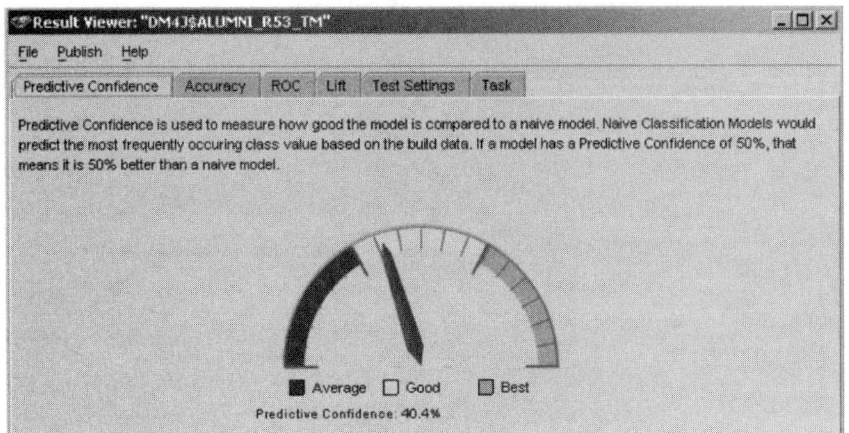

Figure 7.23: *Predictive Confidence Test Metric.*

By viewing the Accuracy tab, we can see what type of mistakes the model made with the test dataset.

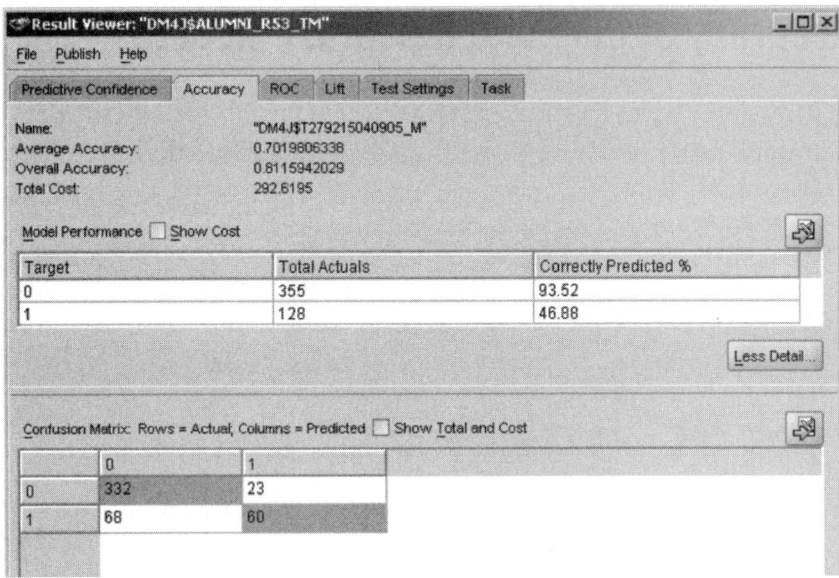

Target	Total Actuals	Correctly Predicted %
0	355	93.52
1	128	46.88

	0	1
0	332	23
1	68	60

Figure 7.24: *Accuracy of the DT Model.*

Here, we can see that the model correctly predicted 60 cases where the target attribute = 1, about 47%. Even though the model got more than half of the predicted targets wrong, can we still expect a higher rate of return on our fund raising campaign using the model?

Results of the Fund Raiser DT Model

We will now look at the model itself to understand how the model makes its predictions. Click Result in the Build section.

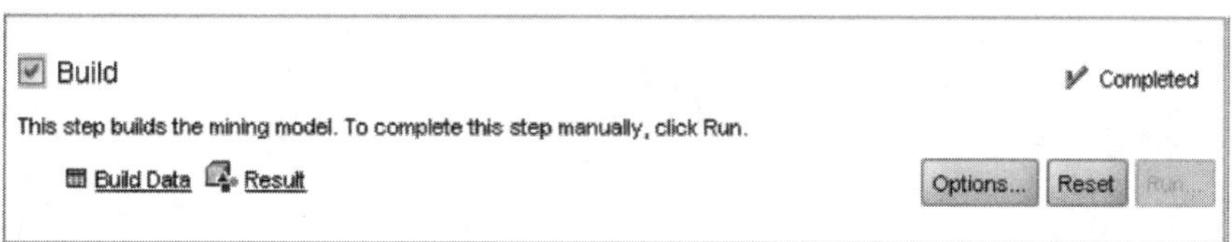

Figure 7.25: *Build Results Section of the DT Activity.*

Next, display the customer segments (each leaf rule), and then highlight which rule predicts those customers likely to respond. Below, we see the rule that predicts that an alumnus responds (predicted value of the target attribute = 1). The non-responders have a predicted value = 0.

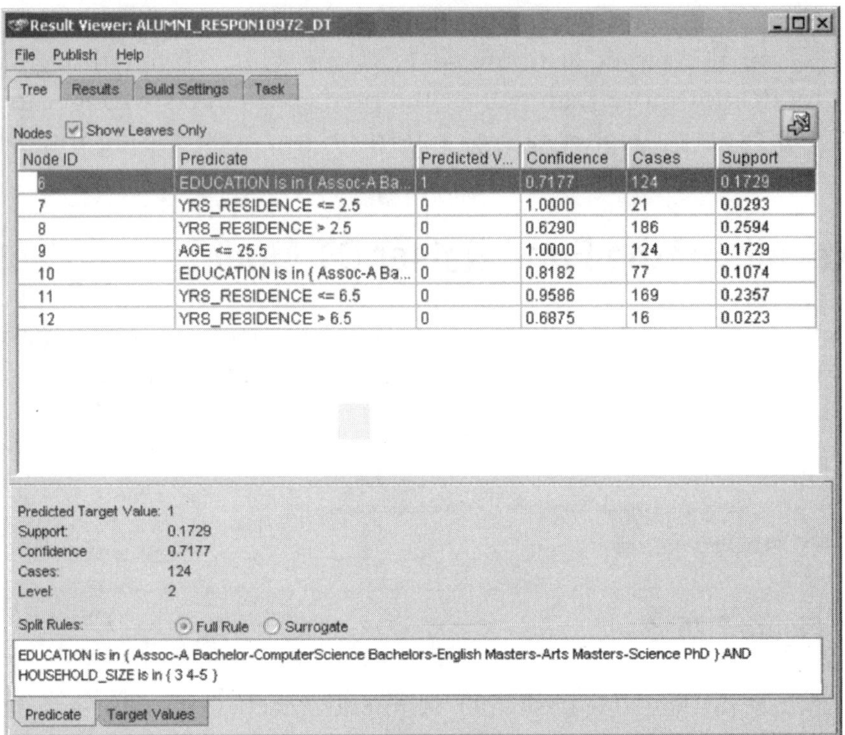

Figure 7.26: *Decision Tree for Fund Raising Classification Model.*

In the Task tab, we can select the model name, which will be used when creating the query for Oracle BI Publisher. In this example the model name is ALUMNI_RESPON10972_DT.

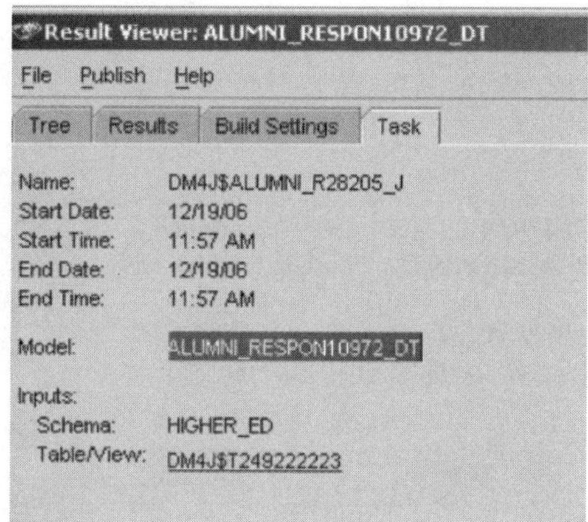

Figure 7.27: *Task Tab Displays the Model Name.*

Using the SQL scoring function PREDICTION_PROBABILITY, select the alumnus ID, predicted value of response to the fund raiser, and the probability of that response. In this example, we set the cut-off probability for a positive response at 0.70.

Test the query in Oracle Data Miner SQL Worksheet, and view the results. You will have selected a subset of alumni expected to respond to your mail-out.

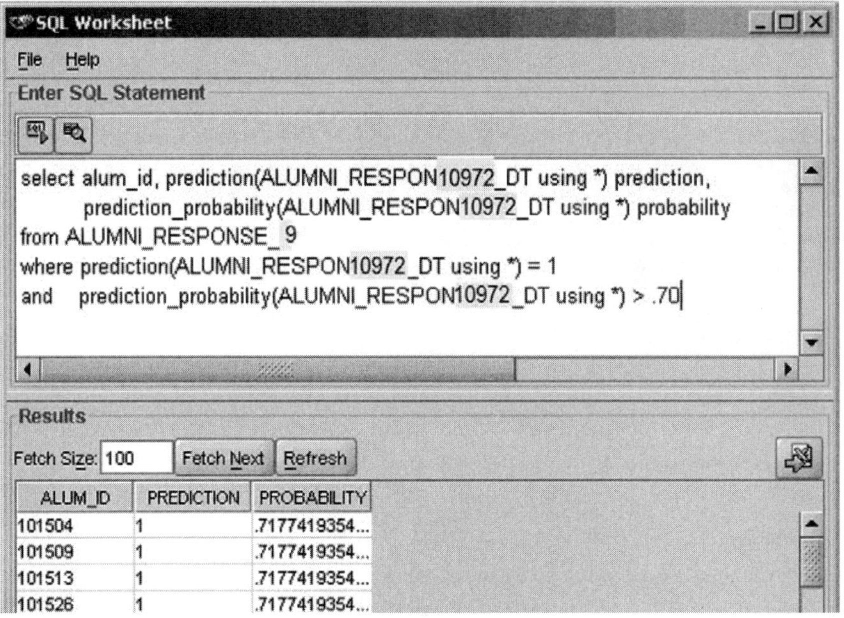

Figure 7.28: *Predict Alumni Likely to Respond.*

Generating XML Data using BI Publisher

Now we will create the form letter in the Word Template Builder for BI Publisher, and paste in the appropriate fields for the alumni name and address, date, and other information. You can further personalize the letter by building business logic into the database and inserting blocks of text as appropriate.

The first step is to create a report based on the SQL query to produce XML containing the data. This data will be used in a Word document.

In the edit report window of BI Publisher Enterprise, paste the query we used to get the alumnus ID, prediction (response or not), and probability (how likely to respond). We are asking for only those alumni who are at least 60% likely to respond.

The data source we created accesses the database where the Oracle Data Mining model and data reside.

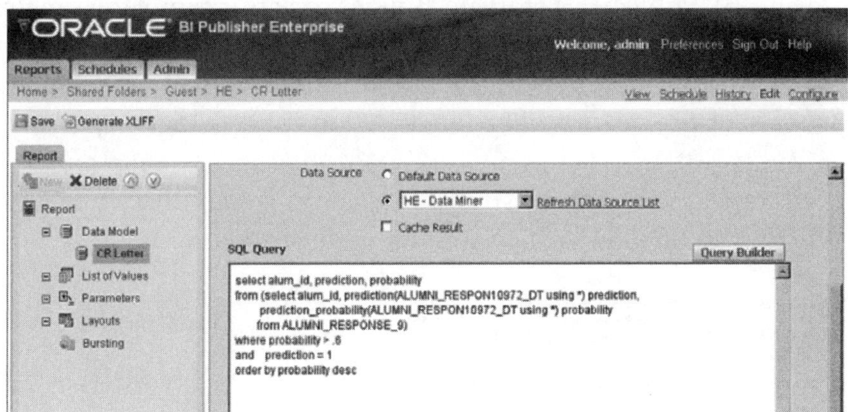

Figure 7.29: *Create XML Data with BI Publisher.*

Next, save the report, and then export the data in XML. Save the file as an xml file so that the data can be accessed in the Template Builder.

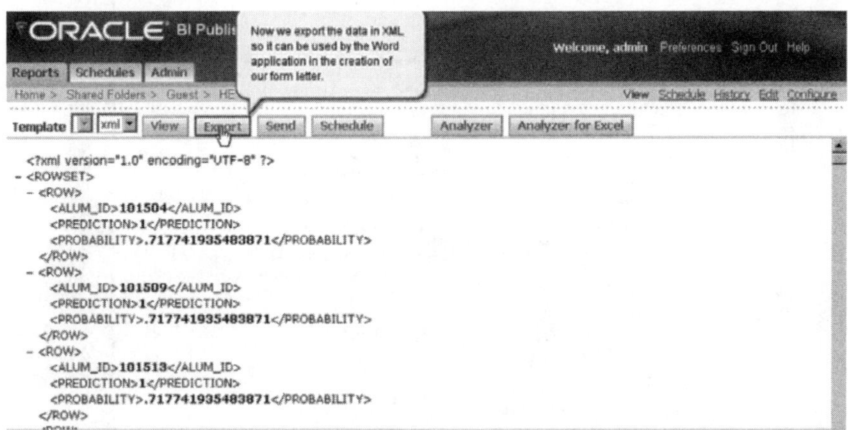

Figure 7.30: *Exporting XML Data.*

Creating a Form Letter with the Template Builder

Using BI Publisher Template Builder, create a template, dragging and dropping the ALUM_ID field from the SQL statement. Only those alumni that the model predicts will respond with sufficient probability will be included in the mailing.

Of course, you will substitute the alumnus name in place of the ID and add the address by joining with another table.

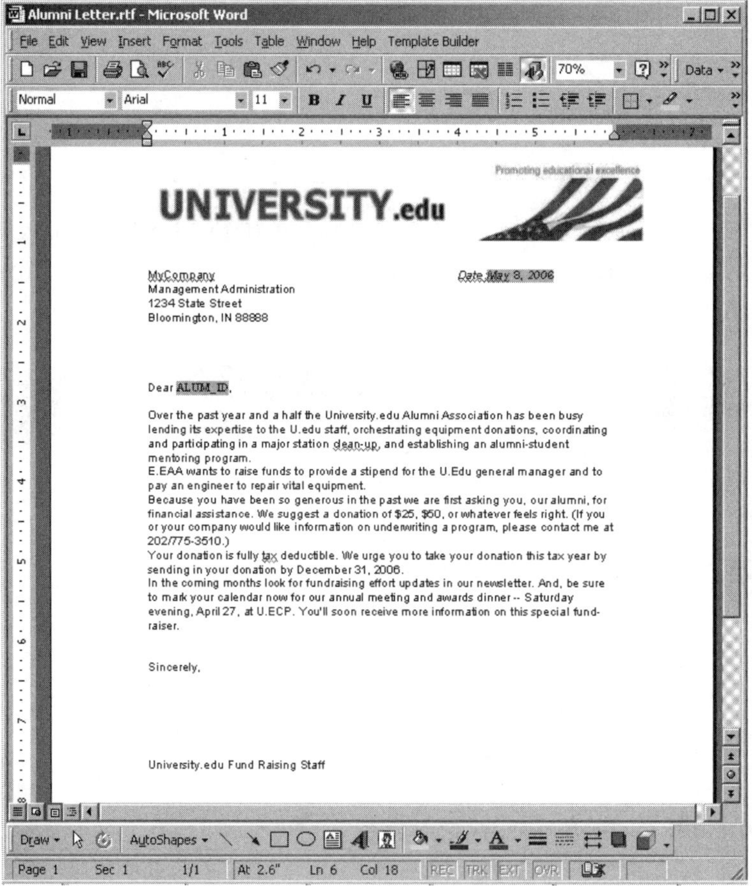

Promoting educational excellence

UNIVERSITY.edu

MyCompany
Management Administration
1234 State Street
Bloomington, IN 88888

Date May 8, 2006

Dear ALUM_ID,

Over the past year and a half the University.edu Alumni Association has been busy lending its expertise to the U.edu staff, orchestrating equipment donations, coordinating and participating in a major station clean-up, and establishing an alumni-student mentoring program.
E.EAA wants to raise funds to provide a stipend for the U.Edu general manager and to pay an engineer to repair vital equipment.
Because you have been so generous in the past we are first asking you, our alumni, for financial assistance. We suggest a donation of $25, $50, or whatever feels right. (If you or your company would like information on underwriting a program, please contact me at 202/775-3510.)
Your donation is fully tax deductible. We urge you to take your donation this tax year by sending in your donation by December 31, 2006.
In the coming months look for fundraising effort updates in our newsletter. And, be sure to mark your calendar now for our annual meeting and awards dinner -- Saturday evening, April 27, at U.ECP. You'll soon receive more information on this special fund-raiser.

Sincerely,

University.edu Fund Raising Staff

Figure 7.31: *Form Letter to Alumni Expected to Respond.*

The next step is to add the document as a layout in Oracle BI Publisher. This is done by uploading the RTF template to BI Publisher.

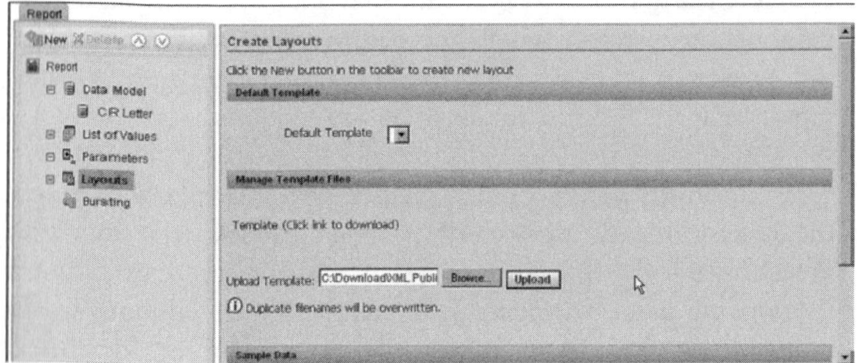

Figure 7.32: *Import Template into Layouts in BI Publisher Enterprise.*

Finally, view the letter in BI Publisher, and print the letters.

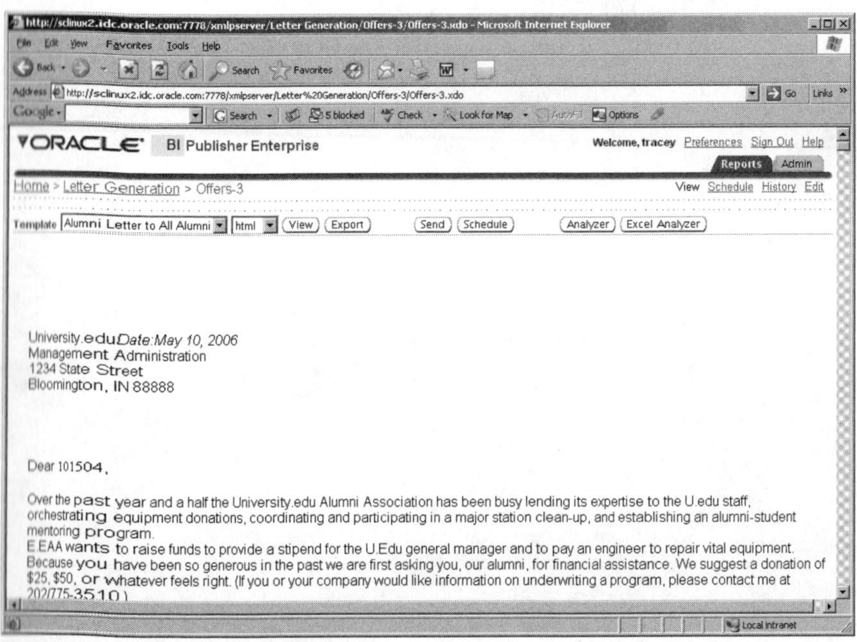

Figure 7.33: *Print the Letters.*

Conclusion

This chapter shows how to utilize Oracle Data Mining with Oracle BI Publisher to generate personalized form letters. We demonstrate ways in which the data mining analyst can leverage the powerful built-in data mining functionality in Oracle to rapidly deploy business intelligence applications.

The important points of this chapter are to explain how to use the Decision Tree algorithms to build models that can predict behavior, saving time and money in fund-raising campaigns and introducing a new domain example for higher education. Data mining queries are then utilized to select customers predicted to respond to an offer. Coupling Oracle Data Mining with BI Publisher enables easily creating personalized letters for reaching the targeted population.

Book Conclusion

This book serves as a general introduction to the Oracle Data Mining tool and the Oracle Data Miner user interface. A step-by-step approach is used to introduce the concepts of data mining and how to use the classification and clustering algorithms to explore patterns in diverse sets of real world examples.

Oracle's highly-rated Data Mining tools are a tremendous asset for developers, analysts, and database administrators. As data accumulates it will become ever more critical that data mining tools be utilized to explore and analyze large quantities of data.

Installing Oracle Data Miner

Appendix

ODM Tutorial

This Tutorial is re-printed with permission from Oracle By Example:

http://www.oracle.com/technology/obe/10gr2_db_single/install/odminst/odminst_otn.htm.

Purpose

This tutorial shows you how to enable the Data Mining option in the Oracle Database 10g Release 2, populate a data mining schema with sample tables, and install Oracle Data Miner.

Time to Complete

Approximately 30 minutes

Topics

This tutorial covers the following topics:

- Overview
- Prerequisites
- Enabling the DMSYS Account
- Load Mining Data into your Database

- Installing Oracle Data Miner
- Summary

Overview

Oracle Data Miner is a graphical user interface for Oracle Data Mining. It provides wizards that can easily be used to perform all data mining operations. Oracle Data Miner helps data analysts find valuable hidden information and makes data mining easier by doing the following:

- Automating data mining and model scoring process.
- Giving hints for the flow of steps in the operations.

Prerequisites

Before you perform this tutorial, you should:

- Perform the Installing Oracle Database 10g on Windows tutorial or have access to an Oracle Enterprise Edition 10g Release 2 Database with the Data Mining option enabled.
- Download and unzip the Data Mining Sample Data from OTN.

Note: It is recommended that you perform the Basic Installation. If you are required to perform a Custom Installation, note that the Oracle Data Mining option is automatically installed with any installation. DO NOT install the Oracle Data Mining Scoring Engine option as that action will disable the Oracle Data Mining option. Also, if you unlock and assign a password to the user DMSYS in step 11 of the database installation instructions, it is not necessary to enter the commands shown in the section below: Enabling the DMSYS account.

Enabling the DMSYS Account

After installing Oracle Database 10g on Windows, you need to enable the Oracle Data Mining administrative function and unlock schema required for the data mining examples.

Open a command prompt window and execute the following commands to unlock the DMSYS account and assign a password.

```
cd <demofilelocation>\DATA MINING Demos\admin
sqlplus sys/<sys_password> as sysdba
ALTER USER dmsys IDENTIFIED BY dmsys ACCOUNT UNLOCK;
```

```
SQL*Plus: Release 10.2.0.1.0 - Production on Thu Jan 26 12:41:04 2006

Copyright (c) 1982, 2005, Oracle.  All rights reserved.

SQL> connect / as sysdba
Connected.
SQL> ALTER USER dmsys IDENTIFIED BY dmsys ACCOUNT UNLOCK;

User altered.

SQL>
```

<demofilelocation> is the path where you unzipped the demo files in step 2 of the prerequisites.

<sys_password> is the password assigned to sys during database installation.

Note: The SH user also needs to be unlocked.

Creating and Configuring A Data Mining Account

Each database user who executes ODM operations must have:

- Default and temporary tablespaces specified
- Permission to access the mining data

Under normal circumstances in a simple training environment, or single-user system, users can share existing default and temporary tablespaces. But, in a production setting with several users, it is better to create separate tablespaces for each user.

The following describes the process to create and configure a data mining account.

Create a new tablespace. To create a new tablespace named dmuser1, execute the following command:

```
CREATE TABLESPACE dmuser1 DATAFILE
'<oracle_base>\oradata\orcl\dmuser1.dbf'
SIZE 20M REUSE AUTOEXTEND ON NEXT 20M;
```

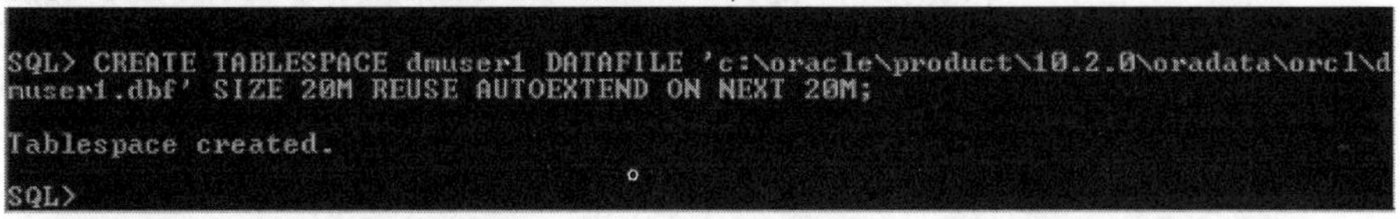

```
SQL> CREATE TABLESPACE dmuser1 DATAFILE 'c:\oracle\product\10.2.0\oradata\orcl\d
muser1.dbf' SIZE 20M REUSE AUTOEXTEND ON NEXT 20M;

Tablespace created.

SQL>
```

Figure A.1: *Create Tablespace Code*

<oracle_base> is the directory where the oracle_home is defined (i.e. c:\oracle\product\10.2.0).

You can create a data mining user named dmuser1 having password dmuser1. Execute the following command:

```
CREATE USER dmuser1 IDENTIFIED BY dmuser1
   DEFAULT TABLESPACE dmuser1 TEMPORARY TABLESPACE temp
   QUOTA UNLIMITED ON dmuser1;
```

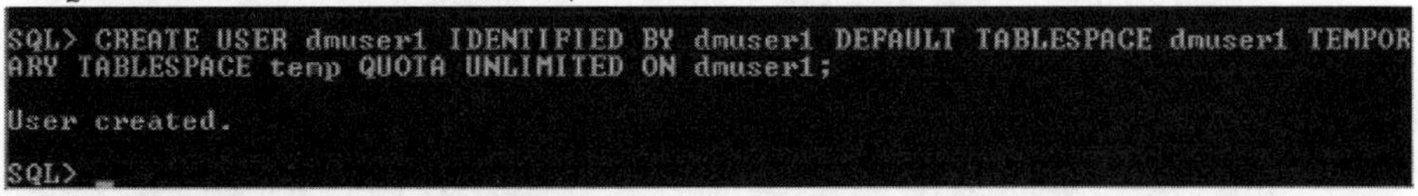

```
SQL> CREATE USER dmuser1 IDENTIFIED BY dmuser1 DEFAULT TABLESPACE dmuser1 TEMPOR
ARY TABLESPACE temp QUOTA UNLIMITED ON dmuser1;

User created.

SQL> _
```

Figure A.2: *Create User Code*

Next, the user must be granted permissions to carry out data mining tasks. Execute the following command:

```
@dmshgrants <sh_password> dmuser1
```

```
SQL> @dmshgrants sh dmuser1
old   1: GRANT create procedure to &DMUSER
new   1: GRANT create procedure to dmuser1

Grant succeeded.

old   1: grant create session to &DMUSER
new   1: grant create session to dmuser1

Grant succeeded.

old   1: grant create table to &DMUSER
new   1: grant create table to dmuser1

Grant succeeded.

old   1: grant create sequence to &DMUSER
new   1: grant create sequence to dmuser1

Grant succeeded.

old   1: grant create view to &DMUSER
new   1: grant create view to dmuser1

Grant succeeded.

old   1: grant create job to &DMUSER
new   1: grant create job to dmuser1

Grant succeeded.

old   1: grant create type to &DMUSER
new   1: grant create type to dmuser1

Grant succeeded.

old   1: grant create synonym to &DMUSER
new   1: grant create synonym to dmuser1

Grant succeeded.

old   1: grant execute on ctxsys.ctx_ddl to &DMUSER
new   1: grant execute on ctxsys.ctx_ddl to dmuser1

Grant succeeded.

Connected.
old   1: GRANT SELECT ON customers TO &DMUSER
new   1: GRANT SELECT ON customers TO dmuser1

Grant succeeded.

old   1: GRANT SELECT ON sales TO &DMUSER
new   1: GRANT SELECT ON sales TO dmuser1

Grant succeeded.
```

Figure A.3: *Running dmshgrants*

<sh_password> is the password assigned to the user SH when the account is unlocked (i.e. SH).

Finally, the schema for the new user can be populated with tables and views constructed from the data in the SH schema. You need to connect as dmuser1. Execute the following commands:

```
connect dmuser1/dmuser1
@dmsh
commit;
```

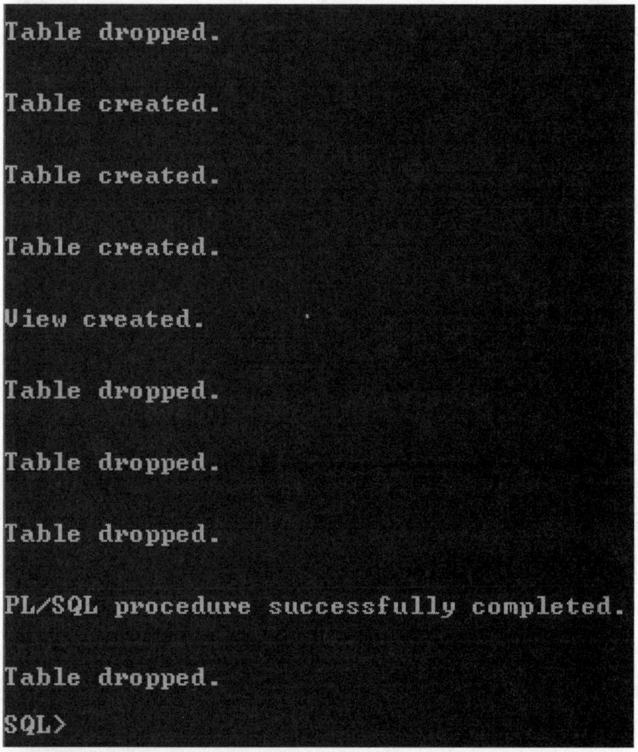

```
Table dropped.

Table created.

Table created.

Table created.

View created.

Table dropped.

Table dropped.

Table dropped.

PL/SQL procedure successfully completed.

Table dropped.
SQL>
```

Figure A.4: *Running dmsh*

Installing Oracle Data Miner

To install Oracle Data Miner, perform the following steps:

1. Download Oracle Data Miner from OTN and unzip into any directory except under your <database oracle home> directory.
2. Double-click <your_path>\bin\odminerw.exe.

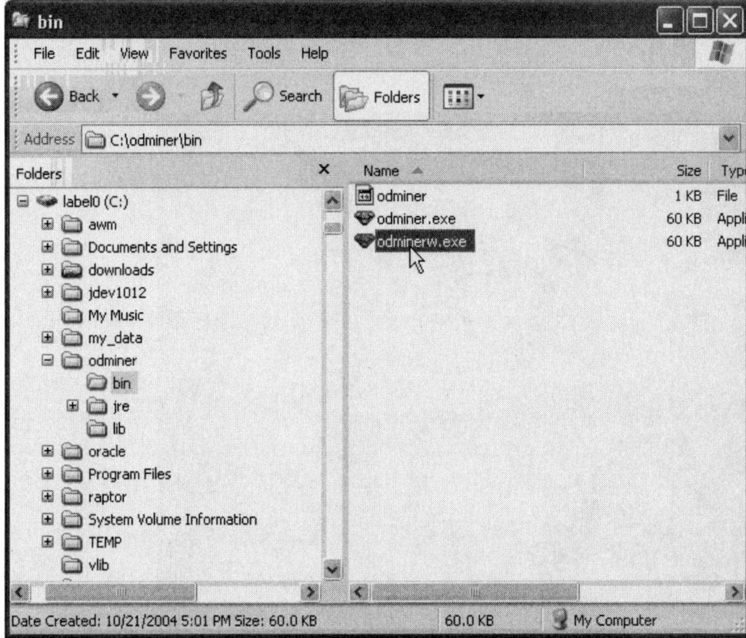

Figure A.5: *Starting Data Miner*

3. You need to create a database connection for the DMUSER1 account you created previously. Enter the following details in the window and click OK.

```
Connection Name: dmuser1_connect
User: dmuser1
Password: dmuser1
Host: <the machine where your Oracle Database is installed>
Port: 1521
SID: orcl
```

Note: The connection name can be anything you want. The Port and SID (Global Database Name) were assigned during the database installation.

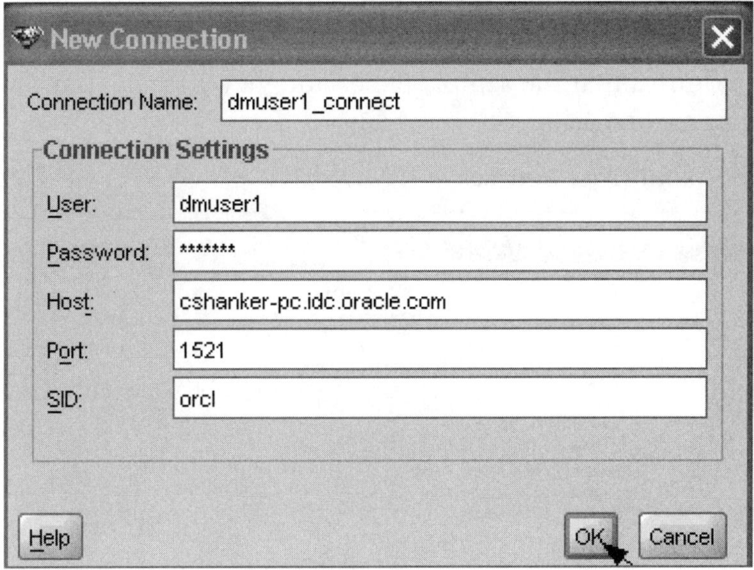

Figure A.6: *Create Database Connection*

4. Once your connection has been created, click OK to open Data Miner.

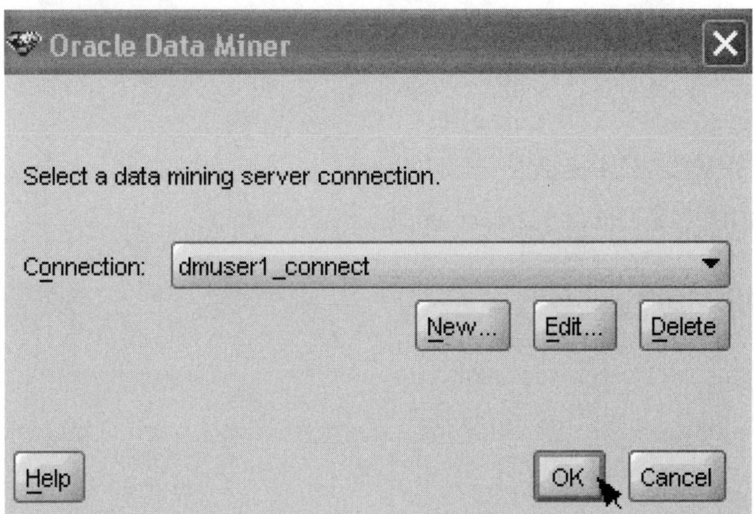

Figure A.7: *Open Data Miner*

5. Confirm that the sample tables and views are in your dmuser1 user schema.

6. Expand Data Sources > DMUSER1 > Views and Tables.

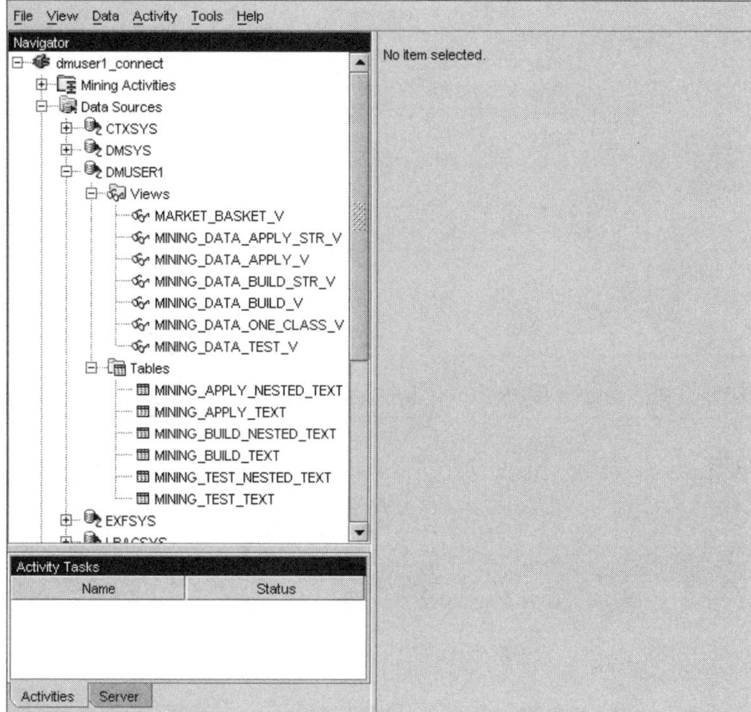

Figure A.8: *Confirm Tables and Views*

Summary

In this tutorial, you learned how to:

- Enable the data mining option in the Oracle Database 10g Release 2 database
- Populate a data mining schema with sample tables
- Install Oracle Data Miner

Script to Create ODM User

Appendix

Scripts

I sometimes found that creating more than one ODM user helped me organize my data mining subjects. I used this script to create ODM users.

```
CREATE USER "ODM" PROFILE "DEFAULT"
     IDENTIFIED BY "PSWD"
     QUOTA UNLIMITED ON "ODM_TBLS"
     ACCOUNT UNLOCK;
GRANT CREATE PROCEDURE TO "ODM";
GRANT CREATE SEQUENCE TO "ODM";
GRANT CREATE SESSION TO "ODM";
GRANT CREATE SYNONYM TO "ODM";
GRANT CREATE TABLE TO "ODM";
GRANT CREATE TYPE TO "ODM";
GRANT CREATE VIEW TO "ODM";
GRANT SELECT ANY DICTIONARY TO "ODM";
GRANT "CONNECT" TO "ODM";
GRANT "DMUSER_ROLE" TO "ODM";
GRANT EXECUTE ON "CTXSYS"."CTX_DDL" TO "ODM";
```

Index

About Dr. Carolyn Hamm

Dr. Carolyn Hamm is a recognized expert in Oracle data warehouse technologies, advanced analytics and Oracle data mining.

Dr. Hamm specializes in Oracle Discoverer, Oracle OLAP and Oracle Data Warehouse Builder, and is an expert in multivariate statistics using SAS and SPSS.

Earning her Ph.D. in Experimental Psychology, Dr. Hamm has spent the past 10 years developing web-enabled data systems for population health, medical management, clinical research, and health plan management. She currently serves on the board of directors for the Oracle Life Science User Group.

She is the Chief of the Decision Support Center, creating a data warehouse and using Oracle data mining tools to identify opportunities to improve the health of military service men and women and to improve the structure and operations of the military health care system in the National Capital Area and the Northeastern United States.

The Decision Support Center, in partnership with Oracle's Data Mining section, was a finalist in DM Review's 2005 World Class Solution Awards in the Business Intelligence category. Dr. Hamm likes to spend her leisure time jet skiing, fishing, scuba diving, and gardening.